38527803

CYBERSOCIETY
2.0

NEW MEDIA CULTURES

Series Editor: Steve Jones

New Media Cultures critically examines emerging social formations arising from and surrounding new technologies of communication. It focuses on the processes, products, and narratives that intersect with these technologies. An emphasis of the series is on the Internet and computer-mediated communication, particularly as those technologies are implicated in the relationships among individuals, social groups, modern and postmodern ways of knowing, and public and private life. Books in the series demonstrate interdisciplinary theoretical and methodological analyses, and highlight the relevance of intertwining history, theory, lived experience, and critical study to provide an understanding of new media and contemporary culture.

Books in this series . . .

CYBERSOCIETY
2.0 Revisiting Computer-Mediated Communication and Community

Steven G. Jones
Editor

SAGE Publications
International Educational and Professional Publisher
Thousand Oaks   London   New Delhi

For information:

SAGE Publications, Inc.
2455 Teller Road
Thousand Oaks, California 91320
E-mail: order@sagepub.com

SAGE Publications Ltd.
6 Bonhill Street
London EC2A 4PU
United Kingdom

SAGE Publications India Pvt. Ltd.
M-32 Market
Greater Kailash I
New Delhi 110 048 India

Printed in the United States of America

Library of Congress Cataloging-in-Publication Data

Main entry under title:

CyberSociety 2.0: Revisiting computer-mediated communication and community / edited by Steven G. Jones.
    p. cm. — (New media cultures ; v. 2)
  Rev. ed. of: CyberSociety. c1995.
  Includes bibliographical references and index.
  ISBN 0-7619-1461-7 (cloth : acid-free paper)
  ISBN 0-7619-1462-5 (pbk. : acid-free paper)
 1. Computer networks—Social aspects. 2. Communication. 3.
Computers and civilization. I. Jones, Steve, 1961-
II. CyberSociety. III. Title: CyberSociety two point zero IV. Series.
  TK5105.5 .C917   1998
  303.48′33—ddc21   98-8984

98 99 00 01 02 03 8 7 6 5 4 3 2 1

Acquiring Editor:	Margaret H. Seawell
Editorial Assistant:	Renée Piernot
Production Editor:	Astrid Virding
Editorial Assistant:	Nevair Kebakian
Typesetter/Designer:	Rose Tylak
Cover Designer:	Ravi Balasuriya

Contents

Preface

To paraphrase Ted Peterson's introduction to the revised edition of his book *Magazines in the Twentieth Century*, almost as soon as this book's predecessor, *CyberSociety: Computer-Mediated Communication and Community*, first appeared, netizens, software developers, hardware manufacturers, social scientists, social critics, and social activists set about making it out of date. When *CyberSociety* was completed late in 1994, the World Wide Web was something I clearly recall talking about with colleagues on-line. Web sites were few and far between, and content was, well, let's only say that it was by and large text with an occasional image thrown in for variety.

As I had expected at that time, though, innovations in CMC (Computer-Mediated Communication), and communication via computers generally, exponentially increased to the point when electronic mail is as common in most countries as a phone call, or, as Adrianne Laird, then one of my undergraduate students, put it, even virtual reality was "just around the corner from commonplace." The Internet still is not so ubiquitous that we all know what it is and how to use it, though, partially due to the fact that the technology still is rapidly changing, that it is not embraced by all, and, most important, because it is still inaccessible to the vast majority of people in the western world, and in other countries it is almost unknown.

CyberSociety 2.0, like its predecessor, is rooted in criticism and analysis of technologies that do presently exist and form the foundation for the media-ready pronouncements by everyone from MIT's Media Lab, to Microsoft, to Nintendo, about the wonders we are about to witness. And, also like its predecessor, *CyberSociety 2.0* will not assist its readers to become more proficient at using any of a variety of tools for computer-mediated communication (CMC). Such assistance can be found in a variety of sources available at most bookstores and libraries and even more readily available on-line.

CyberSociety 2.0 is so named because, as in the world of software engineering where it is common to number versions of revised software sequentially, it builds on its predecessor's foundations. Some parts of those foundations still are present and visible in this book, and have been reengineered, whereas other parts of this book represent entirely new construction. The goal was not to document the changes that have taken place since the first book's writing, just as the goal of this book is not to anticipate what changes will come our way. Instead, the goal of this book, as of its predecessor, is to assist readers to become aware and critical of the hopes we have pinned on computer-mediated communication and of the cultures that are emerging among Internet users. Both books are products of a particular moment in time, and also thereby serve as snapshots of the state of affairs, the concerns and issues, surrounding these new technologies of communication.

I am indebted to the authors whose work appears in these pages. Their enthusiasm about the project and about computer-mediated communication not only constitutes this book but gives it life. They have patience, perseverance, faith, integrity, and diligence, and I will be forever grateful to them.

I am also indebted to Margaret Seawell, my editor at Sage, with whom it is a joy to work, and who is thoughtful, caring, and helpful. Frank Christel, general manager of KWGS-FM at the University of Tulsa remains a good friend and fellow cyberspace explorer who continues to alert me to new Internet-related developments, and whose insight and humor are priceless. The ADN/Academic Computer Center staff at the University of Illinois at Chicago, and my colleague Jim Danowski, have been most helpful in assisting with, and providing, network resources, and I am most appreciative. Emily Walker has been most supportive and helpful, and my colleagues in the Department of Communication at the University of Illinois at Chicago have given friendship, guidance, and intellectual sustenance. The support of Sidney B. Simpson, Jr., Eric Gislason, Larry Poston, and Steve Weaver in UIC's College of Liberal Arts and Sciences has been invaluable and is greatly appreciated. The Computing and Information Resources staff at the University of Tulsa, in particular Reed Davis, Tristia Watson, Cherie Stovall, and Rick Kruse were always helpful and ready to assist. I owe my colleague in the Faculty of Communication at the University of Tulsa, Joli Jensen, far more than words can convey. Her critiques of my work and the insights I gain from conversation with her are a high point of my academic life.

I also wish to thank my mother and father, Jan Reynolds, Eric Cartman, and many net.friends who have provided support and encouragement.

I want to thank Jodi White, whose company I missed on many evenings and weekends while I worked on this book's predecessor, and who must have inwardly cringed when I broached the subject of working on another, but who showed patience, understanding, and pitched in to help me out.

Lastly, I wish to thank Ted Peterson, former Dean of the College of Communication at the University of Illinois at Urbana-Champaign, for his friendship, his teaching, his editing, the music he passed on to me, his handwritten letters, and the lucky penny. I miss him.

For Laza, Boris, and Sofia

Introduction

Steven G. Jones

> *We have never known*
> *Was it you drawing near?*
> *Or me*
> *Pulling close?*

— "Filled," Lynn Canfield / Area, 1987

> *Our concept of cyberspace, cyberculture, and cyber-everything is, more*
> *than we care to realize, a European idea, rooted in Deuteronomy, Socrates,*
> *Galileo, Jefferson, Edison, Jobs, Wozniak, glasnost, perestroika, and the*
> *United Federation of Planets.*

— Neal Stephenson (1994, p. 100)

The Internet, World Wide Web (WWW), Usenet, electronic mail, messaging and bulletin board services (BBSs), intranets; these are the words that probably best define the late 1990s. Electronically distributed, almost instantaneous, communication has for many people supplanted the postal service, telephone, fax machine—in some cases it has supplanted face-to-face communication as well. There are now more than 30 million Internet host computers. Businesses continue to spring forth every day offering Internet access, consulting, design, countless services. Nearly every sector of business has been touched by the Internet. And most any industry involved with delivering anything remotely electronic (and in many cases nonelectronic—on-line grocery delivery services come to mind) to the home, be it cable television, telephone, even electricity itself, has ventured into providing network services. To borrow from Lynn Canfield: Are we pulling close to these technologies, warming to them, or are they drawing nearer and nearer, inexorably encroaching on daily life?

In truth, such dualisms are never actual, and in the late 1990s likely bespeak of millenialism. Accompanying these technological manifestations is an ongoing resurgence in prophecy related to computers and computing. Some portion of that prophecy relates to virtual reality (VR) technology, which promises all flavors of reality on demand but has yet to deliver it. Some of it is associated with the combination of audio and video in the computer that is to lead us to the long-promised connection between the radio, television, computer, and to the combination of the Web and television, a match, one might say, made by those who make and sell couches. Most of the prophecy is simply about the newfound capacity to never be "out of touch." There are fewer comments about the wonders of technology, though, as we've become accustomed to at least the hype. We do find concerns about privacy, protection, safety, and civility; about the new forms of community brought about by CMC, the new social formations I termed "cybersociety."

James Carey (1989) has eloquently argued that prophecy has accompanied the arrival of most every new communication (not to mention other) technology. What Carey and collaborator John Quirk argued is that "electrical techniques (are hailed) as the motive force of desired social change, the key to the re-creation of a humane community, the means for returning to a cherished naturalistic bliss" (p. 115). Perhaps technology's numerous unfulfilled promises have led us to expect less bliss, but expectations for social change and community remain. Evidence of the expectations for social change can be found in the sublimity with which electronic mail and Internetworking are said to be of importance to democracy. As a press release touting the White House's e-mail connection claimed,

> Today, we are pleased to announce that for the first time in history, the White House will be connected to you via electronic mail. Electronic mail will bring the Presidency and this Administration closer and make it more accessible to the people. (Letter from the President and Vice President in announcement of White House electronic mail access, June 1, 1993)

What is meant by "closer"? What is meant by "more accessible"? Our hopes and expectations for community are evident in these terms, and in the everyday discourse on-line, on Usenet, in mail messages and interactive media like Internet Relay Chat (IRC), MUDs and MOOs. More important, these hopes lurk between the lines of that discourse, in the assumptions CMC users make about the connections they have to other users.

To examine those assumptions is to understand fundamentally human needs for contact, control, knowledge, the social and sociological elements of communication, and community. Whereas it is true that the Internet overcomes distance, in some ways it also overcomes proximity. We may eschew some forms of proximal communication (chatting in the hallway at work, for instance) for ones that distance us (as we concentrate on the computer screen and not our environs), even as these technologies make distance seem meaningless. Each essay in this volume provides another glimpse of how the promises of technology and the reality of its use mesh, collapse, and reorganize, and of the forms of cybersociety that are conjoined with that promise.

The "Net"

Cybersociety relies on, of course, the forms of CMC allowed by current computer network structures, and some discussion of those is in order. Excellent written introductions to electronic mail, the Internet, the World Wide Web, and a host of other computer networks, as well as software, are readily available, and I will not cover the ground they do. Each can readily assist with connection to the variety of computer links, experiences and activities described in *CyberSociety 2.0*, and I suggest you use this technology (if you have not already) to experience electronic mail, to examine the bulletin boards, lists, and newsgroups, to "surf" the Web and share the experiences about which the contributors herein write. Unlike many other analyses and studies of contemporary society, one may enter the communities and discourse described in these chapters with relative ease. The issues with which sociologists and anthropologists, among others, traditionally have engaged when conducting their research are part of that discourse, for it becomes necessary to cover ground concerning participant observation, privacy, and biography. The best way to come in contact with those issues is to experience CMC.

As background to the following chapters, though, some introduction to the history of computer-mediated communication is useful. The connections in place for the most widely discussed computer network, the Internet, were formed in the 1960s and early 1970s when the U.S. Department of Defense and several research universities, via DARPA (Defense Advanced Research Program Agency) linked computers. Of course, one may draw deeper connections to older technologies, as do Carey (1989), King, Grinter, and Pickering (1997), and Marvin (1988), for example. The resulting network, Arpanet, allowed for access to each site's computers not only for research but also for communication. The former role took a back seat to the use of Arpanet as a means for researchers to share information by way of electronic messaging. Initially such messaging was in the form we are accustomed to from using the post office; individual messages are sent from one person to another.

Nevertheless, it quickly became clear that messages often contained information to be shared by many users, and thus mailing lists were created. These lists allowed one person to mail one message to a central point from which that message was "bounced" or "reflected" to others who subscribed to the list. Eventually lists became specialized in particular topics, and the terms "bulletin board" and "mailing list" came to have some interchangeability. Bulletin boards, though, generally referred to computers one could reach by dialing through standard phone lines with a computer modem and linking with another computer. The effect of each, board and list, was similar in many ways, as both provided news and information to users and came to be subsumed under the category of "newsgroup." Newsgroups gather the messages posted by users in a centralized fashion and permit interaction with posted messages by way of simple means of reply. Lengthy threads are created by individual messages that generate dozens, even hundreds, of replies. The largest manifestation of newsgroups is known as Usenet, a massive repository of thousands of newsgroups accessible from most any computer with a connection to the Internet. In the 1990s, the creation by Tim Berners-Lee of the World Wide Web, as a means of sharing visual, aural, and textual information, became the most visible, and most talked about, of the Internet's uses.

The Internet essentially serves as the main connecting point for many other networks. It has come to be a "backbone" by which networks link up with each other. It is a decentralized network, and its overall management now occurs via several not-for-profit governing organizations, though day-to-day management (maintenance of network services, allocation of domain names and access, etc.) is managed by a handful of for-profit companies, telecommunications industry giants, and computer networking companies. More important, no one group manages it. Instead, a variety of groups, such as the Internet Society and InterNIC, in concert with industry, circulate information, resolutions, and do research on the network's needs.

There are many purposes the Internet can serve, but the ones with which its users most frequently engage are text-based, even in the case of the World Wide Web. It could be argued, in fact, that the Internet is the latest expression of print-capitalism. Much as newspapers and pamphlets spread word of the New World to Europe, the Internet spreads word of electronic environments.

Technologies continue to converge. Virtual reality (VR) technology and even computer games like Nintendo's and Sega's, for example, provide still more arenas for communication and interaction. Still, textuality and narrative provide an important focus of study for anyone seeking to comprehend the varieties of CMC, and it is important to ask questions about power in relation to them. Who will secure the "master" narrative (if there will be one) concerning CMC? Some say software will enable all users to contribute to, or create, an unlimited amount of narratives and texts.

The notion of self and its relation to community is one that must be taken up critically, and the contributors to *CyberSociety 2.0* do so. Given, for instance, the mutability of identity on-line, where it is possible to post messages anonymously and pseudonymously, how are we to negotiate social relations that, at least in the realm of face-to-face communication, were fixed by recognition of identity? One answer to that question comes in the form of the previously mentioned constraints on CMC users. The developers of Eudora, an electronic-mail software package, for instance, in early versions made it possible to send messages adopting anyone else's name by using their e-mail address. Later versions of Eudora circumvented this software loophole by appending the word "unverified" in parentheses next to the e-mail address of the sender if the message originated without a password.

Still other means of fixing identity and conduct continue to develop, and along with them so does the exercise of power in the social relations being formed via CMC. Such matters speak directly to the creation of community via CMC, as one area of development, that of standards of conduct, is in a sense the development of a moral code, a system of values, akin to the ones that arise and are revised in most social formations. Consequently, the question that needs to be asked is: In these fleeting worlds, how does an individual, much less a community, maintain existence?

That question points to one of the most compelling issues concerning CMC: Who are we when we are on-line? The question becomes even more important as new technologies are developed for creating "bots," "agents," or "alters" that roam the network for us when we are away from our terminals. Perhaps the issue is not, in fact, identity but anonymity, a state difficult, in most ways, to achieve off-line.

The preeminent arena for real-time interaction on the Internet is the MUD, Multi-User Dimension, Dungeon, or Domain (take your pick). In a MUD, many users can interact using a text-based communication system and collaboratively created spaces. We have, in a sense, created virtual worlds since the invention of writing. But rarely have those worlds been created and shared simultaneously among people at such great physical distance from each other. Though text-based, MUD discourse combines elements of the written and spoken, which itself points to the "naturalness" of the environments MUD users create. The spontaneity with which discourse and dialogue can occur affects the text itself, and MUDs are an arena within which users communicate in real time and with little time to construct carefully written texts.

CyberSociety 2.0 is at heart an attempt to understand and probe into these social formations. The contributors probe issues of community, communication, identity, knowledge, information, and power. One reason such work is needed is to understand the framing of reality that CMC brings about. As Mary Chayko (1993) claimed,

> In modern everyday life, it is difficult (and becoming impossible) to definitively classify experience as "real" or "not real"; it is more helpful to determine the degree or "accent" of reality in an event. The frames we once used, conceptually, to set the real apart from the unreal are not as useful as they once were; they are not as sturdy; they betray us. As they become ever more fragile, we require new concepts and under-standings. (p. 178).

The purpose of this book is to provide a few such concepts and under-standings. It also emphasizes that new social formations may require new forms of inquiry, too. How will sociologists, ethnographers, communica-tion scholars, and anthropologists, for instance, grapple with issues re-lated to studying electronic communities? The essays in *CyberSociety* 2.0 are evidence of some answers to that question. They are descriptive, sometimes empirical, sometimes theoretical but not prescriptive. The interest is to understand the everyday life of the network and its citizens, to, as Carey (1993) puts it, engage in "a sociology of border crossing, of migration across the semipermeable membranes of social life that consti-tuted . . . disorderly fronts" (p. 179). In this case the fronts are on our computer screens, beckoning us to go from a place, a "where" of our own boundaries to a less palpable site, a "who knows" that, like any new frontier, is colonized first by our imagination and thought.

References

Carey, J. (1989). *Communication as culture.* Winchester, MA: Unwin-Hyman.

Carey, J. (1993). Everything that rises must diverge: Notes on communications, technology, and the symbolic construction of the social. In P. Gaunt (Ed.), *Beyond agendas* (pp. 171-184). Westport, CT: Greenwood.

Chayko, M. (1993). What is real in the age of virtual reality? "Reframing" frame analysis for a technological world. *Symbolic Interaction, 16*(2), 171-181.

King, J. L., Grinter, R. E., & Pickering, J. M. (1997). The rise and fall of Netville: The saga of a cyberspace construction boomtown in the great divide. In S. Kiesler (Ed.), *Culture of the Internet* (pp. 3-33). Mahwah, NJ: Lawrence Erlbaum.

Marvin, C. (1988). *When old technologies were new.* Oxford, UK: Oxford University Press.

Stephenson, N. (1994, February). In the kingdom of Mao Bell. *Wired, 2*(2), 100.

Other books authored or edited
by Steven G. Jones:

*Virtual Culture: Identity and Communication
in Cybersociety*

*CyberSociety: Computer-Mediated Communication
and Community*

*Rock Formation: Popular Music, Technology and
Mass Communication*

*CyberSociety 2.0: Revisiting Computer-Mediated
Communication and Community*

1

Information, Internet, and Community: Notes Toward an Understanding of Community in the Information Age

Steven G. Jones

It seems that in the few years since the Internet's rise from a network of computers to popular cultural (and commercial) icon, metaphors are no longer necessary for its description. Once it was necessary to point out the Internet's function as an "information highway," to evoke metaphors of movement, speed, control, destination, and voyage. Whether promoting the use of the Internet, as Microsoft did with its "Where do you want to go today?" advertising campaign, or being critical of its development, as is Michael Noll (1997), who stated, "The (information superhighway) has not been as super as many have promised. The many potholes and washed out bridges have jolted our sense of reality" (p. 191), our discussions have been cloaked in the language of transportation and consumerism. Now those metaphors have begun to seem outdated. Yet, they still are necessary insofar as they allow us to place the history of the Internet as a project rather than only technology, to demonstrate the startling parallels between the Internet as "information highway" and the interstate highway system. Both projects were devised, and spurred on, initially by military considerations, by real and imagined world wars, and, more important, as Noll found, by *lulls* during which the military-industrial complex searched for other opportunities for itself. The Internet, like its concrete-and-steel counterpart, the highway system, quickly made its way to the civilian, and, most important, commercial realms.

Phil Patton (1986), in his history of the U.S. interstate system, noted that it was

> the most expensive and elaborate public works program of all time, offer[ing] a vision of social and economic engineering. It was planned to be at once a Keynesian economic driver and a geographic equalizer, an instrument for present prosperity and the armature of a vision of the future. It was at once the last program of the New Deal and the first space program. (p. 17)

The Internet has what seems now long ago become less of a public works program and more of a worldwide experiment in organization for commercial gain. The U.S. government has kept a hand in the project, though less and less of one (even as it seeks to repeat its role by virtue of the next generation Internet). The Internet is the first program of the new New Deal and the *last* space program. Information is to this new New Deal what work, labor, was to FDR's. As the WPA (Works Project Administration), CCC (Civil Conservation Corps), and other programs transformed and cataloged the social and physical landscapes, so too do efforts to organize the Internet, provide access to it, sell it, knit it together with everyday life, transform social relations and cyberspatial landscapes. As the New Deal changed not only our communities but our sense of community, of togetherness, so too does the Internet have consequences for our sense of who we are, who we are among others, and who we want to be. Phil Patton's comment about the effects interstates have had on cities and communities therefore bear especially close scrutiny, as he evoked images of what the information highway also may do to social formations. Highways, Patton (1986) said, have had monstrous side effects. They have often rolled, like some gigantic version of the machines that build them, through cities, splitting communities off into ghettos, displacing people, and crushing the intimacies of old cities.

WhilepromisingtobringuscloserhighwaysinfactcatertooursenseofseparatenessWhile promising to bring us closer, highways in fact cater to our sense of separateness. (p. 20)

Critical to the rhetoric surrounding the Internet use is the promise of a renewed sense of community and, in many instances, new types and formations of community. Computer-mediated communication (CMC), it seems, will do by way of electronic pathways what cement roads were unable to do, namely, connect us rather than atomize us, put us at the controls of a "vehicle" and yet not detach us from the rest of the world.

If that is to be so, it is not premature to ask questions about these new formations. What might electronic communities be like? Most forecasters, like Howard Rheingold (1993), envisioned them as a kind of ultimate flowering of community, a place (and there is no mistaking in these visions that it is place that is at stake) where individuals shape their own community by choosing which other communities to belong to. Rheingold's own attempt to create such a place, "Electric Minds," floundered and ultimately had few users and even fewer financial backers. Interestingly, community, in the case of Electric Minds, was framed as a marketable commodity, and thus one could be forgiven for believing that the Internet is now less of a public works program and more of a global experiment in organization for commercial gain.

Rheingold's (1993) dream, however, and that of those for whom modern society seems, for one reason or another, cold and impersonal lives on. It is a dream rooted in nostalgia for civility and sociability. But it is also struck from a paradox that has long haunted America and the connections to others that the Internet provides also make for a solution to that paradox in a particularly American way: We may forge our own places from among the many that exist, not by creating new places but simply by choosing from the menu of those available, by joining in (and opting out) wherever and whenever we wish. Similarly, Healy (1997) noted that such mobility may "not oblige . . . participants to deal with diversity" (p. 63), thus reinforcing users' biases. Stephen Doheny-Farina (1996), in *The Wired Neighborhood*, expressed it well:

A community is bound by place, which always includes complex social and environmental necessities. It is not something you can easily join.

> You can't subscribe to a community as you subscribe to a discussion
> group on the net. It must be lived. It is entwined, contradictory, and
> involves all our senses. (p. 37)

Thus, another of the many questions we must ask about electronic communities is: What is the nature of individual members' commitments to
them? In the physical world, community members must live together.
When community membership is in no small way a matter of subscribing
or unsubscribing to a bulletin board or electronic newsgroup, is the nature
of interaction different simply because one may disengage with little or
no consequence? As Vilém Flusser (1996) pointed out, there is a sharp
distinction, ontological and spiritual, between "worlds that we ourselves
have designed [and] . . . something that has been given to us, like the
surrounding world" (p. 242). What are the consequences of differences
between temporary and persistent worlds?

Perhaps the most important question for the purposes of this book
is: How do we study computer-mediated community? Indeed, how do
we study community in an information age? Doheny-Farina (1996)
questioned his own sense of community in a warm movie theater on a
cold winter night: "The weather was real," he wrote, "but was the
community? Did I experience community only because I saw a depthless
reflection of it on the screen? Am I constructing a community in the act
of describing it?" (p. 5). As is our experience of community off-line, our
experience on-line is similar. The sense of community is palpable, yet
evanescent. As Fernback (1997) pointed out, "community is a term which
seems readily definable to the general public but is infinitely complex
and amorphous in academic discourse. It has descriptive, normative,
and ideological connotations . . . [and] encompasses both material and
symbolic dimensions" (p. 39). Much, if not all, of the discussion and
debate about CMC and community is taking place among academic
critics—in what ways do our own attitudes, assumptions, hopes and
desires for and about community affect that discourse?

One way scholars may be lulled into a false sense of certainty when
looking for on-line community is based on the ability to "freeze" electronic discourse by capturing text and information it may contain, making external and permanent the memory of it. But how do we ascertain
the interpretive moment in electronic discourse, particularly as it en-
gages both reading and writing? Does the very ability to record it in some
fashion make us feel more certain we can put it under a microscope?

What are the types of interactivity allowed and structured by these new technologies? Is community constituted in conversation and interaction? Berger and Luckmann's (1967) groundbreaking work on the social construction of reality should, at least, make one reluctant to dispute that it is. But if such is the case, what are the consequences for our sense of community whether conversation and interaction are via face-to-face meetings, e-mail, World Wide Web, or other mediated forms?

There should be no mistake about the apperceived "realness" of the reality encountered on-line—Internet users have strong emotional attachments to their on-line activities. Weise (1996), for one, remarked vividly about her introduction to on-line social relationships after moving to a new city and feeling isolated there. E. F. Schumacher (1977) has forcefully argued that "The most 'real' world we live in is that of our fellow human beings" (p. 24). The social construction of the reality that exists on-line is, however, not constituted *by* the networks CMC users utilize, it is constituted *in* the networks. It would be far easier to understand the physical, or hardwired, connections than to understand the symbolic connections that emerge from interaction. To borrow from James Carey, much of our energy has been directed toward understanding the speed and volume with which computers can be used as communication tools. Conspicuously absent is an understanding of how computers are used as tools for connection and community (for what one might term "compunity"). Carey (1989) made clear the distinction between transmission and ritual views: "Communication under a transmission view is the extension of messages across geography for the purposes of control, the . . . case under a ritual view is the sacred ceremony that draws persons together in fellowship and commonality" (p.18). The distinctions between the two views of communication Carey drew are critical to understanding the full range and scope of CMC. It would seem we now have our global village or community and not just via CMC but by way of the many media of communication ever present. Everywhere we go we can "tap into" that community with a cellular telephone, a personal digital assistant, modem, or satellite dish. But connection does not inherently make for community, nor does it lead to any necessary exchanges of information, meaning and sense-making at all. Barnes and Duncan (1992) borrowed from James Clifford: "When we write we do so from a necessarily local setting" (p. 3). The primary acts involved in CMC, whether via e-mail, Usenet, World Wide Web, MUDs and MOOs, are those of reading and writing. Like Walter Ong's (1982) description of authorship, these acts are *intensely* local, for though we may be certain of an audience, we are also unable to verify its existence just as we are unable to verify its interpretation of our writing.

That uncertainty of an "other" interpreting our utterance is central to the act of writing, as Ong (1986) saw it. It also may be central to the desire for control and feedback James Beniger (1986) believed caused the "control revolution." Beniger's thoughts were focused on the rapid technological innovation at the end of the late 19th century that heralded the introduction of basic communication technologies and, he said, restored the economic and political control lost during the Industrial Revolution.

> Before this time, control of government and markets had depended on personal relationships and face-to-face interactions; now control came to be reestablished by means of bureaucratic organization, the new infrastructure of transportation and telecommunications, and system-wide communication via the new mass media. (p. 14)

Or, to put it another way, Nguyen and Alexander (1996) claimed that, "The old mass media were unifying media; they assembled and sustained nations with real-time theater. In cyberspace, there is no center stage; however immense, cyberspace time is intensely decentralizing" (p. 108). Nguyen and Alexander did not thereby claim mass media's superiority to that of CMC, they underscored a need for control, obvious when citizenship, politics, economics, are viewed in relation to geography, at once problematized and solved by transportation and communication.

The issue of geography, to which I will return later in this chapter, is critical not only for an understanding of CMC but for an understanding of the increasingly complicated relationship between mass communication, individuals, and new media technologies. Paul Virilio (1995) noted the shift in social space between a theater play and a film:

> In theater, each member of the audience scattered throughout the auditorium necessarily sees a different play. In the cinema, on the other hand, these same spectators see exactly what the camera has seen, wherever they happen to be sitting; that is, they see *The same film*. (p. 8)

New media like cable broadcasting, and the Internet, and new uses of media, like WWW sites that allow for "personalization," browser "cookies," even grocery store checkout machines that scan and collect buyer data and return coupons directed toward that particular buyer, signal yet another shifting from Virilio's explication of cinema's relation to theater: Now each member of an audience, or a community, can, in fact, see something that is different but *still mass-mediated*. The importance of this cannot be understated. Daniel Dayan and Elihu Katz (1992) defined "media-engendered social structures" that are "not bound by geography," (p. 16) that they compared and contrasted to "The communitas of good neighborliness and shared spirituality" (p. 132) not unlike, in many ways, the Jewish *seder* (pointedly discussed later in this book by Mark Poster in relation to the "cyberjew" e-mail listserve). Media events, like the *seder*, require people in different places, at the same times, to participate in ritual, or ceremonial, events. The comparison is a compelling one, particularly when one considers media events on a global scale. One hardly needs to be reminded of the many such events experienced by the western (and occasionally, and increasingly, nonwestern) world; Apollo 11, the JFK assassination, Princess Diana's death, Live-Aid, and so forth. It is worth asking how often we feel part of a global community compared to a more local one. As our horizons have expanded, have they also collapsed on us with a weight that forces us inward on ourselves? What are the very meanings of "public" and "private" in a world where media events and "personalized" media can coexist?

We continue to face a predicament: How do we attend to the social, economic, and political connections impinging on us, the connections we at once desire (e-mail, telephone, fax, democratic participation, business, etc.) and that nurture our character as public beings and also despise (for they take up more and more of our time and energy and fragment privacy and self among a variety of publics)? Again, control is sought after, but it is not sought for the purposes of power but for the purposes of its inverse, restraint. As Carey (1993) put it, "Human intelligence has lodged itself, extrasomatically, in the very atmosphere that surrounds and supports us. Yet, back at home, we have a surplus of disorder and disarray" (p. 172). The very surfeit of knowledge and information leads toward chaos and ever greater efforts are made at controlling the disorder with Internet information-navigating devices like Netscape, Explorer, Gopher, Lynx, Mosaic, and myriad search engines.

Such disorder and the attempts to control it underscore the mythical investment we have in computer technology. The chaos and confusion generated by the opening of new frontiers led us to devise means of communication and transportation as if those means were one, part and parcel of the same process. Rail and road followed river and stream, to be supplanted by telegraph wire, telephone wire, fiber optic cable. (One ought to wonder what wireless communication as it develops in all its manifestations will truly bring, as the link between communication and transportation, forged by history, dissolves.) Jenkins and Fuller's (1995) chapter on new world narratives in *CyberSociety* provided precisely the analysis needed to make the links between our new media and our history explicit through examination of language and narrative.

It is important, too, for us to not only understand the parallels between new world narratives and CMC narratives but to understand their differences. In a modern world there is a need for control related to structure and homogenization, to the reversal of entropy. Such reversal comes to us in the guise of connections and associations that overcome geography and physical space. Computer-mediated communication will, it is said, lead us toward a new community; global, local, and everything in between. Douglas Schuler (1996) forcefully argued for the need for new communities whose very existence is dependent on communication technology. Schuler's compelling argument rested on the premise that "Computer technology—in concert with other efforts—can play a positive role in rebuilding community by strengthening . . . core values" (p. 34). But the presence of chaos inexorably draws us away from that ideal as the need for control becomes greater and greater. It is most accurate to claim, as Carey (1993) did, that when it comes to proselytizing CMC and community, "these are ideas that people want or need to be true merely because it would be bewildering to be without them" (p. 172). However difficult it may be to create community networks, irrespective of the technology involved, it is more difficult to argue that we would be better off without them.

Now, as we create those communities, indeed even as we talk about them, it may as well be "bewildering" for us to create and learn the norms of on-line worlds, in a way that is itself fragmenting. The learning process may bring people together insofar as such learning is often collaborative, but it is equally as often frustrating and off-putting. The exclusivity, inflexibility, isolation, rigidity, homogeneity, for which Schuler (1996) criticized the "old concept of community" (p. 9) also can take root in computer-mediated ones. Nevertheless, Schuler's enthusiasm for new communities is one shared by many, and it is driven by the sense that we are embarking on an adventure in creating new communities and new forms of community. It is an enthusiasm fueled by the perception that, first, we *need* new communities, and second, that we can create them technologically. Such motives, in turn, arise from what Edward Soja (1989) has called "postmodern geographies," the tensions caused by differentiation and homogenization in the (re)production of space. In the case of CMC, what allows for the reproduction of space is the malleability with which identity can be created and negotiated, an issue several of the authors in *CyberSociety* took up and that contributors to *CyberSociety 2.0* also engage. Consequently, one must question the potential of CMC for production of social space. Could it perhaps *re*produce "real" social relations in a "virtual" medium?

More likely is that social relations emerging from CMC are between the two poles of production and reproduction. Pushing too close to either pole puts at risk whatever new social construction of reality may arise. And yet, any new social formations are at risk of being mythologized and incorporated into the "rhetoric of the electrical sublime" Carey (1989) identified. All media, for instance, have been touted for their potential for education. Radio and television, in particular, were early on promoted as tools for education, and CMC is no different. When radio and TV were introduced, the emphasis was on broadcasting in the public interest, convenience, and necessity. The rhetoric surrounding development of community networks is similar. One should not too hastily dismiss these efforts, but there is need for critical analysis. Internetworking pioneer John Quarterman (1993) has said, "Radio and television produced a different society. Computer networks will, too. Perhaps this time we can avoid a few mistakes" (p. 49). One should, of course, hope so. But one should also ask, "what gets to count as technology and progress?" (Terry & Calvert, 1997, p. 2) as these potentials are set toward realization. It is critical to the success of efforts at building community that one does not obfuscate the power behind decisions that go into planning and organizing media. Who will plan, how will we plan, and how will we account in our planning for unanticipated consequences? Media regulation in the United States has hardly been the most successful enterprise. Why should we believe regulating CMC will be different?

At the heart of comments like Quarterman's (1993) is a pervasive sense that we can learn from the "mistakes" we believe we've made

using older media. Computer-mediated communication (and computers generally) gives us a sense that we can start over and learn from the
past. And of course we have a fundamental need, or at least hope, for
something better to come from future media.

But what exactly are we hoping *for*? The answer to that question is
necessarily linked to questions about who we are hoping to be as a
society, and that, in turn, is tied to issues of identity and discourse. Who
are we when we are on-line? The question becomes even more important
as new technologies are developed for creating "agents," "bots" or
"alters" that roam the network for us when we are away from our
terminals.

The possibility of new social formations is certainly alluring and is
one of those ideas we seem to "want or need to be true." Burnett (1996)
noted,

> While it is true that the Internet is making community contacts possible
> on a far greater scale than previously imagined, the ground rules,
> needs, and desires of people remain very much the same as in earlier
> periods. One must be careful therefore in attributing too much to the
> technologies here, but then again those attributions are part of the
> energizing force behind so much of the activity. (p. 92)

Among those needs is the primacy of the visual, the tendency toward the
image, and to fill that need technologies for virtual (or, as I have noted in
an earlier article, Jones, 1993), what is primarily *visual*) reality is being
developed, with the energy Burnett (1996) ascertains. What is most interesting, though, is that virtual reality is hardly less "bewildering" than
nonvirtual reality. The systems of cultural significance and methods of
social control in on-line worlds in some instances parallel ones we are
already accustomed to and in some instances they do not. In all instances,
though, they do form a new matrix of social relations. What impulses
those formations are propelled by is an important matter and should not
be overlooked. Cybersocieties are not organized simply for the transmission of information, nor do they "have to do something nontrivial with
the information they send and receive" (Licklider & Taylor, 1968, p. 21).
In fact, much of what is done with CMC is trivial. It is possible, as
Chesebro and Bonsall (1989) noted, that CMC may "promote efficiency
at the expense of social contact" (p. 221). Nevertheless, it is unlikely that

many in contemporary society find the values explicit in Chesebro and Bonsall's statement antagonistic. Should all communication be for the purpose of social contact? Not likely. What is compelling about CMC, though, is that it brings us a form of efficient social contact: It rolls efficiency and social contact into one.

I believe that an important point, for it speaks to the issue of community formation in a postmodern world. CMC allows us to customize our social contacts from fragmented communities and to plan, organize, and make efficient our social contacts. Few have studied this phenomenon comprehensively (and to be successful it requires truly multi-disciplinary approaches), though a step in the right direction was taken by Linda Harasim, editor of the anthology *Global Networks.* Harasim (1993) found that social communication is a primary component of CMC and is well able to organize thoughts about the use of CMC around social, rather than solely, work functions. Nevertheless, none of those contributing to the anthology she edited probed satisfactorily into the nature of CMC's social use, preferring to claim, in the final analysis, that we simply seek community by whatever means it is available.

This is true, particularly insofar as we seek community in other places as it dissolves in the spaces we physically inhabit. That dissolution is what caused Schuler (1996, and others like him but not involved in CMC, Robert Bellah, for instance) to call for the rebuilding of communities. It should not be a surprise that technology has found a useful tool for that rebuilding. Forceful arguments about the ways technology shapes social relations have been made by numerous social scientists and philosophers, including Lewis Mumford (1934) and Marshall McLuhan. Mumford in particular noted a shift in society's interests, away from the abstraction of time and space and toward a desire to *use* space and time. CMC gives us a tool with which to use space for communication.

CMC, of course, is not just a tool; it is at once technology, medium, and engine of social relations. As Terry and Calvert (1997) noted,

> Defining technology strictly in terms of objects, such as tools, machines, and appliances, implies fundamental (but ultimately illusory) distinctions between the technology, its designer, and its user. In this formulation of the term, technology, then, has been described as neutral and autonomous, having no inherent or built-in moral or political qualities. In other words a tool can be used for good or for bad. (p. 3)

CMC not only structures social relations, it is the space within which the relations occur and the tool individuals use to enter that space. Consequently it is more than the context within which social relations occur (though it is that, too) for it is commented on and imaginatively constructed by symbolic processes initiated and maintained by individuals and groups, via software and hardware designed and modified by numerous people. Likely this is the genesis of the "consensual hallucination" for which William Gibson coined the term *cyberspace*. The emphasis is on "consensual" rather than "hallucination" in regard to that conception of space, for it is no more hallucinatory to think of space in CMC than it is to think of spaces beyond our immediate perception.

But is it even possible to pin down space to any particular definition? As Benedikt (1991) correctly observed, "space, for most of us, hovers between ordinary, physical existence and something other" (p. 125). Where we find it hovering is, as Edward Soja (1989) noted, in

> socially produced space, [where] spatiality can be distinguished from the physical space of material nature and the mental space of cognition and representation, each of which is used and incorporated into the construction of spatiality but cannot be conceptualized as its equivalent. (p. 120)

The importance of CMC and its attendant social structures lies not only in interpretation and narrative, acts that can fix and structure and are ones with which CMC users are constantly engaged but in the sense of mobility with which one can move (narratively and otherwise) through the social space. Mobility has two meanings in this case. First, it is clearly an ability to "move" from place to place without having physically travelled. But, second, it is also a mobility of status, class, social role, and character. Like the boulevardiers or the denizens of Nevsky Prospect described by Marshall Berman (1982) the citizens of cyberspace (or the "net" as it is commonly called by its evanescent residents) "come here to see and be seen, and to communicate their visions to one another, not for any ulterior purpose, without greed or competition, but as an end in itself" (p. 196). The difference between those on the Net and those on the street is encompassed in a distinction made by Edward Soja (1989). "Just as space, time, and matter delineate and encompass the essential qualities of the physical world, spatiality, temporality, and social being can be seen as the abstract dimensions which together comprise all facets of human existence" (p. 25). In cyber-space, spatiality is largely illusory in its apperception (at least until Gibson's accounts of its visualization are realized), and temporality is problematized by the instantaneity of CMC and the ability to roam the Net with "agents," software constructs that are automated repre-sentatives able to retrieve information, interact on the Net, or both. What is left is social being, and that too is problematic. Is the social actor in cyberspace mass mediated, a mass mediator, a public figure, or a private individual, engaged in close, special interrelation? As Soja saw it in a summary of the dialectic between space and social life,

> The spatio-temporal structuring of social life defines how social action and relationship (including class relations) are materially constituted, made concrete. The constitution/concretization process is problematic, filled with contradiction and struggle (amidst much that is recursive and routinized). Contradictions arise primarily from the duality of produced space as both outcome/embodiment/product and me-dium/presupposition/producer of social activity. (p. 129)

No matter how ill defined the space of cyberspace, the space that we occupy as social beings is as affected by CMC. As Gillespie and Robins (1989) saw it, "New communications technologies do not just impact upon places; places and the social processes and social relationships they embody also affect how such technological systems are designed, imple-mented and used" (p. 7).

Soja's (1989) comments and the questions that arise from them speak to the heart of the many contradictions and problems embodied in CMC. On the one hand, it appears to foster community, or at least the sense of community, among its users. On the other hand, it embodies the imper-sonal communication of the computer and of the written word, the "kind of imitation talking" Walter Ong (1982, p. 102) aptly described. In that fashion, CMC wears on its sleeve the most important dichotomy Joli Jensen identified in her book *Redeeming Modernity*. Jensen (1990) wrote that traditional life supposedly "was marked by face-to-face, intimate relationships among friends, while modern life is characterized by dis-tant, impersonal contact among strangers. Communities are defined as shared, close, and intimate, while societies are defined as separate, distanced, and anonymous" (p. 71). Can CMC be understood to build communities and form a part of the conduct of public life, as other forms of communication seem to, or does CMC problematize our very notions of community and public life? CMC may yet be the clearest evidence of James Beniger's (1987) "pseudo-community," part of the "reversal of a centuries-old trend from organic community—based on interpersonal relationships—to impersonal association integrated by mass means" (p. 369). Even if it is, the most important question is: How is it that a mass medium can be so closely related to (in some cases equated with) a community?

A danger in our assessment of cyberspace and cyberspatial social relations is the implacability of Carey and Quirk's "mythos of the electronic revolution" previously mentioned. For instance, Michael Benedikt (1991) has claimed that in cyberspace, "to which every computer is a window, seen or heard objects are neither physical nor, necessarily, representations of physical objects but are, rather, in form, character and action, made up of data, of pure information" (pp. 122-123). It is important to remind oneself that computer data are essentially binary information based on the manipulation of strings of ones and zeros, themselves no more "physical" than our imagination allows them to be. In the operation of an audio compact disc player the compact disc's bits of information are decoded by the player and converted to sound waves representative of (and analogous to) the sound waves encoded during recording. The sound retains "high fidelity," faithfulness to that which was recorded, thanks largely to the enormous quantities of information encoded by the disc. The more information, the higher the fidelity, but the limit is finite: No amount of information will make the original, recorded sound. In the operation of cyberspatial social relations, bits of information are decoded by users and converted to analogues of mediated and interpersonal social relations. The danger lies in the sense that cyberspatial social relations maintain "high fidelity" to those analogues. First, there is no prerequisite for such a homology. Second, any presupposition of a homology also assumes and fixes the rebirth of prior social relations, engineered along with the machines that make them palpable.

The importance of the disappointment engineered communities have brought cannot be understated. We can no more "build" communities than we can "make" friends; or, at least, as David Harvey (1989) pointed out, "the potential connection between projects to shape space and encourage spatial practices . . . and political projects . . . can be at best conserving and at worst downright reactionary in their implications" (p. 277). Harvey followed Heidegger up to his connections to fascism, a condition the Internet generally has avoided (at least socially), but his points, particularly as they concern political life, ought to be heeded by CMC users. Definitions of community largely have centered around the unproblematized notion of place, a "where" that social scientists can observe, visit, stay and go, engage in participant observation. They have relied, as Lotfalian (1996) claimed, on terms

> that refer to group dynamics such as assimilation, acculturation, adaptation, and participation [and] to the opposite: expulsion, expatriation, and exile. [On-line] the terms used for indicating communities are different, such as posting, cross-posting, reading, lurking, and flaming, which don't imply being part of a whole. (p. 118)

Traditionally, the observations of social scientists largely have been formed by examination of events, artifacts, and social relations within distinct geographic boundaries. The manifestation of political struggle as boundaries shift, break apart, and re-form largely has been overlooked and is hard in some sense to "look at," for, as Lotfalian noted, on-line groups "interact in a mode that is hieroglyphic," a mode in which "the object of interaction is treated as confrontation, and it is rhizomatic in the sense that there is no beginning and no end" (p. 118). Sandy Stone's (1991) definitions of virtual communities and virtual space are most helpful, as for her they are, "incontrovertibly social spaces in which people still meet face-to-face, but under new definitions of both 'meet' and 'face' . . . [V]irtual communities [are] passage points for collections of common beliefs and practices that united people who were physically separated" (p. 85). Thus cyberspace hasn't a "where" (though there are "sites" or "nodes" at which users gather). Rather, the space of cyberspace is predicated on knowledge and information, on the common beliefs and practices of a society abstracted from physical space. Part of that knowledge and information, though, lies in simply knowing how to navigate cyberspace. But the important element in cyberspatial social relations is the sharing of information. It is not sharing in the sense of the *transmission* of information that binds communities in cyberspace. It is the *ritual* sharing of information (Carey, 1989) that pulls it together. That sharing creates the second kind of community Carey identified as arising from the growth of cities during the late 19th and early 20th century, the one formed by imaginative diaspora—cosmopolitans and the new professionals who lived in the imaginative worlds of politics, art, fashion, medicine, law and so forth. These diasporic groups were twisted and knotted into one another within urban life. They were given form by the symbolic interactions of the city and the ecology of media, who reported on and defined these groups to one another, fostered and intensified antagonisms among them, and sought forms of mutual accommodation. (p. 178)

Such a formation is recurring in the discourse within CMC and without it, in the conversations its participants have on-line and off and in the media coverage of electronic communication, electronic communities, and virtual reality.

The Community
Along the Highway

In *The Postmodern Condition* geographer and theorist David Harvey (1989) referred frequently to "time-space compression: . . . processes that so revolutionize the objective qualities of space and time that we are forced to alter, sometimes in quite radical ways, how we represent the world to ourselves" (p. 240). Harvey found such compression central to understanding the now commonplace (and perhaps dated) concepts of the world as a "global village" or "spaceship earth." As part of his analysis of shifts in the history of capitalism, he identified a change in spatial organization from feudal to Renaissance Europe. As regards the former, he wrote,

In the relatively isolated worlds . . . of European feudalism, place assumed a definite legal, political, and social meaning indicative of a relative autonomy of social relations and of community inside roughly given territorial boundaries. . . . External space was weakly grasped and generally conceptualized as a mysterious cosmology populated by some external authority, heavenly hosts, or more sinister figures of myth and imagination. (pp. 240-241)

Meaghan Morris (1992) has criticized Harvey's reduction of complex problems to simple dualities. In particular, Morris wrote,

> Global problems are posed with a sense of urgency verging on moral panic, but then existing practical experiments in dealing with these on a plausible scale are dismissed for the usual vices ("relativisim," "defeatism"), reclassified as what they contest ("postmodernism"), or altogether ignored. (pp. 271-272)

Still, at least two points Harvey made are important for the study of CMC and community. First, external space is in some sense no more firmly grasped today, though it is conceptualized in a variety of ways linked to objective representation via maps, photographs, and other visual media. Second, the relative autonomy of which Harvey (1989) spoke has given way since the Renaissance "to the direct influence of [the] wider world through trade, intra-territorial competition, military action, the inflow of new commodities, of bullion and the like" (p. 244). Social isolation becomes a difficult proposition for any contemporary community. Computer-mediated communities are in a sense "practical experiments" dealing with "global problems," and Morris's critique was all the more sharp as she pointed out Harvey's fallacy that "geographically 'global' space requires a philosophically *transcendent* space of analysis" (p. 273). Which of these spaces, if any (or all), is to be addressed in studies of CMC?

It is clear that studies of community have embedded a similar fallacy. The study of community followed a course similar to that which Harvey (1989) described and Morris critiqued as it evolved from attempts to describe and "write" communities in an isolated (almost antispatial) fashion to attempts to grapple with the complexities of overlapping and interlinked communities.

Assessing the history of community studies, one finds that space was understood less as socially produced and more as that which produced social relations. So, for instance, Stacey (1974) identified the threads running through definitions of community in the sociological study of community. These include territory, social system, and sense of belonging. The first element, territory, however, is meant as a boundary within which a community maintains the other two elements. Similarly, Bell and Newby (1974) identified a variety of elements present in most definitions of community; social interaction based on geographic area, self-sufficiency, common life, consciousness of a kind, and possession of common ends, norms, and means. Bell and Newby also included ideas about social systems, individuality, totality of attitudes and process as commonalities in approaches to community studies.

The most useful deconstruction of conceptions of community came from Effrat (1974) who categorized three main ones:

1. Community as solidarity institutions
2. Community as primary interaction
3. Community as institutionally distinct groups

Effrat's categories betray not only a western, sociological bias (which she admits), as a branch of an "instrumentalist" perspective, based on involvement and interaction. The roots may well be in the Chicago School of Sociology, but the concepts are easier to measure than those of community, which are best qualitatively described. Such a perspective stems also from one of the earliest community studies, Lloyd Warner's (1963)*Yankee City*, which Warner claimed would cross-sectionally represent American communities. The desire driving these studies is that of the social scientist who seeks to generalize from conditions of study as close to the "laboratory" as possible. Schuler (1996) similarly identified what he termed "core values of the new community": conviviality and culture; education; strong democracy; health and well-being; economic equity, opportunity, and sustainability, and; information and communication (pp. 12-13). I cannot imagine one would argue against these generalized categories. But it is difficult to define them and measure them in life on-line and off-line. And it is equally difficult to determine their place in the relation between the self and others. In terms of Etzioni's (1991) "I and We" paradigm, based on

> the idea that both individual and community have a basic moral standing; neither is secondary or derivative. To stress the interlocking, mutually dependent relationship of individual and community, and to acknowledge my mentor, Martin Buber, I refer to this synthetic position . . . (the We signifies social, cultural and political, hence historical and institutional forces, which shape the collective factor—the community). (p. 137)

Etzioni set out three criteria with which to focus community: scope, substance, and dominance (pp. 144-149). Each criterion focused too, in its way, on the argument Calhoun (1980) made that,

> We need to develop a conceptualization of community which allows
> us to penetrate beneath simple categories . . . to see a variable of social
> relations. The relationship between community as a complex of social
> relationships and community as a complex of ideas and sentiments has
> been little explored. (p. 107)

The former has been an element of CMC study from the start. Some of the
earliest ideas about CMC recognize that computer-mediated community
will affect our considerations of space. As Licklider and Taylor saw it in
1968,

> What will on-line interactive communities be like? In most fields they
> will consist of geographically separated members, sometimes grouped
> in small cluster and sometimes working individually. They will be
> communities not of common location, but of *common interest.* In each
> geographical sector, the total number of users . . . will be large enough
> to support extensive general-purpose information processing and stor-
> age facilities . . . life will be happier for the on-line individual because
> the people with whom one interacts most strongly will be selected more
> by commonality of interests and goals than by accidents of proximity.
> (pp. 30-31)

The relation between "fields" and "interests" is not questioned in that
article, nor is the connection between "common interest" and Calhoun's
concept of "community as a complex of ideas and sentiments" followed
up, but of greater importance is the belief that "accidents of proximity"
lead one to be unhappy. Serendipity in its usual sense plays no part in
either world Licklider and Taylor described, only a kind of will to interact
among others with (undefined) "common interests" is operational. Yet
geography does play a role, for it at the very least serves as the site and
center of machines that they state will serve us as we escape the social
constraints location has placed on us.

Jan Walls (1993) in an essay on global networks attempted to subdi-
vide community into those that are "relationship-focused" and those
that are "task-focused." That subdivision only provides insight into the
functions of particular user groups rather than into the connections
between users and hardly accounts for Calhoun's (1980) conception of
community. Howard Frederick (1993) borrowed from Harasim's (1993)
concept of "networlds" and Rheingold's (1993) notion of "virtual com-

munities" to identify "nonplace" communities. None of these all-too-brief forays into CMC and community hit the mark. What is missing is the concomitant conceptualization of space and the social, the inquiry into connections between social relations, spatial practice, values, and beliefs. The ability to create, maintain, control space (whatever we call it—virtual, nonplace, networld) links us to notions of power and necessarily to issues of authority, dominance, submission, rebellion, and cooptation, notions Etzioni established as primary criteria and concerns of community. Just because the spaces with which we are now concerned are electronic, there is not a guarantee that they are democratic, egalitarian, or accessible, and it is not the case that we can forego asking in particular about substance and dominance.

Concerns about these issues not only have been underrepresented in the study of CMC. They also have been lost in community studies. In his classic study of communities and social change in America, Thomas Bender (1978) critiqued community sociology as the study of "locality-based action" that emphasizes territory at the expense of culture:

> The identification of community with locality and communal experiences with rather casual associations has quietly redefined community in a way that puts it at odds with its historical and popular meaning . . . drain[ing] the concept of the very qualities that give the notion of community cultural, as opposed to merely organizational, significance. (p. 10)

For Bender, communities are defined not as places but as social networks, a definition useful for the study of community in cyberspace for two reasons. First, it focuses on the interactions that create communities. Second, it focuses away from place. In media that shift not only the sense of space but the sense of place, decentering (though not removing) the consideration of territory is necessary to permit entry of notions of power and its analysis.

Pseudo-Community and the Decentering of Place

Several authors, most notably James Beniger (1987) and Scott Peck (1987), have written about pseudo-community, "the great societal transformations of the 19th century . . . a sharp drop in interpersonal control of individual behavior: from traditional communal relationships (*gemeinschaft*) to impersonal, highly restricted association or *gesellschaft* . . . from face-to-face to indirect or symbolic group relations" (Beniger, 1987, p. 353). Beniger borrowed from Ferdinand Tonnies's (1967) work to bring the distinctions between *gemeinschaft* and *gesellschaft* into a discussion of mass-mediated discourse. For Beniger, a pseudo-community is one in which impersonal associations constitute simulated personalized communication, what he calls "a hybrid of interpersonal and mass communication" (p. 369). His and Peck's criticisms of pseudo-community centered on the insincerity (or inauthenticity) of communication it represents and the goals toward which that communication may be directed. It is natural that such criticisms ought to be part of an awareness of CMC, for it is, to say the least, difficult to judge sincerity in electronic text. Howard Rheingold (1993) asked the appropriate questions: Is telecommunication culture capable of becoming something more than what Scott Peck calls a "pseudo-community," where people lack the genuine personal commitments to one another that form the bedrock of genuine community? Or is our notion of "genuine" changing in an age where more people every day live their lives in increasingly artificial environments? New technologies tend to change old ways of doing things. Is the human need for community going to be the next technology commodity? (pp. 60-61). What, for instance, does it mean for off-line community if on-line community really is a substitute for off-line community? Research is beginning to suggest that it is not a substitute (Cody et al., 1997) and that personal traits on-line are very like ones off-line—those who are able to make fast friendships off-line do so on-line and vice versa. But it is not at all clear that on-line communities are therefore inconsequential.

A most important question to ask is whether or not our notions of the "genuine" are changing. One of the measures of genuine community ought to be its relationship to action (political or otherwise). As Charles Taylor (1992) noted in *The Ethics of Authenticity*, political powerlessness feeds alienation from community. Does participation in on-line communities increase or decrease individual's feelings of power? Is it a technology that embodies Taylor's ethic, as its users spin off identities, or one that technologizes and reduces that ethic, by problematizing identity and, with it, authenticity? To answer that question it is necessary to define just what would constitute on-line political and personal action.

The connections between computer-mediated community and the social and political worlds' users are part of off-line are unclear, much like the connections between advertising and consumer behavior or television and its direct effects. Moreover, it is important not to slide by questions of access to computer-mediated communities, as they are related to power. As Robert Doolittle (1972) has noted, the rhetorical and political elements that most often constitute communities include common understandings that action and effort will lead to the realization of achievements for the common good. The situation in which we find computer-mediated communities at present is that their very definition as communities is perceived as a "good thing," creating a solipsistic and self-fulfilling community that pays little attention to political action outside of that which secures its own maintenance. Community and power do not necessarily intersect, but such solipsism is a form of power itself, wielded by those who occupy the community. Anne Branscomb (1993) has pointed out, "More important than the substance of the legal rules that are likely to arise governing electronic communications is the question of what group will determine which laws or operating rules shall apply" (p. 99). Part of what is already occurring is the creation of multitechno or cultural groups that determine operating rules for their own domain. But what is occurring in addition as the Internet and other computer networks sprout commercial nodes is the agglomeration of capital and its concomitant pressures on groups that already have power. Oscar Gandy, Jr. (1995), pointed out in a well-written and sharply critical essay titled "It's Discrimination, Stupid!" that the creation and identification of communities based on common interests often is based on the classification of people "in terms of their abilities and disabilities, and increasingly in terms of their medical status" (p. 43) and just as often by automated procedures that rely on information gathering, marketing, and statistical analysis. The arguments those groups (and others) often marshal to persuade government, industry, and citizens that computer networks must remain "free" are based on the very idea that it is only for lack of constraint that community could exist via CMC, but the arguments are often, at best, self-serving and, at worst, exploitative. Community itself is a structuring concept and a strong one given the almost primordial pull of symbolic force the word *community* continues to have. It is as useful for industry as it is for society.

Community as
Culturally-Constructed Category

Creating and maintaining community has traditionally been valued as a commendable goal. Bell and Newby (1974) wrote that " 'community' was thought to be a good thing, its passing was to be deplored, feared and regretted" (p. 21). That theoretical inheritance was brought, and left behind, by modernism and in some ways is thus part of postmodernism too. Its importance is clear from the continued rhetorical use of community in social planning and the strength of persuasion the term *community* contains. In her book *Redeeming Modernity*, Joli Jensen (1990), borrowing from Robert Nisbet, identified "the community/society dichotomy [that] references social relations," and claimed that "what is at stake in this dichotomy, in American social thought, is the issue of connection— how we are to link up to each other in America" (p. 71). Jensen's questions about the ties that bind us ought to be asked in light of CMC. How is computer-mediated communication to link us up?

We have some answers insofar as links already have been made and others are envisioned. The scholarly literature examining CMC is expanding, as scholars in various fields probe and examine the nature of this form of communication. What can be learned from these forays that seek to assess not only the present state of CMC but its future?

Several threads, or categories, emerge from a close reading of the literature, predicated on the notion of CMC's effects on social relations. The CMC, it is claimed, will

1. create opportunities for education and learning;
2. create new opportunities for participatory democracy;
3. establish countercultures on an unprecedented scale;
4. ensnarl already difficult legal matters concerning privacy, copyright, and ethics; and
5. restructure man and machine interaction.

The unifying principal among these claims is that organizational change will precipitate their occurrence. As Carolyn Marvin (1988) noted in her brilliant study of the earliest electrical communication devices, *When Old Technologies Were New*, assumptions about technological change tell us what we believe the technology is supposed to do, which in turn reveals much about what we believe *we* are supposed to do. It would seem, then, that rather than reinvent or recreate social relations or even reexamine culturally constructed definitions of community we already have, we believe we are supposed to reorganize social relations around a new technology.

The most important reorganization is the force with which the ideal of face-to-face communication is brought to the center of arguments about the structure of communication technology. Some evidence of this is found in the use of terms like *interactivity* to describe (and promote) new technology that allows for user feedback. As Rafaeli (1988) saw it,

> Interactivity is generally assumed to be a natural attribute of face-to-face conversation, but it has been proposed to occur in mediated communication settings as well.
>
> [I]nteractivity is an expression of the extent that in a given series of communication exchanges, any third (or later) transmission (or message) is related to the degree to which previous exchanges referred to even earlier transmissions. . . . This complex and ambitious definition misrepresents the intuitive nature of interactivity. In fact, the power of the concept and its attraction are in the matter-of-factness of its nature. The common feeling is that interactivity, like news, is something you know when you see it. (pp. 110-111)

Rafaeli went on to criticize the use of interactivity as a "buzzword," but does not overlook a fundamental question: Why should face-to-face communication serve as an ideal? The most likely answer is that it is a form of communication we identify and associate with community, with *gemeinschaft*, and face-to-interface communication we associate with the impersonal communication Beniger (1987) decried has led to "pseudo-community."

Yet Michael Schudson (1978) has noted that,

> When we criticize the reality of the mass media, we do so by opposing it to an ideal of conversation which we are not inclined to examine. We are not really interested in what face-to-face communication is like; rather, we have developed a notion that all communication *should* be like a certain model of conversation, whether that model really exists or not. (p. 323)

Computer-mediated communication permits us the "feeling" that Rafaeli emphasized, but we are too media-savvy to be misled to believe that CMC has achieved the face-to-face ideal. Indeed, Schudson noted, the face-to-face ideal is

> in part a consequence of mass media. . . . First, the mass media have contributed to making the "egalitarian" criterion of ideal communication more prominent and more possible to realize. . . . The mass media have had a second effect in making the conversational ideal more frequently realizable. (p. 326)

We have been accustomed to imagining an "other," and most often not as an individual but rather as a group, be it an audience, a market, or a community. That is the context of mass media consumption and, as Foster (1997) found, of CMC: "The context of CMC necessarily emphasizes the act of imagination that is required to summon the image of communion with others who are often faceless, transient, or anonymous" (p. 25). Healy (1997) called the Internet a "middle landscape" that allows individuals to exercise their impulses for both separation and connectedness" (p. 66). We thus totter between belief that CMC will, to borrow from Marshall McLuhan, "retribalize" us by providing for us a technologized, but nevertheless ideal, form of communication we have found lacking and belief that our interaction will become mechanized and hollow, without the "richness" of face-to-face conversation. It is important to note that even in face-to-face interaction much of what is most valuable is the absence of information, the silence and pauses between words and phrases. Cohen (1985) also critiqued the idyllic (and often romantic) view of face-to-face interaction:

> The idea that, in small-scale society, people interact with each other as "whole persons" is a simplification. They may well encounter each other more frequently, more intensively and over a wider range of activities than is the case in more anonymous large-scale milieux. But this is not to say that people's knowledge of "the person" overrides their perception of the distinctive activities (or "roles") in which the person is engaged. (p. 29)

We are reassured by the belief that the reality our eyes perceive in face-to-face communication is more real (or less manipulable) than other media by which we perceive reality. That belief reasserts itself in the understanding we have that what mediated reality lacks is sufficient "richness" to convey nonmediated reality. Each belief fuels the bias toward filling cyberspace with information and gives rise to two distinct ideas: First, unused space is wasteful and, second, more information is desirable and better. The trend in CMC, as in other areas of computing, has been to provide greater speed and more levels of organization to cope with that bias, and CMC has been viewed from the perspective of organizational communication scholarship for quite some time. That perspective brings a bias, which I will examine in a moment. Regarding community most directly, though, the bias most readily discernible is toward the removal of boundaries. And yet, as Cohen (1985) noted, it is "boundary [that] encapsulates the identity of the community" (p. 12). Face-to-face interaction does not necessarily break down boundaries, and to adopt it as an ideal will likewise not necessarily facilitate communication, community building, or understanding among people.

Computer-Mediated Communication and Organization

Although the study of organizational communication has begun to intersect with community studies, particularly in the field of health communication, it has long had connections to CMC. Much of the literature that examines CMC is from an organizational perspective, from studies of the introduction of computers in the workplace. The work of Ron Rice (1984, 1987, 1989; Rice & Love, 1987; Rice & McDaniel, 1987) as well as that of Lee Sproull and Sara Kiesler (1991) is exemplary and developed ideas about the changes electronic mail brings to organizations. The main body of their scholarship examined patterns of interaction and communication through telecommuting, teleconferencing, e-mail, and the like, and asked questions about management, work, and the future of traditional organizational structures unbound from "the conventional patterns of who talks to whom and who knows what" (Sproull & Kiesler, 1991, p. 116).

There are two key elements to this form of analysis of CMC. First, it assumes that distance and space are to be centrally overcome and controlled, not in the sense that an individual is to control them but in the sense that a technology centrally and universally used will permit "almost unlimited access to data and to other people" (Sproull & Kiesler,

1991, p. 116). Almost in the same breath, however, Sproull and Kiesler argued for centralized oversight and control of access, claiming,

> It is up to management to make and shape connections. The organiza-
> tion of the future will depend significantly not just on how the technol-
> ogy of networking evolves but also on how managers seize the oppor-
> tunity it presents for transforming the structure of work. (p. 123)

The issue, however, is less changes to "the structure of work" and more the control of access to information and people. That access is based on two principal assumptions about the use of computers found in many analyses of CMC: (a) Computers cut across or break down boundaries, and (b) computers break down hierarchies. Both of these assumptions are based on the idea that modifications to present social systems and reactions to social concerns can be best achieved by using a new technology on old problems. It is not unusual to find such assumptions when any new technology is put to use, as Marvin (1988) noted. Similarly, Hiltz and Turoff (1978) noted in relation to electronic mail that there is a tendency to view new technology as simply a more efficient method or tool for confronting or improving an existing technology or situation.

And yet computers just as easily create boundaries and hierarchies. As Andrew Ross (1990) pointed out in a terrific essay, there is a "tendency to use technology to form information elites" (p. 15), and evidence of such formations can be found in the romanticizing of the hacker as a countercultural hero, in the elevation of privacy as a critical issue for computer users and in the fervor with which PGP (Pretty Good Privacy) and other data encryption devices are being adopted, as mechanisms for access to encryption keys are being sought by government agencies.

The speed with which we may form new hierarchies and reorganize existing ones, particularly such as those formed in interactive text media, does little to mitigate the fact that they are indeed present. They may rise and fall more quickly, but they are just as ubiquitous. Howard Rheingold (1993) went so far as to determine that computer-mediated communities will "grow into much larger networks over the next twenty years" (p. 58) but does not question or examine how that growth will be accompanied by structuring and hierarchies created within networks.

Indeed, it is difficult to understand just how hierarchy and community can coexist via CMC, in part because of the seemingly anarchic (or at least unstructured) nature of many computer networks. A common denominator linking hierarchy and community is identity, not only in terms of one's sense of self but also in terms of one's sense of others. The CMC provides ample room for identity but not for its fixing and structuring. Ross (1990) noted that, "Access to digital systems still requires only the authentication of a signature or pseudonym, not the identification of a real surveillable person, so there exists a crucial operative gap between authentication and identification" (p. 24). As others have pointed out, from varied perspectives on CMC (MacKinnon, 1995; Turkle 1995), one can have multiple identities in cyberspace; moreover, one can shift identities rather easily, taking on characteristics of others' identities. Issues of identity ought to be front-and-center with those of community as CMC develops. As Cheney (1991) correctly claimed, "one's identity is somehow related to the larger social order. However [there is] disagree[ment] . . . on what kind of relationship this entails" (p. 10). Most important is that identity is related directly to the increase in size of social organizations. The necessity to "keep track" of individuals by way of Social Security numbers and other bureaucratic devices that connect an individual to a larger entity makes identification a matter of organization too, rather than only a matter of self-definition. Cheney's comment that "there has been a transformation of the term 'identity' from its 'sameness' meaning to its 'essence' meaning" (p. 13) is significant precisely because identity as mediated in cyberspace carries no essential meanings. Alliances based on a "sameness" may form and dissolve. Yet the ideas Cheney borrowed from Burke that assisted him to develop a definition of identity "associated with the individual that must draw upon social and collective resources for its meaning" (p. 20) do not apply equally in CMC, as it is possible to use similar resources to develop and structure meaning but without the affective alliances Cheney implied are necessary.

Rheingold (1993) attempted to define how identity will be constructed via CMC:

> We reduce and encode our identities as words on a screen, decode and unpack the identities of others. The way we use these words, the stories (true and false) we tell about ourselves (or about the identity we want people to believe us to be) is what determines our identities in cyberspace. The aggregation of personae, interacting with each other, determines the nature of the collective culture. (p. 61)

One might suppose the same is true about the aggregation of particular traits that determine the nature of the individual. Nevertheless, the symbolic processes Rheingold elided through use of such words as *encode* and *unpack* (words that are also part of the language of computer software) are fraught with unproblematized assumptions about the work humans perform in search of their own identities and those of others. Interaction ought not be substituted for community, or, for that matter for communication, and to uncritically accept connections between personae, individuals and community is inadvisable. An important point to remember is one that Wellman (1997) made, that many of our on-line relationships are embedded in one's off-line. The increased use of technology in the workplace and in school means that CMC in many ways exists side-by-side with social relationships already formed and that relationships formed only on-line develop differently or just more slowly than others.

It will be unfortunate if we do not make attempts to understand CMC as a social technology alongside other social activities and relationships and if we uncritically accept that CMC will usher in the great new era that other media of communication have failed to bring us. It is not, as virtual reality pioneer Jaron Lanier said in an interview, that television has failed us because it "wasn't planned well enough" ("Virtual Reality," 1992, p. 6), it is that organization and planning are not necessarily appropriate processes for constructing or recapturing the sense of community for which we are nostalgic. Thomas Bender (1978) sharply criticized those who seek "to recapture community by imputing it to large-scale organizations and to locality-based social activity regardless of the quality of human relationships that characterize these contexts" (p. 143). Instead, Bender found community in the midst of a transformation and asked us to heed his call that we not, by way of our nostalgia, limit definitions of community to that which "seventeenth-century New Englanders knew" (p. 146).

Of course, it is difficult to imagine what new on-line communities may be like, and it is far easier to use our memories and myths as we construct them. As Willson-Quayle (1997) put it in regard to democracy, "the effect of computer technology on democratic politics will be more a matter of degree rather than kind" (p. 241). Likely the same is true for its effect on community. What is important to understand is that the construction we are undertaking is peculiar and particular to the computer. Because these machines are seen as "linking" machines (they link information, data, communication, sound, image, through the common language of digital encoding), they inherently affect the ways we think of linking up to each other, and thus they fit squarely into our concerns about community. Media technologies that largely have been tied to the "transportation" view of communication mentioned earlier were developed to overcome space and time. The computer, in particular, is an "efficiency" machine, purporting to ever increase its speed. But unlike those technologies, the computer used for communication is a technology to be understood from the "ritual" view of communication, for once time and space have been overcome (or at least rendered surmountable) the spur for development is connection, linkage. Once we can surmount time and space and "be" anywhere, we must choose a "where" at which to be, and the computer's functionality lies in its power to make us organize our desires about the spaces we visit and stay in. Such organizational work is not easy, and it will take extra effort to not simply let others organize those desires for us.

The manner in which we seek to find community, empowerment, and political action all embedded in our ability to use CMC is troubling. No one medium, no one technology, has been able to provide those elements in combination, and often we have been unable to find them in any media. CMC has potential for a variety of consequences, some anticipated, some not. A critical awareness of the social transformations that have occurred and continue to occur with or without technology will be our best ally as we incorporate CMC into contemporary social life.

References

Barnes, T. J., & Duncan, J. S. (1992). *Writing worlds.* New York: Routledge.

Bell, C., & Newby, H. (1974). *The sociology of community.* London: Frank Cass and Company, Ltd.

Bender, T. (1978). *Community and social change in America.* New Brunswick, NJ: Rutgers University Press.

Benedikt, M. (1991). Cyberspace: Some proposals. In M. Benedikt (Ed.), *Cyberspace* (pp. 119-224). Cambridge: MIT Press.

Beniger, J. (1986). *The control revolution.* Cambridge, MA: Harvard University Press.

Beniger, J. (1987). Personalization of mass media and the growth of pseudo-community. *Communication Research, 14*(3), 352-371.

Berger, P. L., & Luckmann, T. (1967). *The social construction of reality.* New York: Anchor.

Berman, M. (1982). *All that is solid melts into air.* New York: Simon & Schuster.

Branscomb, A. W. (1993). Jurisdictional quandaries for global networks. In L. M. Harasim (Ed.), *Global networks* (pp. 57-80). Cambridge: MIT Press.

Burnett, R. (1996). A torn page, ghosts on the computer screen, words, images, labyrinths: Exploring the frontiers of cyberspace. In G. Marcus (Ed.), *Connected* (pp. 67-98). Chicago, IL: University of Chicago Press.

Calhoun, C. J. (1980). Community: Toward a variable conceptualization for comparative research. *Social History, 5,* 105-129.

Carey, J. (1989). *Communication as culture.* Boston, MA: Unwin Hyman.

Carey, J. (1993). Everything that rises must diverge: Notes on communications, technology and the symbolic construction of the social. In P. Gaunt (Ed.), *Beyond agendas* (pp. 171-184). Westport, CT: Greenwood.

Cheney, G. (1991). *Rhetoric in an organizational society: Managing multiple identities.* Columbia: University of South Carolina Press.

Chesebro, J. W., & Bonsall, D. G. (1989). *Computer-mediated communication.* Tuscaloosa: University of Alabama Press.

Cody, M. J., Wendt, P., Dunn, D., Pierson, J., Ott, J., & Pratt, L. (1997, May). *Friendship formation and creating communities on the Internet: Reaching out to the senior population.* Paper presented at the Annual Meeting of the International Communication Association, Montreal, Canada.

Cohen, A. (1985). *The symbolic construction of community.* London: Tavistock.

Dayan, D., & Katz, E. (1992). *Media events: The live broadcasting of history.* Cambridge, MA: Harvard University Press.

Doheny-Farina, S. (1996). *The wired neighborhood.* New Haven, CT: Yale University Press.

Doolittle, R. J. (1972). *Speech communication as an instrument in engendering and sustaining a sense of community in urban and poor neighborhoods: A study of rhetorical potentialities.* Unpublished doctoral dissertation, Pennsylvania State University, University Park.

Effrat, M. P. (1974). *The community: Approaches and applications.* New York: Free Press.

Etzioni, A. (1991). *The responsive society.* San Francisco: Jossey-Bass.

Fernback, J. (1997). The individual within the collective: Virtual ideology and the realization of collective principles. In S. G. Jones (Ed.), *Virtual culture* (pp. 36-54). London: Sage.

Flusser, V. (1996). Digital appartition. In T. Druckrey (Ed.), *Electronic culture,* (pp. 242-245). New York: Aperture Foundation.

Foster, D. (1997). Community and identity in the electronic village. In D. Porter (Ed.), *Internet culture* (pp. 23-38). New York: Routledge.

Frederick, H. (1993). Computer networks and the emergence of global civil society. In L. M. Harasim (Ed.), *Global networks* (pp. 283-296). Cambridge: MIT Press.

Gandy, O., Jr. (1995). It's discrimination, stupid! In J. Brook & I. A. Boal (Eds.), *Resisting the virtual life* (pp. 35-48). San Francisco: City Lights Books.

Gillespie, A., & Robins, K. (1989). Geographical inequalities: The spatial bias of the new communications technologies. *Journal of Communication, 39*(3), 7-18.

Harasim, L. M. (Ed.). (1993). *Global networks.* Cambridge, MA: The MIT Press.

Harvey, D. (1989). *The condition of postmodernism.* Cambridge, MA: Blackwell.

Healy, D. (1997). Cyberspace and place: The Internet as middle landscape on the electronic frontier. In D. Porter (Ed.), *Internet culture* (pp. 55-72). New York: Routledge.

Hiltz, S. R., & Turoff, M. (1978). *The network nation: Human communication via computer.* Reading, MA: Addison-Wesley.

Jenkins, H., & Fuller, M. (1995). Nintendo and new world travel writing: A dialogue. In S. Jones (Ed.), *CyberSociety: Computer-mediated communication and community* (pp. 57-72). Thousand Oaks, CA: Sage.

Jensen, J. (1990). *Redeeming modernity.* Thousand Oaks, CA: Sage.

Jones, S. (1993). A sense of space: Virtual reality, authenticity and the aural. *Critical Studies in Mass Communication, 10*(3), 238-252.

Licklider, J. C. R., & Taylor, R. W. (1968). The computer as a communication device. *Science & Technology, 76,* 21-31.

Lotfalian, M. (1996). A tale of an electronic community. In G. Marcus (Ed.), *Connected* (pp. 117-156). Chicago, IL: University of Chicago Press.

MacKinnon, R. C. (1995). Searching for the Leviathian on Usenet. In S. G. Jones (Ed.), *CyberSociety: Computer-mediated communication and community* (pp. 112-136). Thousand Oaks, CA: Sage.

Marvin, C. (1988). *When old technologies were new.* Oxford, UK: Oxford University Press.

Morris, M. (1992). The man in the mirror: David Harvey's "condition" of post-modernity. *Theory, Culture & Society, 9,* 253-279.

Mumford, L. (1934). *Technics and civilization.* New York: Harcourt, Brace & World.

Nguyen, D. T., & Alexander, J. (1996). The coming of cyberspacetime and the end of the polity. In R. Shields (Ed.), *Cultures of Internet* (pp. 99-124). London: Sage.

Noll, A. M. (1997). *Highway of dreams.* Mahwah, NJ: Lawrence Erlbaum.

Ong, W. (1982). *Orality and literacy.* New York: Methuen.

Patton, P. (1986). *Open road.* New York: Simon & Schuster.

Peck, M. S. (1987). *The different drum: Community-making and peace.* New York: Simon & Schuster.

Quarterman, J. S. (1993). The global matrix of minds. In L. M. Harasim (Ed.), *Global networks* (pp. 35-56). Cambridge: MIT Press.

Rafaeli, S. (1988). Interactivity: From new media to communication. *Sage Annual Review of Communication Research, 16,* 110-134.

Rheingold, H. (1993). A slice of life in my virtual community. In L. M. Harasim (Ed.), *Global networks* (pp. 57-80). Cambridge: MIT Press.

Rice, R. E. (1984). *The new media, communication, research, and technology.* Beverly Hills, CA: Sage.

Rice, R. E. (1987). Computer-mediated communication and organizational innovation. *Journal of Communication, 37*(4), 65-94.

Rice, R. E. (1989). Issues and concepts in research on computer-mediated communication systems. In J. A. Anderson (Ed.), *Communication yearbook, Vol. 12* (pp. 436-476). Newbury Park, CA: Sage.

Rice, R. E., & Love, G. (1987). Electronic emotion: Socioemotional content in a computer-mediated communication network. *Communication Research, 14,* 85-108.

Rice, R. E., & McDaniel, B. (1987). *Managing organizational innovation: The evolution from word processing to office information systems.* New York: Columbia University Press.

Ross, A. (1990). Hacking away at the counterculture. *Postmodern Culture, 1*(1), 1-43.

Schudson, M. (1978). The ideal of conversation in the study of mass media. *Communication Research, 12*(5), 320-329.

Schuler, D. (1996). *New community networks.* New York: ACM Press.

Schumacher, E. F. (1977). *A guide for the perplexed.* New York: Harper & Row.

Soja, E. (1989). *Postmodern geographies: The reassertion of space in critical social theory.* London: Verso.

Sproull, L., & Kiesler, S. (1991, September). Computers, networks, and work. *Scientific American, 265*(3), 116-123.

Stacey, M. (1974). The myth of community studies. In C. Bell & H. Newby (Eds.), *The sociology of community* (pp. 13-26). London: Frank Cass and Company, Ltd.

Stone, A. R. (1991). Will the real body please stand up?: Boundary stories about virtual cultures. In M. Benedikt (Ed.), *Cyberspace* (pp. 81-118). Cambridge: MIT Press.

Taylor, C. (1992). *The ethics of authenticity.* Cambridge, MA: Harvard University Press.

Terry, J., & Calvert, M. (1997). *Processed lives.* New York: Routledge.

Tonnies, F. (1967). *Community and society.* Lansing: Michigan State University Press.

Turkle, S. (1995). *Life on the screen.* New York: Simon & Schuster.

Virilio, P. (1995). *The art of the motor.* Minneapolis: University of Minnesota Press.

Virtual reality: A new medium and a new culture. (1992, November). *Communique,* p. 6.

Walls, J. (1993). Global networking for local development: Task focus and rela-
    tionship focus in cross-cultural communication. In L. M. Harasim (Ed.),
    Global networks (pp. 153-166). Cambridge: MIT Press.

Warner, L. (1963). *Yankee city.* New Haven, CT: Yale University Press.

Weise, E. R. (1996). A thousand aunts with modems. In L. Cherny & E. R. Weise,
    Wired women, (pp. vii-xv). Seattle, WA: Seal.

Wellman, B. (1997). An electronic group is virtually a social network. In S. Kiesler
    (Ed.), *Cultures of the Internet* (pp. 179-205). Mahwah, NJ: Lawrence Erlbaum.

Willson-Quayle, J. (1997). Cyberspace democracy and social behavior: Reflections
    and refutations. In J. E. Behar (Ed.), *Mapping cyberspace: Social research on the
    electronic frontier* (pp. 229-244). Long Island, NY: Dowling College Press.

2

The Emergence of On-Line Community

Nancy K. Baym

Early scholarship on computer-mediated communication (CMC) was oriented toward organizational uses of computing. The primary questions asked were how CMC could enhance work processes such as group decision making. Conducted primarily in organizations and laboratories, this research generally argued that computers are inherently inhospitable to social relationships. Scholarship has finally caught up with what many users of CMC had long known: Social relationships thrive on-line and have since the beginning of interactive computing. For many observers and participants the word "community" seemed appropriate for the new social realms emerging through this on-line interaction, capturing a sense of interpersonal connection as well as internal organization. Its use has turned out to be more loaded than some of us foresaw. As Fernback (1997) pointed out, "community is a term which seems readily definable to the general public but is infinitely complex and amorphous in academic discourse. It has descriptive, normative, and ideological connotations . . . [and] encompasses both material and symbolic dimensions" (p. 39). Despite—or perhaps because of—the term's intuitive appeal, these normative and ideological connotations have made its use controversial in the academic and popular work surrounding CMC.

It is impossible to assess how many Internet participants consider themselves part of on-line communities, but many clearly invest strong feelings in Usenet newsgroups, mailing lists, chat rooms, MUDs, MOOs, and other forms of on-line groups. Writers who position themselves as participants as well as observers often emphasize emotion in their use of "community." In what is surely the most widely read book on the subject, Rheingold (1993) described virtual communities as "social aggregations that emerge from the Net when enough people carry on those public discussions long enough, with sufficient human feeling, to form webs of personal relationships" (p. 5). Weise's (1996) essay about her introduction to on-line social life exemplifies the emotion-laden sense of belonging people can find. Having just moved to a new city, working nights, and socially isolated, Weise described herself as coming "to the community with a cry of pain, feeling alone and bereft, and these women I did not know sat down beside me and offered comfort, told their own stories" (p. xi). With explicitly familial affection, she titles her tale "A Thousand Aunts With Modems."

Many critics would read Weise's story as grounds to fear on-line community—in life conditions that offered her no locally grounded sense of belonging, on-line interactions with people she might never meet filled that need. The dominant concern underlying most criticism of on-line community is that in an increasingly fragmented off-line world, on-line groups substitute for "real" (i.e., geographically local) community, falling short in several interwoven regards. Lockard (1997), for instance, argued that, "to accept only communication in place of a community's manifold functions is to sell our common faith in community vastly short" (p. 225). The most serious charges against on-line communities are their homogeneity and lack of moral commitment. Most of the Internet is organized by interests, allowing people to form groups based on similarity. Because participants can leave with a mere click, on-line communities "do not oblige their participants to deal with diversity" (Healy, 1997, p. 63). The homogeneity of the Net is further enhanced by the obvious, yet often ignored, fact that most of the world's population have no Internet access and likely never will. The Internet serves less than "one percent of the adult global population" and remains "unknown and irrelevant to daily life in the world-at-large" (Lockard, 1997, p. 228). Healy (1997) and Stratton (1997) located the romance of

Internet community in a nostalgia for the homogenous small town. Stratton wrote that, "the American mytholigization of the Internet as a community represents a nostalgic dream for a mythical early modern community which reasserts the dominance of the white, middle-class male and his cultural assumptions" (p. 271). Lockard (1997) put it more bluntly: "if the offline/black streets have turned mean, go plug into on-line/white optic fiber" (p. 228).

In other words, these critics recast the much lauded levelling of race, social status, and class in CMC (e.g., Hiltz & Turoff, 1978; Kiesler, Siegel, & McGuire, 1984; Rheingold, 1993) as an evasion of the moral responsibility to confront the problems these categories raise off-line (Tabbi, 1997). "Real" community entails more than "the voluntary association of like-minded individuals" (Healy, 1997, p. 61). Doheny-Farina's (1996) statement on community exemplifies these critics' connotations:

> A community is bound by place, which always includes complex social and environmental necessities. It is not something you can easily join. You can't subscribe to a community as you subscribe to a discussion group on the net. It must be lived. It is entwined, contradictory, and involves all our senses. (p. 37)

From this point of view, rather than singing the praises of on-line community, we should be worried that this alternative to an increasingly difficult real world will have deleterious consequences on morality and ethics off-line (Robins, 1995).

These arguments are in essence about whether or not on-line groups deserve the label "community" and how these groups (whatever they should be called) will affect off-line communities. These issues deserve debate. However, there are at least two prior questions on which these debates should be based. First, does on-line community really serve as a substitute for off-line community in any meaningful way? Some evidence points in the opposite direction. Cody et al. (1997) and Joe (1997) have presented research suggesting that those who are lonely off-line remain so on-line, whereas those who plunge into on-line interactions also are highly sociable off-line. For most users, then, on-line communities might well bring community to times when they were previously alone, in effect creating more community without affecting their off-line lives. It is quite likely that on-line time replaces work and television more than time spent with others. Furthermore, as community networks

demonstrate, on-line communities can be used to enhance geographically local communities (e.g., Doheny-Farina, 1996; Schuler, 1996). In
short, whereas theory abounds, we do not have empirical grounds on
which to assess how (or if) on-line community affects off-line community.

The second question is: What occurs on-line that leads some people
to experience them as communities in the first place? Whereas common
interest may well be at play, it is not enough to generate a sense of
community. As anyone who subscribes to multiple mailing lists or reads
several newsgroups can attest, they differ considerably in how much
they feel like a community. Furthermore, some participants in an on-line
group may experience it as community whereas others don't (Ito, 1997).
For all the concern about on-line community, we still have very little
systematic understanding of what happens within on-line groups. This
chapter presents an emergent model of on-line community, which moves
us toward answering this second question.

Though not a direct influence, this model (first proposed in Baym,
1995b) is in line with several recent applications of Benedict Anderson
(1983) to CMC (e.g., Jones, 1997; Stratton, 1997; Tepper, 1997). Anderson
argued that all communities beyond the primal face-to-face are imagined, a process enabled by mass media. Rather than asking whether
on-line communities are authentic, CMC scholars influenced by Anderson have argued for looking at "the style in which they are imagined"
(Anderson, 1983, p. 6). I argue here that an on-line community's "style"
is shaped by a range of preexisting structures, including external contexts, temporal structure, system infrastructure, group purposes, and
participant characteristics. In ongoing communicative interaction, participants strategically appropriate and exploit the resources and rules
those structures offer. The result is a dynamic set of systematic social
meanings that enables participants to imagine themselves as a community. Most significant are the emergence of group-specific forms of
expression, identities, relationships, and normative conventions. To
ground and elaborate each of these points, I integrate my research on the
Usenet newsgroup rec.arts.tv.soaps (r.a.t.s.) with others' analyses of
other on-line groups.

The research reported here comes from a 3-year ethnographic study
of rec.arts.tv.soaps (r.a.t.s.), the newsgroup devoted to the recreational
discussion of daytime soap operas. Usenet links millions of users in an

enormous stream of topical chatter known as newsgroups. There are more than 13,000 hierarchically organized "newsgroups," each of which (at least ostensibly) operates as an open forum for the discussion of a specific interest. The most popular topic by far is sex, but most every other topic shows up somewhere. Discussion takes the form of asynchronous electronic letters (posts), identical to e-mail, which are sent by users from their sites and automatically distributed to the thousands of Usenet sites receiving the group. As I've argued elsewhere (Baym, 1996), the discourse in these posts is a hybrid of interpersonal and mass communication as well as oral and written language. Sites offering Usenet access were once restricted primarily to universities, research laboratories, high-tech companies, and the government, but the recent boom in commercial Internet providers now allows anyone with a computer, a modem, a phone line, and adequate disposable income to participate. In September, 1997, Usenet carried a daily average of 682,144 messages (Erol's, 1997). People access newsgroups through Internet accounts using web browsers or one of a number of programs called "newsreaders" to read the messages and to write their own.

In the early 1990s, when the data considered here were collected, r.a.t.s. consistently ranked as one of the 15 highest-traffic newsgroups, carrying approximately 150 new messages each day (B. Reid, 1993). In the time since, the Internet's traffic has increased exponentially, sex groups have outpaced all the others, and r.a.t.s. has split into three groups: rec.arts.tv.soaps.abc, rec.arts.tv.soaps.cbs, and rec.arts.tv.soaps. misc. These three offshoot groups now carry a daily average of 436 posts—196, 112, and 128 messages, respectively—(Tile.net, 1997). Although soap opera discussion obviously continues to thrive on-line, the three groups that were once r.a.t.s. account for only about 0.06% of Usenet messages.

Sources of Influence on CMC

Several researchers interested in task-oriented uses of CMC have suggested that CMC patterns emerge unpredictably out of complex interactions among five factors: the external contexts in which the use of CMC is set, the temporal structure of the group, the infrastructure of the computer system, the purposes for which CMC is used, and the characteristics of the group and its members (Contractor & Seibold, 1993;

Hollingshead & McGrath, 1995; Seibold, Heller, & Contractor, 1994; Steinfield, 1986). I now address each of these sets of variables.

External Contexts

All interaction, including CMC, is simultaneously situated in multiple external contexts. Rather than disappearing when one logs on, the preexisting speech communities in which interactants operate provide social understandings and practices through and against which interaction in the new computer-mediated context develops. The CMC use always is nested in the national and international cultures of which its participants are members. From this they draw a common language (usually but not always English), common ways of speaking, and a good deal of shared understandings. Turkle (1995) pointed to one kind of shared understanding that enables the possibility of on-line community. She argued that as contemporary computers have gained "personalities," their longtime users have come to share a cultural willingness to engage computerized space as real. Dyrkton (1996) offered a provocative counteranalysis, arguing from his experience of e-mail in Jamaica that some worldviews preclude psychological comfort with on-line interaction. A more specific external context is the overwhelmingly American, generally well-educated, predominantly white, economically comfortable substrata of the population with access to and knowledge of computers who dominate the Internet (and on whom Turkle's research seems to focus). This no doubt limits the extent to which diverse people are thrown together through Usenet interaction, as the previously noted critics argued persuasively.

The immediate situations through which participants come to have their computer network access also can influence the interaction. When the participants in a computer-mediated group are all employees of the same organization or all undergraduates at a large state university, the influences of those subcultures on communication will inevitably remain strong. In short, participants' communicative styles are oriented around common social practices before they even enter into CMC, practices that are unlikely to be supplanted by computer mediation (Contractor & Seibold, 1993).

A sense of the ways in which contexts may affect interaction can be gained from a glance at three contexts surrounding r.a.t.s. These include

the Internet environment, the external environments from which participants draw group-relevant resources, especially the culture of soap
opera fans, and the environments through which the participants gain
Usenet access. The Internet environment provides a terrain in which the
paths of individual participants may cross outside of the group; they
may meet in other newsgroups, on IRC (Internet Relay Chat), through
e-mail, and so on. The broader context of the Internet also provides some
of the group's vocabulary, including an extensive catalogue of acronyms
(among them, IMHO for "In My Humble Opinion" and BTW for "By
The Way"). Many of these acronyms first appeared in collaborative
amateur presses run within fan cultures as early as the 1920s (H. Jenkins,
personal communication, October 13, 1992). R.a.t.s. also adopts
behavioral norms from Usenet culture, including conventions about
when to quote previous messages when responding to them and how to
edit those quotes. I will return to norms and vocabulary in the discussion
of emergent social meanings in CMC.

Although it is nearly impossible to determine the demographics of
Usenet participants, there is little question that they are predominantly
male. Savicki, Lingenfelter, and Kelley (1996), working with the large
Project-H database of Usenet newsgroups, found 73% of their sample
posters were male. The r.a.t.s. participants, in contrast, are overwhelmingly female. This is, no doubt, due to the fact that they are also participants in soap opera fan culture (or fandom), a predominantly female
subculture. This external subculture of soap opera fandom is of fundamental importance to the interaction on r.a.t.s. It provides a wealth of
resources and practices with which participants organize their talk.
Being a soap opera fan involves more than faithful viewing. Soap fans
are especially involved viewers, many have watched the same shows for
more than 20 years. They support an entire soap opera industry, including not just the production of the soaps but also several magazines,
merchandising operations, dozens of fan clubs, prime-time awards
shows, celebrity public appearances, charity events across America, and
even cruises with the stars. Fans vary in the extent to which they take
advantage of all of these options. When hundreds of these fans are
brought together, as they are on r.a.t.s., information drawn from all these
sources is pooled. One communicative practice on r.a.t.s. that emerges
as a direct consequence of soap fandom is the sharing of news culled
from these many resources. By the same token, one of the concerns the

soap press has raised about the Internet is its potential to diffuse false rumors (thereby ensuring a continuing role for the official press). Another informative communication practice on r.a.t.s., which is directly related to soap operas, is the daily "updates" that retell in extraordinary detail what happened on the shows (see Baym, 1995c for a more extensive discussion of updates).

In addition to providing informative practices, the context of soap opera fandom also provides interpretive practices that are central to the communication in r.a.t.s. These include identifying with characters, bringing the real world to bear on interpreting storylines, speculating on the meaning of soap opera events, and criticizing the show. Interpretation of the characters' behavior and psyches is the most common activity on r.a.t.s. (Baym, 1993). Soap operas present communities of as many as 40 characters, many of whom have been on the shows for years. The fans find most characters interesting, they identify with some, they hate others, they love hating some. Of importance, they come to care about what happens to them, and they see and interpret the story through characters' perspectives (Livingstone, 1990). In order to interpret character psyches and see things from their perspectives, participants must draw on their own interpersonal and emotional experiences as well as other areas of expertise. Because soap characters live in a world where life is focused always on the personal, the familial, the relational, and, above all, the emotional, viewers must bring their own knowledge of these realms to bear on interpretation. The viewers' relationship with characters, the viewers' understanding of social-emotional experience, and soap opera's narrative structure, in which moments of maximal suspense are always followed by temporal gaps, work together to ensure that fans will use the gaps during and between shows to discuss with one another possible outcomes and possible interpretations of what has been seen (Allen, 1985; Ang, 1985; Brunsdon, 1989; Geraghty, 1991; Nochimson, 1992). When fans use r.a.t.s. for such discussions, they rely on preexisting practices of soap fandom.

A third context that influenced r.a.t.s. at the time this study was conducted was that participants accessed r.a.t.s. through personal accounts that they almost always obtained through student status or through their places of employment. This work context influenced some of the shared significance in the group. Responses to funny posts, for example, often referred to the work environment, as with "I was laughing so hard everybody knew I wasn't working." Furthermore, participants' perception of one another as educated (a recurrent theme in surveys I conducted) was surely connected to this context.

Temporal Structure

Many researchers have pointed out that the temporal structure of CMC can be either synchronistic or asynchronistic. Walther (1996, p. 29) even went so far as to posit this distinction as one of CMC's "two structural properties" (the other being partial cues). With synchronistic communication, all participants are on-line simultaneously and read and respond to one another immediately. On the Internet, this is exemplified by Multi-User [Object Oriented] Domains (MUDs/MOOs) and Internet Relay Chat (IRC). With asynchronistic communication, participants need not be on-line simultaneously and can read and respond at different times, as is the case in newsgroups and mailing lists. Hollingshead and McGrath (1995) expanded this dichotomy to include three more ways the interaction can be temporally structured. First, the group may meet only once, for a limited time, communicating either synchronistically or asynchronistically. Second, the group can carry out a series of meetings, again either synchronistically or asynchronistically. Third, the group can carry on a continual asynchronistic meeting over an extended time period. Differences in temporal structures influence the availability of immediate feedback, the opportunity to compose and rewrite messages before sending them, how many members of a group are participating at any given time, the meanings of some verbal and nonverbal phenomena (such as pauses), and other variables that directly affect a group's communication patterns (e.g., Baym, 1996; Werry, 1996).

The temporal structure of r.a.t.s., as with all Usenet newsgroups (and on-line mailing lists), is that of an ongoing asynchronistic meeting. Messages are stored at each site for a time period left to the system administrators to decide, usually no longer than a couple of weeks. Until the old messages are removed, readers can check in at their convenience to read or respond to what has arrived. The fact that things can be read and responded to at one's own leisure makes it possible for more people to participate and for people to contemplate and edit their messages before sending them. It also allows people to respond to multiple messages at once.

The temporal structure of r.a.t.s. is also affected by the fact that its use is situated in office environments. Because most r.a.t.s. participants access the group while at work, most messages are written during working hours, Monday through Friday, whereas far less traffic is generated during evenings and weekends. The temporal structure of participation also is affected by the temporal structure of the soap operas. Because there are five new episodes each week and the stories continually evolve, it is only relevant to respond to posts for a few days. Most responses on r.a.t.s. are posted within 48 hours of the original post (Baym, 1994). Temporal norms of relevance are an important dimension of temporal structure that remains unexamined in CMC scholarship. The evidence from r.a.t.s. suggests that such norms may be related to the external contexts in which interaction is situated.

System Infrastructure

As the differences in possible temporal structures suggest, computer network infrastructures shape interaction in many ways. Seibold et al. (1994) argued that systems differ in three general ways: physical configurations, system adaptability, and level of user friendliness. Physical configuration includes such variables as how many computers there are, how they are spatially dispersed, and the speed of the system. System adaptability includes such variables as the capacity for anonymous entries and the system's programmability. User friendliness incorporates the dimensions of ability to support multiple tasks, flexibility and ease-of-learnability, and others. A difference in any one of these many features modifies the possibilities available to users as they develop organized communicative systems.

R.a.t.s. is highly influenced by the structure of Usenet and the newsreaders through which it is read and written. It is beyond the scope of this chapter to fully explain the structure of Usenet or newsreaders; the reader is referred to any of the many popular guides to the Internet. Here I want to address a few salient features of Usenet and of the newsreaders that influence emergent social patterns in Usenet groups. The observation that there are reduced nonverbal cues in CMC has been made so often it's become banal, but it remains (however temporarily) a defining feature of CMC systems (Culnan & Markus, 1987; Walther, 1996; Walther & Burgoon, 1992). This quality was what led early researchers to conceptualize CMC as a socially-impaired space, but, as I will address, this paucity of face-to-face cues has resulted in innovative alternatives rather than a lack of expressivity.

Usenet shapes both the temporal structure and the participant structure of interaction. It shapes temporal structure because it is a continual asynchronous medium. Another element of the temporal structure attributable to Usenet infrastructure is the fact that most posts are distributed to the other sites within a matter of minutes or hours, though some sites may not receive messages for days. Responses to messages thus may come within minutes or as far away as days. At some sites, replies may arrive before the original posts. Coherent threads of conversation span days or weeks. Usenet also shapes the participant structure of its interaction. Usenet links millions of people, any of whom can read anything posted to any group received at their site. Because anyone can read or participate, all Usenet interaction is fundamentally multiparty and public.

The interaction on Usenet also is shaped by the many newsreader programs that are used to read and post to the groups. Whereas early newsreaders often forced participants to read posts in chronological (rather than topical) order, the threaded newsreaders that have become standard allow people to select which posts they want to read from a menu organized by subject and identifying posters. Three especially significant features of newsreaders are the headers they automatically attach to the top of all posts, the quotation system they provide, and the possibility for readers to select which posts they read.

The headers convey information about the sender, the subject of the message, the time the message was sent and more. This information can be, and is, used by newsreaders to sort messages and by participants to decide what to read and what to skip. The quotation system most newsreaders provide makes it easy for posters to quote previous messages when they respond to them. Quoted material is automatically marked, usually with a ">" at the start of each line. Responses then can be embedded directly into the original message at relevant points. This system, along with the use of subject identification in the headers, allows posts to be explicitly linked. Without these features of newsreaders, it would be difficult to navigate the flood of seemingly disconnected messages. Finally, the identification of subject and sender in newsreader menus allows users to avoid topics or messages from particular individuals. For a fuller discussion of how Usenet's structure affects practice in r.a.t.s., the reader is referred to Baym (1995a). A nice analysis of the effects of synchronous infrastructure on IRC discourse can be found in Werry (1996).

Group Purposes

Organizational theorists have been the most direct in addressing group purposes. Hollingshead and McGrath (1995) proposed the most articulated perspective, arguing that task types have prior structures that affect communication processes. Drawing on an earlier formulation by McGrath (1984), they claimed that tasks vary in whether they require that the group generate ideas or plans, choose amongst answers or solutions, negotiate conflicting views or conflicting interests, or execute performances in competition with opponents or external standards. These four task types differ in whether or not each requires "the transmission of information among members of the group, or also requires the transmission of values, interests, personal commitments and the like" (p. 51). The task at hand thus influences the extent to which the individuals are involved or invested in what they say in CMC, as well as influencing more obvious factors, such as the topics that will be raised.

As the term *task* suggests, this typology refers to explicit goals of the type one would give to small work groups. Recreational CMC also is organized around purposes, though goals will vary in how explicit they are. Role playing MUDs probably have the most explicit goals around which the group must organize. For example, Ito (1997) wrote of "gaining experience points, loots and levels" (p. 90). Usenet groups are created to serve the vague explicit purpose of "discussing" particular topics, but that entails specific purposes that often remain implicit. Analysis of the communicative practices on r.a.t.s. reveals that their talk is aimed toward several purposes. Some are influenced by the external context of soap opera fandom. Others emerge within the group's interaction.

A common finding in work on soap opera fans is that the opportunity to discuss soap operas with others is a valued incentive to watch (Rubin & Perse, 1987), and having others with whom to discuss the soap opera increases the extent to which people expect to gain pleasure from soap opera viewing (Babrow, 1989). The primary goal around which interaction is constructed on r.a.t.s. is to enhance the pleasure of soap opera involvement. As I suggested in my discussion of the context of soap fandom, enhancing soap opera pleasure through talk, whether computer mediated or not, involves practices of collaborative interpretation and distributing information. The fact that collaborative interpretation of soap operas involves sharing perspectives on socio-emotional issues creates non-soap opera concerns toward which participants orient. Discussion often evolves beyond the soap opera to tackle these issues more directly. At these times, r.a.t.s. serves as a forum for the discussion and negotiation of private issues difficult to discuss publicly. The topics that have been addressed in these extended discussions range from corporal punishment, sexual abuse and assault, wife beating, and racism to engagements, weddings, and pregnancies. The use of r.a.t.s. as a forum for talking about issues beyond the soap opera, issues that often are highly personal and emotionally charged, shows that whereas some purposes are predetermined, others can emerge within a group's inter-action. For those who engage in this personal talk over extended periods of time, maintaining friendships and acquaintances becomes another purpose of the interaction. Some of the purposes of r.a.t.s., then, are to provide information about what has happened and what will happen on the shows, to interpret the shows, to negotiate private issues in a public space and to sustain relationships. While some purposes of a CMC group may be given, this discussion shows that the complete list of purposes is a question for empirical analysis.

Participant Characteristics

Group and member characteristics are the final factor that has been argued to affect CMC outcomes. One important group characteristic is size, which can vary from three to thousands. Other important group characteristics are composition, members' joint interactional history, and whether or not the group is hierarchically structured (Baron, 1984; Hollingshead & McGrath, 1995; Seibold et al., 1994). Individual members differ in their degrees of training in the medium, ability and task expe-rience, experience with new technologies, and attitudes toward technol-ogy (Hollingshead & McGrath, 1995; Seibold et al., 1994). Participant perceptions in particular are privileged as important determinants of communicative outcomes, as Dyrkton (1996) and Turkle (1995) dis-cussed in a cultural context. In an organizational context, Steinfield (1986) found that participant perception of the medium was a major determinant of whether or not people used it socially. Those most likely to use the computers socially perceived them as high in social presence. The participants in r.a.t.s. are involved in the group voluntarily. Many work on computers daily and they are quite adept at using them for interpersonal communication. Like the millions of others who use com-puters socially, r.a.t.s. participants often view the computer as a "play-ground" (E. M. Reid, 1991). Finally, as the work by Cody et al. (1997) and

Joe (1997) suggest, participants differ in a sociability that transcends communicative medium. Though I had no means of assessing r.a.t.s. participants' off-line sociability, one can imagine that a group with more sociable participants would be more likely to foster a sense of community.

R.a.t.s. was a large group even before it split, with several hundred people posting each month. In 1993 its estimated readership was 41,000 (B. Reid, 1993). Tile.net's current estimates are more conservative, placing the readership of each offshoot group around 10,000 (Tile.net, 1997). Exact readership figures are impossible to attain, and there is no way to distinguish people who read all messages every day from those who peek in once and never return. Participants are distributed geographically throughout the United States and Canada. A handful of people participate from Europe, Australia, and New Zealand. Their jobs are diverse. There are students, nurses, secretaries, engineers, scientists, teachers, and others. Thus, although they may share a common interest and sociocultural contexts, these participants would never interact were they not on-line. Several interactants, however, enter r.a.t.s. with preexisting acquaintances from other Usenet groups.

The participants on r.a.t.s., as I have said, are mainly women, though there are many men involved. Savicki et al. (1996) found that the gender balance of newsgroups does have a modest correlation with language patterns (though they stress that there were clearly many other factors at play). Groups with more men used slightly more fact-oriented language and calls for actions, whereas those with fewer men were more likely to self-disclose and try to prevent or reduce tension. Herring (1994, 1996) has described an on-line female style she called "supportive/ attenuated." This style "idealizes harmonious interpersonal interaction" (1996, p. 137). In this style, "views are presented in a hedged fashion, often with appeals for ratification from the group" (1996, p. 119). Herring's description matches well the disagreement styles of r.a.t.s. participants, as documented in Baym (1996). In contrast, however, Witmer and Katzman (1997) found that women in their sample from the Project-H database were somewhat more likely to flame than were men. In r.a.t.s. there is a social taboo against insulting one another, and participants explicitly value friendliness, supporting the findings of Savicki et al. and Herring. Gender affects the topics discussed as well; the personal issues raised, for example, are often those that particularly affect women.

Because r.a.t.s. participants have diverse experiences, each brings unique resources to the group. The relevance of those resources depends, of course, on the twists of soap opera storylines. Those with knowledge of law, for instance, were able to debate whether it was wise for an attorney on *All My Children* to seek an "order of protection" rather than a "restraining order" against her psychotic ex-husband. Those who read the soap opera press are able to bring the resources of inside information. Those who watch daily and have time may post regular updates of the shows. As the soap operas cover a range of personal topics, participants differ in what relevant life experiences they can bring to the interpretive process. Finally, participants span a wide range of writing skill, wit, and insight. Together, participants' knowledge, opinion, experience, and skill provide more than enough resources to transform soap opera viewing into a collaborative communal enterprise.

Summary

There are at least five sources of impact on CMC, each of which affects a given group's communication. Each of those sources—external contexts, temporal structure, system infrastructure, group purposes, and participant characteristics—is itself comprised of variables. Furthermore, these already-complicated factors affect one another in ways that may not be expected, as when the external context of soap operas influences norms of temporal relevance or group purposes. Finally, the discussion of purposes in r.a.t.s. demonstrates that which aspects of the five categories of influence are relevant in a group may be emergent rather than predictable. It may not be possible to specify the specific factors that will combine to affect CMC outcomes in a particular group in advance of actual interaction, let alone what the impact of those factors will be. Research on CMC must attend to these factors if the findings are to be comparable with those of other studies and the complexities and differences of on-line communities understood.

Appropriation

The idea that CMC groups are emergent was shared by Contractor and Seibold (1993). In their work on Group Decision Support Systems (GDSS), they drew on Giddens to argue that participants appropriate rules and resources from preexisting sources of influence through social interaction. They based appropriations in members' perceptions of the group's rules for structuring discussion and in the content and pattern of group interaction. Structuration theory and self-organizing systems theory were used to explain that the group members' interactive appropriation of the preexisting rules and resources creates structure beyond what already exists. The generative mechanism of a group's structure lies in the recursive interplay between structure and interaction. The patterns of appropriation that emerge in computer-mediated groups may attain stability, may occur cyclically, or may fluctuate, depending on the fit between the factors of temporal structure, external contexts, communicative purposes, and participant characteristics. The notion of "appropriation" is apt. Rather than seeing participants in CMC as operating in ways dictated by the available resources or rules, appropriation implies that participants pick and choose from what is available, at times using things in unexpected ways, at times not using some of the possibilities.

Contractor and Seibold (1993) left the specifics of "appropriation" vague. The scholar looking to see how, in general, groups appropriate what is offered and transform possibilities into social structures is left without precise pointers on where to look or what to look for in search of "appropriation." Answers to these questions can be found in the growing body of work in many of the social sciences that approaches culture as a system dynamically recreated through the interplay between preexisting structures and the practices of everyday life (Ortner, 1984). This practice perspective runs through the work of the French sociologist Bourdieu (1977) and many scholars of language socialization, including Miller and Hoogstra (1992), Ochs (1988), and Schieffelin (1990). These scholars have used ethnography to record and interpret the concerns toward which members of a culture orient their interaction and the ways in which they use cultural resources, especially language, to achieve and validate cultural meanings. This work has shown that even the most mundane interactions require that people draw on preexisting resources endowed with social meanings that create and invoke event types, identities, relationships, and norms. Culture is continually recreated and modified through the communicative use of resources to invoke social meanings.

Using a theory of off-line culture to explain on-line groups entails a presumption that they operate in comparable fashions. Given that the question here is what qualities of on-line groups make people want to describe them in the language of off-line community, it only makes sense to turn to models of off-line life. The practice theory of culture is especially applicable because of its focus on communicative interaction, the primary (and arguably the only) characteristic on- and off-line communities share. This thumbnail sketch of the practice approach suggests that the researcher interested in computer-mediated groups' appropriation of resources needs to view the communicative creation of social meaning as central to the appropriation process. The work I discussed in the first section focused on preexisting structures. Those structures do not make a group. Social organization emerges in a dynamic process of appropriation in which participants invoke structures to create meanings in ways that researchers or system designers may not foresee. Those innovative uses may in turn influence the structures. As Lemos (1996) wrote in his analysis of the French computer network Minitel, technology "takes on a 'life' of its own or is taken over and made to come alive by the diverse forces of social interaction" (p. 35). In the next section, I turn to the creation of social meaning through everyday computer-mediated interaction.

Emergent Social Meanings

All interaction, including that which is task-oriented, conveys social meaning and thus creates social context (Goodwin & Duranti, 1992; Watzlawick, Beavin, & Jackson, 1967). The social meanings created in CMC have been the focus in studies of Bulletin Board Systems (BBS), local networks, IRC, MUDs and MOOs, mailing lists, and Usenet. This research showed that the members of these groups creatively exploit the systems' features in order to play with new forms of expressive communication, to explore possible public identities, to create otherwise unlikely relationships, and to create behavioral norms. When, and if, these emergent features develop into stable group-specific understandings, the group gains the potential to be imagined as a community. The specific categories of on-line social meaning I discuss here are exemplary; I do not mean to suggest they are the only ways to categorize on-line social meanings nor that they include all possible on-line social meanings. I will now review each of these four facets of the creation of community in more detail, suggesting how each might be related to the factors of external context, temporal structure, system infrastructure, group purposes, and participant characteristics.

Forms of Expression

The computer medium is often used to diffuse forms of expressive communication that are usually associated with face-to-face communication (Fox, 1983; Dorst, 1990). Fox found that computerized networks in a high school were quickly taken over as a way to share jokes and riddles. The success of the Usenet group rec.humor also shows this transmission of expressive communication via CMC. Nevertheless, Fox went beyond arguing that CMC was used for expressive purposes, proposing (with remarkable foresight) that eventually the medium could lead to the development of new forms of expressive communication. Bakhtin (1986) was among those to argue that as groups develop over time, they generate group-specific meanings. Eventually, new forms of speech, or genres, unique to that community evolve. Cherny's (1995) analysis of "ElseMOO" is one demonstration of how new expressive forms are created and conventionalized into unique linguistic "registers" as part of the interactive process in computer-mediated communities.

Smiley faces, graphic icons built out of punctuation marks, are the most famous kind of new expressive cue. The potential for "emoticons" to facilitate community is seen in their collection in "smiley face dictionaries." Compiled by users, the dictionaries catalogue those emoticons actually in use as well as dozens of purely silly ones meant to represent things as obscure as buck-toothed vampires. That the repertoire of smiley faces is codified into folk dictionaries and circulated informally among users indicate that users are aware that their communities have group-specific forms of expression and take active roles in the codification of those expressions. Besides these emoticons, there are other ways to express nonverbal information. For instance, participants use asterisks or capital letters for emphasis (e.g., Baym, 1995c; Danet, 1995) and explicit verbal descriptions of behavior. Because people being funny in CMC can't hear their audience's laughter (or lack thereof), the amused often describe themselves as "rolling on the floor laughing," sometimes abbreviated to ROFL. Movements in the fictional spaces of computer-mediated role play games may be described in great detail (Danet & Ruedenberg, 1992). Other expressively loaded innovations include new acronyms and vocabulary, new kinds of jokes, and new categories of talk all together.

Users of r.a.t.s. adapt these communicative innovations from other CMC contexts and also create their own forms of expression. The response to humorous posts mentioned above, "I laughed so hard everybody knew I wasn't working," is one such r.a.t.s.-specific convention. Another r.a.t.s.-specific expressive innovation is the acronym IOAS, meaning "it's only a soap" and repeated like a mantra at times when the show is particularly unrealistic or otherwise frustrating. Acronyms are just part of the group-specific vocabulary that has emerged. Soap opera characters are nicknamed, for example. *Days of Our Lives* Marlena became "Big Bird" whereas Carly was renamed "Camel Lips." The day the character of Natalie on *All My Children* was fatally injured in a car accident her moniker was changed from "Nat" to "Splat." Like the smiley-face dictionaries, lists of nicknames are often compiled and posted to the group or e-mailed to confused newcomers. Again, the active collection and codification of the group's expressive forms demonstrates the self-reflexivity of computer-mediated community.

R.a.t.s. also has developed unique forms of jokes. "Soap opera laws," for instance, enumerate common narrative devices, such as "if you only have sex once you will get pregnant." The posing of "unanswered questions" in the *All My Children* discussion likewise finds its humor in drawing attention to the absurdity of the soap opera world and demonstrating competence in reading the soap opera genre (Baym, 1995c). New categories of communication also are found in r.a.t.s., some borrowed from Usenet culture. These include the "updates," which retell the soap operas, "spoilers," which preview what will happen on the shows, "predictions," guesses about what will happen on the show, and "TAN"'s, discussions tangential to the topic of soap operas. Tepper (1997) wrote about the sociopolitically loaded practice of "trolling" in one Usenet group, where asking obviously stupid questions became a form of joke used to distinguish group insiders from outsiders. Cherny's (1995) examination of "whuggling" in ElseMOO is particularly intriguing as it suggests the extent to which individual participants' interpretations of these group-specific genres may vary.

These innovative forms of expression that occur as part of the creation of computer-mediated culture are related to each of the factors discussed earlier. The external context of being "on the Net" provides familiarity with a range of alternative expressive forms. External cultural norms about the expression of affect suggest when their use might be appropriate. The temporal structure of CMC groups allows them time to develop needs for forms of expression (needs that will be influenced by the group's purposes) and time to codify particular forms. The system infrastructure may disable many conventional forms of expression, but it also offers the tools and links to build new forms. Finally, participant characteristics provide the creativity that generates and chooses among emergent forms of expressive communication.

Identity

CMC is often anonymous, but, given a little time, people create on-line identities. Many analyses have focused on how anonymous users can switch genders, appearances, sexual orientation, and countless other usually integral aspects of the public self as well as take on multiple identities (e.g., Carpenter, 1983; McRae, 1997; Myers, 1987b; E. M Reid, 1991, 1995; Stone, 1995; Turkle, 1995). In general, the work on on-line identity demonstrates a scholarly fascination with how anonymity can be used to invent alternative versions of one's self and to engage in untried forms of interaction, theoretically problematizing the notion of "real self." E. M. Reid (1991) wrote that IRC "users are able to express and experiment with aspects of their personality that social inhibition would generally encourage them to suppress." Stone (1995) and Turkle (1995) both connected this to a postmodern condition, in which identities have become more fragmented and flexible. Even in systems that are not anonymous, however, identities are actively and collaboratively created by participants through communicative practice.

The obvious starting point in creating an identity is the choice of a name. Myers (1987a) wrote that names are "transformed into trade-marks, distinctive individual smells by which their users are recognized as either friends or enemies within an otherwise vague and anonymous BBS communication environment" (p. 240). Anonymous CMC systems give people the chance to name themselves (Myers, 1987b; E. M. Reid, 1991). Other systems attach real names, as do many Usenet newsreaders, but users still may sign their messages with names they have chosen for themselves. Bechar-Israeli (1995) offered an analysis of one user's name choice that demonstrates the playful and performative nature of on-line naming. Walther and Burgoon (1992), studying a CMC system that was not anonymous, found that participants still developed nicknames and used embellished signatures. Taking a social-information-processing perspective, Walther and Burgoon suggested that the creative enhance-ment of naming counteracts the inordinately high levels of uncertainty about one another in computer-mediated space. This is further supported by reports that names are also enhanced in order to define identity in other disembodied communication media, including Citizens Band (CB) radio (Dannefer & Poushinsky, 1977; Kalcik, 1985) and urban subway graffiti (Castleman, 1982). Kalcik noted that in choosing an on-air name, CB users had a choice between trying on alternative personae or just being themselves. She wrote, "In discussing handles and identities, then, some significant aspects of the CB community include the choice between . . . the possibility of fantasy and real identities and their separation, or the maintenance of both side by side" (p. 102).

Both Dannefer and Poushinsky (1977) and Myers (1987b) found that participants highly valued their anonymity and protected it by carefully guarding the release of private information. For Myers this meant that none of his subjects would fill out his surveys accurately. Although initially frustrating, his further interviews and observations revealed the significance of this seemingly useless data. Such information, he concluded, is excluded from discussion because of the expressive freedoms that accompany anonymity. One active New Orleans BBS participant, who goes by the name "Andromeda X," told him "I keep my identity secret not because I am afraid of the contact with the people I meet in BBS but because anonymity is part of the magic" (1987b, p. 259).

Judging from the scholarly attention paid to anonymous CMC interaction and its uses in identity play, one would think most on-line interaction is anonymous and few people ever interact as themselves. The reality seems to be that many, probably most, social users of CMC create on-line selves consistent with their off-line identities. E. M. Reid (1991) wrote of "net romances" in which people meet and fall in love over the IRC. The CB users Kalcik (1985) studied had chosen to meet face-to-face and thus had given up their potential anonymity. Hellerstein (1985) also discussed CMC interactants who seem to interact as "themselves." In r.a.t.s., people usually use their own names. Some take on nicknames, but most who use nicknames also promulgate their real names within the same messages. One prominent r.a.t.s. personality, for instance, uses her initials as a name, but her full name appears in the headers. The use of real names is no doubt partly due to the general Usenet tendency toward the use of real names. Nevertheless, participants on r.a.t.s. actively discourage anonymity, suggesting that the Usenet is not the only influence on the creation of r.a.t.s. identities. When a person's e-mail address is a seemingly random collection of letters and numbers and there is neither a name nor a signature, people will often ask for a name when they respond. I argue that this aversion to anonymity is related to the nature of soap opera discussion and the emergent purposes of the group. As I have suggested, r.a.t.s. functions in part as a public sphere in which people can discuss what are normally private socio-emotional issues. The soap opera is continually assessed for socio-emotional realism, which entails a good deal of self-disclosure from participants on highly personal topics. The use of real names helps to create an intimate environment in which this kind of disclosure can be voiced.

This intimate environment also makes it appropriate for people to build identities through explicit self-disclosure, as when a much-beloved poster who calls herself "Granma" revealed that she is a grandmother, a college undergraduate, and, among other attributes, a former stripper. Granma even shared with the group her joy and excitement when the daughter she had given up for adoption years ago came, with her own daughter, to live with her. Participants also individualize themselves by taking on different roles within the group. As I discussed elsewhere (Baym, 1993), only a few participants can take on the role of updater for a particular day's episodes. Some create roles for themselves by creating new genres of post, as did the man who invented the AMC "unanswered questions."

Another means of creating identity, one that is related to naming, is the creation of a "signature file." Signature files (or "sig files") are attached automatically to the bottom of posts by the sender's newsreader. They usually include a name, an e-mail address (and now a World Wide Web address). Other components often included are quotations, company disclaimers, and illustrations created using punctuation marks and letters. Illustrations may show bicycles in the signature files of cyclists, longhorns in the case of University of Texas sports fans, or stylized representations of one's name. Signature files, because they appear in the body of each post from a given sender, are one of the most immediate and visually forceful cues to identity.

Through these practices, participants are able to interactively create identifiable personalities for themselves in this potentially anonymous terrain. The creation of social identities is clearly related to the interplay between the factors discussed in the previous section. The temporal structure of the group affects the ability to build identity. Without sufficient time, none of the practices of identity formation discussed here can occur. In an analysis relevant to Usenet, Walther (1996) reported that synchronocity can be especially important in impression management, as participants can have more strategic control over the representations of themselves, especially when CMC is the only link between participants. Individual identities also must be understood in terms of their own temporal structures; one of the most important distinctions between posters is the frequency with which they write. Most people write less than twice a month; a few write several times each week (Baym, 1993). Furthermore, some people who write only a few times each month may participate long enough for their cumulative contribution to forge them an individual role in the community.

External contexts and group purposes also affect the formation of identity. This is seen in r.a.t.s. when anonymity is discouraged and self-disclosure encouraged as a result of the context of the soap opera and the practical goals that its discussion entails. The ability to be anonymous or to append signature files depends on the system infrastructure. Anonymous systems will offer a greater range of potentials. Nevertheless, even in systems that are not anonymous, identity is creatively constructed through the use of enhanced naming, signature files, self-disclosure, and role adoption. The personalities themselves come, of course, from the idiosyncratic qualities of participant characteristics. The extent to which people use CMC as a means to invent new personae, to recreate their own identities, or to engage in a combination of the two, and the ways in which they do so, are issues central to the construction of a computer-mediated social world. At the same time, these social contexts and constraints on on-line identity should be considered in discussions of the seemingly endless freedoms available to on-line selves.

Relationship

Not only can CMC participants have identities, they can have relationships with other participants. In some cases, people go into CMC with preexisting face-to-face relationships, as is the case when colleagues in the same office use CMC (Baron, 1984; Seibold et al., 1994; Steinfield, 1986). In other cases, people know one another from prior computer-mediated interactions in different contexts. Myers (1987b) found that many of the people on his BBS already had established relationships on other BBSs. Subscribers to multiple electronic mailing lists or readers of multiple Usenet newsgroups know that even in a network as vast as the Internet, the same people cross paths repeatedly.

People also construct new relationships within computer-mediated groups. Parks and Floyd (1996) conducted a randomized e-mail survey of Usenet participants and found that almost two-thirds of them (60.7%) had established a personal relationship through Usenet. Women were somewhat more likely than men to have established on-line relationships, but the best predictors were the duration and frequency of posting to a particular newsgroup. Though most of the relationships their subjects reported were not profoundly intimate, they displayed "moderate" levels of commitment to these friendships (as measured with a standard scale used to assess commitment in face-to-face relationships).

The work of Myers (1987b) and Hellerstein (1985) suggest that some of the heavier CMC users thrive on the relational possibilities of the medium. The heavy users of the University of Massachusetts system Hellerstein studied said their primary use of the system was to communicate with friends. They reported spending more time in computer-mediated social interaction than on the phone or in face-to-face communication. Myers found two kinds of experts among his heavy users, one technologically astute, the other relationally astute, both of whom dominated the message flow. What he called the "social experts," those who focused on relational concerns within the group, gained their power from their ability to nurture and direct the flow of on-line relationships. They saw the computer as a community and the communication networks as based on social relationships. They interpreted the communication content as the expression of values and saw the result of communication as the creation of roles. My analysis of r.a.t.s. interaction (Baym, 1994) demonstrated that the heaviest posters on the subject of *All My Children* were more likely than lighter users to attend to interpersonal alignment of the interaction. They are more likely, for example, to use people's names when they respond to their messages and to explicitly acknowledge others' perspectives.

People who form on-line relationships usually move them to at least one additional channel. Parks and Floyd (1996) found that 35.3% of their respondents used the telephone, 28.4% used the postal service, and a full third (33.3%) carried their relationships into face-to-face interaction. Hellerstein (1985) found this relational movement off-line in her work as well. On r.a.t.s., people often arrange local get-togethers or meetings when one participant is visiting an area where others live. A few of the r.a.t.s. participants in my town, for instance, met every few months for lunch, to watch a few episodes of *All My Children* together or to meet a visiting r.a.t.s.ter.

Though it generally has been treated as a negative consequence of CMC, even the seemingly antirelational practice of flaming can be reinterpreted as a kind of sporting relationship. Myers (1987a, p. 241) described flaming as a kind of play. Though Myers didn't make the comparison, flaming might be compared to forms of ritual insults that are popular in children's peer groups and serve to define them as members of that group (Bronner, 1988). This is demonstrated by one of Myers' BBS users who wrote to a new user, "it is lots of fun to insult each other but don't get involved." Flaming is a gendered form of relationship to be enjoyed at an emotional distance (Myers described as the "chest-thumping display of on-line egos"). Flaming is highly rare and explicitly discouraged in r.a.t.s. where, as I will describe, civility is the norm.

Relational development between CMC participants also is related to the five factors of external contexts, system infrastructure, temporal structure, group purposes, and participant characteristics. External contexts, such as the physical locations of the participants, clearly limit people's ability to meet or the likelihood that they are already acquainted. The external context of other networked interactions similarly affects whether or not participants already may know one another when they enter a group. System infrastructure provides the links across which relationships can form. As with the development of expressive communication and identities, relational development depends on the presence of a conducive temporal structure. In CMC, as in real life, relationships take time to build. Because the purpose of r.a.t.s. is to discuss soap operas, a process that, as I have shown, involves a fair amount of self-disclosure and discussion of private issues, creating friendly relationships becomes one of the emergent purposes of the group. The influence of participant characteristics on relational formation is seen in part in Myers's finding that the most relationally oriented users' perception of the computer was as a place in which relationships can thrive. The extent to which social relationships develop on-line seems to be influenced in part by the presence of a relatively few heavy users whose perceptions of the medium lead them to encourage the creation of interpersonal bonds in ways that may be quite subtle. The gender balance of a group also may influence how many relationships form as well as the discourse forms in which they manifest. CMC relationships often develop into face-to-face relationships that then can play back into the computer-mediated relationships. The extent to which CMC groups appropriate the medium as a relational forum, and the ways in which they do so, are important issues in the social construction of computer-mediated societies.

Behavioral Norms

Ongoing CMC groups tend to develop behavioral norms as well as shared significances, personalities, and relationships. Some norms span wide groupings of CMC users. For instance, Myers (1987b) wrote that "there is widespread acknowledgment of a national BBS community—with both positive and negative norms of behavior" (p. 264). Werry (1996) discussed IRC norms. There are also norms that span Usenet. McLaughlin, Osborne, & Smith (1995) derived a seven-category "taxonomy of reproachable conduct on Usenet" drawing on posted reproach sequences in Usenet groups and the introductory Usenet postings distributed across the network. They identified norms regarding the incorrect use of technology, bandwidth waste, networkwide conventions, newsgroup-specific conventions, ethical violations, inappropriate language, and factual errors.

Norms also develop at the group-specific level, as the fourth category of McLaughlin et al. (1995) indicates. Usenet groups that discuss television shows and movies often have a norm that the word *spoilers* should be included in the subject lines of posts that give away the story ahead of time. This enables those who don't want the show spoiled by this advanced information to avoid such posts. The system programmers and the participants in each subculture also can create unique normative standards (Hellerstein, 1985). Users continually reinforce the norms by creating structural and social sanctions against those who abuse the groups' systems of meaning (Mnookin, 1996; E. M. Reid, 1991). Groups have differing norms about sanctioning itself. Smith, McLaughlin, and Osborne (1997) found considerable variation across groups in the tone of reproaches for netiquette violations.

I already have mentioned a number of normative conventions that have been imported into r.a.t.s. All of the Usenet netiquette is used in the group. Quotations are used, edited, and correct sources attributed, all in keeping with Usenet standards. Identities are represented relatively accurately. Emoticons are used to avoid misunderstandings. I also have discussed norms that have evolved within the group. The taboo against flaming others is one such norm, and this applies even when reprimanding others for their behavior. The group's temporal norm of relevance, which makes it inappropriate to post responses more than 4 or 5 days after the original message was posted, is another emergent norm. As I demonstrate in my analysis of message features of disagreements and agreements in r.a.t.s. (Baym, 1996), these norms are pervasive, manifesting in a group's (often subtle) language patterns.

The final r.a.t.s. norm I want to discuss is related to soap operas and represents a particularly organized innovation on the part of the participants. Because all soap operas are discussed in r.a.t.s., but few if any participants follow every soap opera, the need arose to identify which soap opera a post addresses. The group responded to this need by conventionalizing acronyms to designate each soap opera and using them at the start of every subject line. Participants can use these designations to automatically delete messages on soap operas they don't follow. This rule of netiquette, more than any other on r.a.t.s., is systematically enforced. Those who omit the soap abbreviation in their subject lines, whether through ignorance or negligence, are likely to be chastised both publicly and through e-mail.

The norms that develop on r.a.t.s., and, I suggest, in any other group, are directly related to the purposes of the group. It is to meet the needs of the community, needs both given and emergent, that standards of behavior and methods of sanctioning inappropriate behavior develop. The taboo on flaming in r.a.t.s. and friendliness of disagreement, for instance, functions to keep r.a.t.s. a safe environment for the kinds of self-disclosures and expressions of opinion involved in interpreting soap operas. The system is clearly an influence on emergent norms; indeed many of the norms revolve around the appropriate use of the system possibilities. Systems also provide different kinds of means to enforce norms. On systems like AOL's "folders," where posting is moderated, inappropriate messages simply can be yanked before they ever appear. In Usenet's unmoderated groups, in contrast, people turn, in effect, to shaming people into compliance by drawing attention to their violations. The external contexts influence norms by providing preexisting standards and by providing the concerns around which normative systems develop. The r.a.t.s. norm of temporal relevance is related to the external context of soap opera fandom, resulting from the soap opera's continu-

ally evolving story structure. The temporal structure, as always, provides time to develop norms but also becomes subject to norms itself. In
ongoing groups, norms will develop about how to use time, and these
emergent temporal structures further structure interaction. Finally, participant and group characteristics, including gender, play a role in determining what behaviors people will and won't tolerate.

Emergent Community

This discussion has shown that participants in CMC develop forms of
expression that enable them to communicate social information and to
create and codify group-specific meanings, socially negotiate group-
specific identities, form relationships that span from the playfully
antagonistic to the deeply romantic and that move between the network
and face-to-face interaction, and create norms that serve to organize
interaction and to maintain desirable social climates. Interaction does not
work on its own. The resources on which participants draw when they
compose their messages, and the rules that shape what they can do, come
from a variety of outside sources. The factors of temporal structure,
external contexts, system infrastructure, group purposes, and participant and group characteristics have been put forward as the most salient
preexisting forces on the development of computer-mediated community. These forces influence one another in affecting emergent social
dimensions of the group.

Dorst (1990, p. 183) concluded that CMC "is an extremely active
folkloric space, in which social and cultural forces operate and register."
The social and cultural forces I've examined here often emerge into
stable patterns within a group. It is these stable patterns of social meanings, manifested through a group's ongoing discourse, that enable participants to imagine themselves part of a community. To say a sense of
community emerges from stable social meanings is not to say that those
meanings are never contested. To the contrary, ongoing challenges are
an intrinsic part of social life in most on-line communities. Stivale (1997)
and Connery (1997), for instance, wrote of newcomers questioning on-
line group meanings that they have not been socialized to share. Connery
put his faith in these questioning newcomers, suggesting they prevent
the fossilization of the community by undermining the authority that
comes from elitism, arguing that "the freedom of the group as a public
sphere can only be revitalized by unruly newcomers who flout the
conventions and the authorities which inevitably evolve in long-lived

groups" (p. 177). An on-line group's continued ability to sustain a sense of community surely depends on the dynamic flexibility with which it negotiates these challenges.

It is also quite possible, of course, that some groups will never generate a stable set of social meanings nor offer a sense of group-specific community. There are countless reasons community might not emerge on-line. There may be inadequate interaction to sustain the development of group-specific meanings. A group whose participants remain highly task or topic-oriented might choose not to develop socially. In some groups, such as the Indian culture newsgroup Mitra (1997) analyzed, the core social meanings within the group may become battlefields, resulting in an openly divisive group offering little, if any, sense of community (though I imagine each faction within the group might feel a sense of community enhanced by its opposition to the others).

What, if anything, can we take from the analysis here in trying to assess the worth or the impact of on-line communities? One of this emergent model's central implications is that it is fundamentally reductionist to conceptualize all "virtual communities" as a single phenomenon and hence to assess them with a single judgement. R.a.t.s. is out there with countless thousands of on-line groups that vary tremendously. Some groups are surely bad for off-line life, but there's certainly no reason to believe that most are. The research I have reviewed and the model I have proposed suggest that on-line groups are often woven into the fabric of off-line life rather than set in opposition to it. The evidence includes the pervasiveness of off-line contexts in on-line interaction and the movement of on-line relationships off-line. There is far more to be understood about the many complex interactions between on-line and local community before writing off either one.

References

Allen, R. C. (1985). *Speaking of soap operas.* Chapel Hill: University of North Carolina Press.

Anderson, B. (1983). *Imagined communities: Reflections on the origin and spread of nationalism.* London: Verso.

Ang, I. (1985). *Watching Dallas: Soap opera and the melodramatic imagination.* New York: Routledge.

Babrow, A. S. (1989). An expectancy-value analysis of the student soap opera audience. *Communication Research, 16,* 155-178.

Bakhtin, M. M. (1986). *Speech genres & other late essays.* Austin: University of Texas.

Baron, N. S. (1984). Computer-mediated communication as a force in language change. *Visible language, 18*(2), 118-141.

Baym, N. K. (1993). Interpreting soap operas and creating community: Inside a computer-mediated fan culture. *Journal of Folklore Research, 30,* 143-176.

Baym, N. K. (1994). *Communication, interpretation, and relationships: A study of a computer-mediated fan community.* Unpublished doctoral dissertation, University of Illinois, Urbana-Champaign.

Baym, N. K. (1995a). From practice to culture on Usenet. In S. L. Star (Ed.), *The cultures of computing* (pp. 29-52). Oxford, UK: Basil Blackwell.

Baym, N. K. (1995b). The emergence of community in computer-mediated communication. In S. G. Jones (Ed.), *CyberSociety: Computer-mediated community and communication* (pp. 138-163). Thousand Oaks, CA: Sage.

Baym, N. K. (1995c). The performance of humor in computer-mediated communication. *Journal of Computer-Mediated Communication* [On-line], *1*(2). Available: http://207.201.161.120/jcmc/vol1/issue2/baym.html

Baym, N. K. (1996). Agreement and disagreement in a computer-mediated group. *Research on Language and Social Interaction, 29,* 315-346.

Bechar-Israeli, H. (1995). From (Bonehead) to (cLoNehEAd): Nicknames, play and identity on Internet relay chat. *Journal of Computer-Mediated Communication* [On-line], *1*(2). Available: http://207.201.161.120/jcmc/vol1/issue2/bechar.html

Bourdieu, P. (1977). *Outline of a theory of practice.* Cambridge, UK : Cambridge University Press.

Bronner, S. J. (1988). *American children's folklore.* Little Rock, AK: August House.

Brunsdon, C. (1989). Text and audience. In E. Seiter, H. Borchers, G. Kreutzner, & E. Warth (Eds.), *Remote control: Television, audiences, and cultural power* (pp. 116-129). New York: Routledge.

Carpenter, T. (1983, September 6). Reach out and access someone. *The Village Voice,* pp. 9-11.

Castleman, C. (1982). *Getting up: Subway graffiti in New York.* Cambridge: MIT Press.

Cherny, L. (1995). *The MUD register: Conversational modes of action in a text-based virtual reality.* Unpublished doctoral dissertation, Stanford University, Palo Alto, CA.

Cody, M. J., Wendt, P., Dunn, D., Pierson, J., Ott, J., & Pratt, L. (1997, May). *Friendship formation and creating communities on the Internet: Reaching out to the senior population.* Paper presented at the Annual Meeting of the International Communication Association, Montreal, Canada.

Connery, B. A. (1997). IMHO: Authority and egalitarian rhetoric in the virtual coffeehouse. In D. Porter (Ed.), *Internet culture* (pp. 161-180). New York: Routledge.

Contractor, N. S., & Seibold, D. R. (1993). Theoretical frameworks for the study of structuring processes in group decision support systems: Adaptive structuration theory and self-organizing systems theory. *Human Communication Research, 19*(4), 528-563.

Culnan, M. J., & Markus, M. L. (1987). Information technologies. In F. M. Jablin, L. L. Putnam, K. H. Roberts, & L. W. Porter (Eds.), *Handbook of organizational computing: An interdisciplinary perspective* (pp. 420-443). Newbury Park, CA: Sage.

Danet, B. (1995). Playful expressivity and artfulness in computer-mediated communication. *Journal of Computer-Mediated Communication* [On-line], *1*(2). Available: http://207.201.161.120/jcmc/vol1/issue2/genintro.html

Danet, B., & Ruedenberg, L. (1992, October). *"Smiley" icons: Keyboard kitsch or new communication code?* Paper presented at the Annual Meeting of the American Folklore Society, Jacksonville, FL.

Dannefer, W. D., & Poushinsky, N. (1977). Language and community: CB in perspective. *Journal of Communication, 27,* 122-126.

Doheny-Farina, S. (1996). *The wired neighborhood.* New Haven, CT: Yale University Press.

Dorst, J. (1990). Tags and burners, cycles and networks: Folklore in the telectronic age. *Journal of Folklore Research, 27,* 179-190.

Dyrkton, J. (1996). Cool runnings: The coming of cybereality in Jamaica. In R. Shields (Ed.), *Cultures of Internet: Virtual spaces, real histories, living bodies* (pp. 49-57). London: Sage.

Erol's (1997). *Usenet Statistics (1997/09/16–1997/09/17)* [On-line]. Available: http://thereisnocabal.news.erols.com/feedinfo (Accessed September, 17, 1997).

Fernback, J. (1997). The individual within the collective: Virtual ideology and the realization of collective principles. In S. G. Jones (Ed.), *Virtual culture* (pp. 36-54). London: Sage.

Fox, W. S. (1983). Computerized creation and diffusion of folkloric materials. *Folklore Forum, 16,* 5-20.

Geraghty, C. (1991). *Women and soap opera.* Cambridge, MA: Polity.

Goodwin, C., & Duranti, A. (1992). Rethinking context: An introduction. In A. Duranti & C. Goodwin (Eds.), *Rethinking context: Language as an interactive phenomenon* (pp. 1-42). Cambridge, UK: Cambridge University Press.

Healy, D. (1997). Cyberspace and place: The Internet as middle landscape on the electronic frontier. In D. Porter (Ed.), *Internet culture* (pp. 55-71). New York: Routledge.

Hellerstein, L. N. (1985). The social use of electronic communication at a major university. *Computers and the Social Sciences, 1,* 191-197.

Herring, S. (1994). Politeness in computer culture: Why women thank and men flame. In M. Bucholtz, A. C. Liang, L. Sutton, & C. Harris (Eds.), *Cultural performances: Proceedings of the third Berkeley women and language conference* (pp. 278-293). Berkeley, CA: Women and Language Group.

Herring, S. (1996). Posting in a different voice: Gender and ethics in computer-mediated communication. In C. Ess (Ed.), *Philosophical approaches to computer-mediated communication* (pp. 115-145). Albany: SUNY Press.

Hiltz, S. R., & Turoff, M. (1978). *The network nation: Human communication via computer.* Reading, MA: Addison-Wesley.

Hollingshead, A. B., & McGrath, J. E. (1995). The whole is less than the sum of its parts: A critical review of research on computer-assisted groups. In R. Guzzo & E. Salas (Eds.), *Team effectiveness and decision making in organizations* (pp. 46-68). San Francisco: Jossey-Bass.

Ito, M. (1997). Virtually embodied: The reality of fantasy in a multi-user dungeon. In D. Porter (Ed.), *Internet culture* (pp. 87-110). New York: Routledge.

Joe, S. K. (1997, May). *Socioemotional use of CMC: Self-disclosure in computer-mediated communication.* Paper presented at the Annual Meeting of the International Communication Association, Montreal, Canada.

Jones, S. G. (1997). The Internet and its social landscape. In S. G. Jones (Ed.), *Virtual culture* (pp. 7-35). London: Sage.

Kalcik, S. (1985). Women's handles and the performance of identity in the CB community. In R. Jordan & S. Kalcik (Eds), *Women's folklore, women's culture* (pp. 99-108). Philadelphia: University of Pennsylvania Press.

Kiesler, S., Siegel, J., & McGuire, T. W. (1984). Social psychological aspect of computer-mediated communication. *American Psychologist, 39*(10), 1123-1134.

Lemos, A. (1996). The labyrinth of Minitel. In R. Shields (Ed.), *Cultures of Internet: Virtual spaces, real histories, living bodies* (pp. 33-48). London: Sage.

Livingstone, S. M. (1990). Interpreting a television narrative: How different viewers see a story. *Journal of Communication, 40,* 72-85.

Lockard, J. (1997). Progressive politics, electronic individualism and the myth of virtual community. In D. Porter (Ed.), *Internet culture* (pp. 219-232). New York: Routledge.

McGrath, J. E. (1984). *Groups: Interaction and performance.* Englewood Cliffs, NJ: Prentice Hall.

McLaughlin, M. L., Osborne, K. K., & Smith, C. B. (1995). Standards of conduct on Usenet. In S. G. Jones (Ed.), *CyberSociety: Computer-mediated community and communication* (pp. 90-111). Thousand Oaks, CA: Sage.

McRae, S. (1997). Flesh made word: Sex, text, and the virtual body. In D. Porter (Ed.), *Internet culture* (pp. 73-86). New York: Routledge.

Miller, P. J., & Hoogstra, L. (1992). Language as a tool in the socialization and comprehension of cultural meanings. In T. Schwartz, G. White, & C. Lutz (Eds.), *New directions in psychological anthropology* (pp. 83-101). New York: Cambridge University Press.

Mitra, A. (1997). Virtual commonality: Looking for India on the Internet. In S. G. Jones (Ed.), *Virtual culture* (pp. 55-79). London: Sage.

Mnookin, J.L. (1996). Virtual(ly) law: The emergence of law in LambdaMOO. *Journal of Computer Mediated-Communication* [On-line], 2 (1). Available: http://207.201.161.120/jcmc/vol2/issue1/lambda.html

Myers, D. (1987a). A new environment for communication play: On-line play. In G. A. Fine (Ed.), *Meaningful play, playful meaning* (pp. 231-245). Champaign, IL: Human Kinetics.

Myers, D. (1987b). "Anonymity is part of the magic": Individual manipulation of computer-mediated communication contexts. *Qualitative Sociology, 19*(3), 251-266.

Nochimson, M. (1992). *No end to her: Soap opera and the female subject.* Berkeley: University of California Press.

Ochs, E. (1988). *Culture and language development.* Cambridge, UK: Cambridge University Press.

Ortner, S. B. (1984). Theory in anthropology since the sixties. *Comparative Studies in Society and History, 26*(1), 126-166.

Parks, M. R., & Floyd, K. (1996). Making friends in cyberspace. *Journal of Communication, 46*(1), 80-97.

Reid, B. (1993, August 6). *Usenet readership report for July, 1993.* news.lists.

Reid, E. M. (1991). *Electropolis: Communication and community on Internet Relay Chat.* Unpublished Master's thesis, University of Melbourne, Australia.

Reid, E. (1995). Virtual worlds: Culture and imagination. In S. G. Jones (Ed.), *CyberSociety: Computer-mediated communication and community* (pp. 164-183). Thousand Oaks, CA: Sage.

Rheingold, H. (1993). *Virtual communities.* Reading, MA: Addison-Wesley.

Robins, K. (1995). Cyberspace and the world we live in. In M. Featherstone & R. Burrows (Eds.), *Cyberspace/cyberbodies/cyberpunk: Cultures of technological embodiment* (pp. 135-156). London: Sage.

Rubin, A. M., & Perse, E. M. (1987). Audience activity and soap opera involvement: A uses and effects investigation. *Human Communication Research, 14*(2), 246-268.

Savicki, V., Lingenfelter, D., & Kelley, M. (1996). Gender language style in group composition in Internet discussion groups. *Journal of Computer-Mediated Communication* [On-line], 2(3). Available: http://207.201.161.120/jcmc/vol2/issue3/savicki.html

Schieffelin, B. (1990). *The give and take of everyday life.* Cambridge, UK: Cambridge University Press.

Schuler, D. (1996). *New community networks: Wired for change.* Reading, MA: Addison-Wesley.

Seibold, D. R., Heller, M. A., & Contractor, N. S. (1994). Group decision support systems (GDSS): Review, taxonomy, and research agenda. In B. Kovacic (Ed.), *Organizational communication: New perspectives* (pp. 143-168). Albany: SUNY Press.

Smith, C. B., McLaughlin, M. L., & Osborne, K. K. (1997). Conduct control on Usenet. *Journal of Computer-mediated Communication* [On-line], 2(4). Available: http://207.201.161.120/jcmc/vol2/issue4/smith.html

Steinfield, C. W. (1986). Computer-mediated communication in an organizational setting: Explaining task-related and socioemotional uses. In M. L. McLaughlin (Ed.), *Communication yearbook, Vol. 9* (pp. 777-804). Beverly Hills, CA: Sage.

Stivale, C. J. (1997). Spam: Heteroglossia and harassment in cyberspace. In D. Porter (Ed.), *Internet culture* (pp. 133-144). New York: Routledge.

Stone, A. R. (1995). *The war of desire and technology at the close of the mechanical age.* Cambridge: MIT Press.

Stratton, J. (1997). Cyberspace and the globalization of culture. In D. Porter (Ed.), *Internet culture* (pp. 253-276). New York: Routledge.

Tabbi, J. (1997). Reading, writing, hypertext: Democratic politics in the virtual classroom. In D. Porter (Ed.), *Internet culture* (pp. 233-252). New York: Routledge.

Tepper, M. (1997). Usenet communities and the cultural politics of information. In D. Porter (Ed.), *Internet culture* (pp. 39-54). New York: Routledge.

Tile.net. (1997) *Newsgroup descriptions* [On-line]. Available: http://tile.net/news (Accessed September 17, 1997).

Turkle, S. (1995) *Life on the screen: Identity in the age of the Internet.* New York: Simon & Schuster.

Walther, J. (1996). Computer-mediated communication: Impersonal, inter-personal and hyperpersonal interaction. *Communication Research, 23*(1), 3-43.

Walther, J. B., & Burgoon, J. K. (1992). Relational communication in computer-mediated interaction. *Human Communication Research, 19*(1), 50-88.

Watzlawick, P., Beavin, J., & Jackson, D. (1967). *Pragmatics of human communication: A study of interactional patterns, pathologies, and paradoxes.* New York: W.W. Norton.

Weise, E. R. (1996). A thousand aunts with modems. In L. Cherny & E. R. Weise (Eds.), *Wired women,* (pp. vii-xv). Seattle: Seal.

Werry, C. C. (1996). Linguistic and interactional features of Internet Relay Chat. In S. Herring (Ed.), *Computer-mediated communication: Linguistic, social, and cross-cultural perspectives* (pp. 47-63). Amsterdam: John Benjamins.

Witmer, D., & Katzman, S. (1997). On-line smiles: Does gender make a difference in the use of graphic accents? *Journal of Computer-Mediated Communication* [On-line], 2(4). Available: http://207.201.161.120/jcmc/vol2/issue4/witmer1.html

3

Designing Genres
for New Media:
Social, Economic,
and Political Contexts

Philip E. Agre

Portrayals of a digital future are too often monolithic:
everything will be digital, everyone will be wired, all
media will converge into one, and the physical world will wither away.
This kind of monolithic story is wrong, I think, and particularly unfortunate when it comes to the future of communications media. In fact,
perhaps the most distinctive feature of the unfolding digital present is a
proliferation of new media and new forms of communicative interaction:
the Web, CD-ROMs, economical printing on demand, cellular telephones, messaging pagers, fax machines, MUD's (Multi-User Domains),

AUTHOR'S NOTE: This chapter is based on a manifesto for a course on conceptual design
for new media, taught to communication undergraduates at the University of California,
San Diego beginning in 1996.

optical scanners, voice mail, and many other media have become wide-spread in recent times, and more will be marketed soon. Perhaps these media will undergo a shakeout, leading back to the relatively homogeneous days of yore. But more likely, I think, media will continue to multiply. Everybody's daily life will include a whole ecology of media; some of these will be voluntarily chosen, and others will be inescapable parts of life in public spaces and the workplace.

As media proliferate and change, the task of designers becomes more difficult. By *designers* I mean to include everyone—authors, composers, performers, public speakers, letter writers, editors, and others—who make decisions about the format and content of communications media, whether for others' purposes or their own. More indirectly, I also mean to include the people—librarians, publishers, book sellers, programmers, critics, anthologists, and others—who operate the distribution channels that connect the producers and the users of media products. Designing for media, and particularly for new media in which stable conventions have yet to be established, requires many kinds of efforts—research, experimentation, rational choice, iteration of prototypes, and learning from the work of others. Many skills enter into the process. In this chapter I want to focus on a single theme: the design of genres that fit into the activities of the audience one hopes to reach. Design for new media, I want to argue, requires some rational understanding of who are using the materials, what they are doing with them, and how they fit into an overall way of life. Such elaborate ideas about the audience might not have been necessary in the old days, when media were few and their uses evolved slowly. That is not so today, and it is not just possible but crucial for designers to learn what is known about the uses of media and to contribute to such knowledge themselves.

My analysis will be divided into four parts. I will begin by sketching some of the processes by which communities conduct their cognitive lives together. In the second part, I will present a framework for media design based on inquiry into the role of genres in people's activities, followed by some examples. Putting these concepts to work will result in a vast space of potential genres and uses of media. The third part, therefore, will describe some of the economic forces that tend to select among these various potentialities, and the fourth part will sketch some of the democratic values that might guide concerned citizens and professionals in shaping the media infrastructures and policies of the future. Nothing is inevitable, not even in technology, and some of the choices we might make about communications media right now are much better than others.

How Communities Think

Every artifact is, in its own way, a collaborative construction of far-flung networks of people. Sometimes this is obvious: A car is built by hundreds or thousands of people organized by markets and hierarchies. But sometimes it is not obvious at all: Words, sentences, conversations, speeches, memos, papers, and meetings are likewise "built" by enormous networks of people. Bakhtin (1975/1981) described some of these phenomena as they manifest themselves in literary texts; this article offers some first thoughts on the machinery through which collective voices arise in real life.

Let us define a "community" to be a set of people who occupy analogous locations in social or institutional structures. This is not the ordinary use of the term "community," and it will take a moment to explicate it fully. First some examples. The following are all communities:

- ◆ The people who manage the parking lots on American university campuses
- ◆ The Republicans who ran for elected offices in the 1994 elections
- ◆ The business people who are implementing "reengineering" programs
- ◆ The children in a particular grade school classroom
- ◆ The fire fighters who drive a given model of fire truck
- ◆ The folks who live in a given political jurisdiction

The "locations" in these examples vary widely. They are notable for their relationships: Virtually every parking lot manager has a community of parkers and a police department to contend with, virtually every Republican candidate has a Democratic opponent to contend with, and so forth. Everyone might belong to a variety of different communities, and these communities can be defined in broader or narrower terms (the community of San Diego residents versus the community of California residents, drivers of Mack fire trucks versus all fire fighters, etc.). The locations might correspond to formal institutional titles or they might not; but in every case they correspond to a relatively stable universe of structural relationships, and this is what makes them "locations."

We can readily observe some patterns among these communities. The community members have certain interests in common, as well as some interests that conflict. These shared and conflicting interests are "objective" in the sense that they are imposed by the institutions. This is distinct from the question of how the people themselves understand their interests in a subjective way.

Another pattern is that the members of a community are frequently in ongoing communication with one another. This is clear enough when the members are routinely brought together into a shared physical space. But it is also true when the members' physical locations are distant. One purpose of clubs, unions, clinic meetings, Friday evening drinking groups, and professional societies is to bring the members of a community together periodically. It is by no means inevitable, however, that the members of a community will interact. Nor is it inevitable *how* they will interact. I will call these things the community's "forms of association." Observe that a community can exhibit elaborate forms of association without any two of its members ever being in the same place—they can associate over the phone, through talk radio, through magazines, through the Internet, through the efforts of a small number of outsiders who carry news of one another from place to place, and so on. Numerous modalities of association may be combined in customary ways. Forms of association are contingent—they could be different from what they are—and they are historical—they arise through concrete processes that leave their marks. And, of course, they are relational—they depend in crucial ways on the ensemble of relationships that constitute a given location.

This is very abstract, so let us make it concrete through a day in the life of a manager. Managers the world over have highly developed forms of association. These forms of association vary by country, sector, social status, and so forth, but they bear family resemblances due to the basic workings of bureaucracy. Managers live dangerous lives—in some sense anyway. Credit and blame are constantly being assigned for large, complicated processes over which nobody has full control (Jackall, 1988). Decisions must be made that depend on more information than any single individual could ever master, and they must be articulated and defended in terms that orient to a constantly shifting set of political alliances. It is not surprising, then, that managers exhibit a powerful orientation to the experience and thinking of others in their community. University campus parking lot managers are well aware of the practices on other campuses. They maintain an elaborate topography of these campuses; they know which ones are considered to be on the cutting edge of parking lot management. If one campus decides to try setting parking prices according to a market-based allocation mechanism, for example, then all of the others will be watching. This "watching" will be subserved by a variety of mechanisms, many of them well institutional-ized: consultants, newsletters, rumor mills, and so on.

In many ways this is a good system because it permits people to put their heads together. It is what Hutchins (1995) called "distributed cognition": thinking that is distributed across a network of people rather than just being located in one person's head. If you ask how the Univer-sity of Walla Walla made its decision about how to charge for parking spaces, you cannot formulate a serious answer without appealing to some collective construct, such as the community of university campus parking lot managers. It is worth noting that this picture forces us to revise, or at least amend, the picture of the economics of knowledge in the newly influential work of Hayek (1945). Hayek depicted the econ-omy as a sprawling network of people who know their own local conditions extremely well, all dealing with one another through the arm's-length mediation of the price system. But the reality is more complicated than this. Of course, people are arranged in some kind of social network. But they also put their collective heads together in ways that have more regularity than Hayek's extreme localism can admit. These collective minds do have their economics, and money certainly changes hands in the conferences and newsletter subscriptions that subserve the process, but this whole architecture is not just a sprawling mass, and it is not just a "spontaneous order" of localized market arrangements.

The analysis to this point also makes clear what the majority of Internet discussion groups are really for. Even those of us who use the Internet intensively have been influenced by journalistic representations, which have focused disproportionately on those areas of the Net to which journalists can easily gain access—especially Usenet. The concern with "rudeness on the Internet" derives partly from that bias. What this concern ignores is the thousands of discussion groups for professions and subprofessions and subsubprofessions of all sorts. These forums are where the real action is sociologically. Imagine if every community—in the sense of the term I am using here: the people who share a certain institutional location—had its own Internet discussion group. Of course, various factors will influence whether the people in a given community would actually benefit from an Internet discussion group:

- How numerous they are
- How often they have questions that pertain to that particular location
- How fast the world around them is changing
- The forms of association that they have in common
- How much conflict is currently going on in the institutional relationships that define the location
- How much conflict is going on among the community members themselves
- Whether they share a common language
- What kind of access to the technology they have
- Whether they have access to sufficiently compatible systems, and so on

Nonetheless, it is worth investigating how we might use technology to support the collective cognition of particular communities. First, however, it will be helpful to examine the physiology of collective cognition in greater detail.

The Physiology of Collective Cognition

In my analysis so far, I have made it sound as though everyone in a community plays an equivalent role in the community's collective thinking. But this is rarely the case. The actual division of cognitive labor in a given community will depend on many aspects of its relationships and its history, and these will have to be studied concretely in each case. Nonetheless, some patterns do recur. The particular patterns I have in mind are driven by change in the community's environment and pertain to the role of innovators and leaders. Innovation in professions often (but not always) is surrounded by an ideology according to which brilliant individuals come up with "new ideas" through hard work, innate genius, sparks of creativity, and so forth, so that one might regard it as mysterious that someone else did not come up with the same "new ideas" years or decades or centuries earlier. My experience has been that it rarely works this way. Instead, innovators are people who (as common idioms put it) "see which way things are going" and "get ahead of the curve." As the world changes, everyone in a given community is going to face a common problem. And in practice, particular individuals position themselves as the thought leaders in relation to those changes.

The thought leader's role is to get on top of an issue: see it coming, gather positions and arguments about it, network with people who are relevant to it in various ways, and articulate it in terms that supply useful raw materials for individual community members' own thinking in their own situations. This, of course, is not an easy task, and the social capital that these people accumulate is usually well earned. The conditions that permit individuals to play this thought leader role vary, and different people bring different strengths and strategies to the job. Networking helps; if you notice the same issue coming up repeatedly in conversations with community members, and if the community members do not realize how common the issue is, then that is an opportunity to do a service for both oneself and the community. Although original thinking on the matter is an advantage, all that is needed to be helpful is to assemble everyone else's thinking in some useful form.

Thought leaders accumulate capital in a variety of ways. Some of these are straightforwardly financial, for example, the money they earn for books and magazine articles, as consulting fees, or through grants. But the capital can take other forms. Most especially, community members' willingness to commit resources to expose themselves to a synthesis of thinking on an emerging issue gives the thought leaders an opportunity to expand their professional networks in the course of organizing conference panels and the like. This social capital then is convertible into other forms of capital in a wide variety of ways, usually unforeseen but usually unsurprising. Professional communities have routinized much of this process: Whole genres of writing and interaction are devoted to it and whole publications are often devoted to uncompensated articles written by people trying to establish themselves as thought leaders.

It is rare for anybody to be taught the "moves" through which one accumulates capital in these worlds or the "moves" through which various kinds of capital are converted into one another in the course of a career. People go through whole careers without quite understanding the process, whereas other people have a highly cultivated instinct for it. Why is this? Part of the reason pertains to social class: If you watched your parents live their lives through the associational forms of distributed cognition through which thought leaders acquire capital, then you will probably grow up with a tacit awareness of the phenomena and a powerful head start in learning the skills.

But it is not all a matter of social class. Some people who did not grow up around successful professionals have good professional skills mentors in college—this is one purpose of public higher education. Others succeed in apprenticing themselves to masters of the craft in their jobs (Lave & Wenger, 1991). Others get the idea in one world by working through rough analogies to processes of distributed cognition and capital accumulation through thought leadership in worlds with different class structures—local politics, labor unions, social competition through parties and the like, street gangs and organized crime, civic associations, churches, support groups, lodges, social movement organizing, and so on. My point, though, is that not enough people ever get these things explained to them and that this is a powerful and remediable force for social inequality.

In sketching the physiology of communities' collective cognition, I have tacitly opposed two extreme models: one in which all community members play the same role, communicating amongst themselves equally and symmetrically, and one in which a thought leader is the sole go-between among all the community members. The reality includes the vast range of associational forms through which community members circulate bits and pieces of thinking among themselves. In Orr's (1996) celebrated studies of photocopier repair technicians, these associational forms involved "war stories" about ugly copier repair problems. Business people engaged in public controversies circulate stories as well, but they do so within a different practice based on public relations; the stories are all crafted to provide support for an agenda of "messages" that the community (having done the necessary solidarity work within its own forums) wishes to get across to particular publics. (A "public," in the language of public relations, is precisely another community that stands in a specific structural relation to one's own, for example, a company's publics might include customers, regulators, neighbors, activists, journalists, and union officials.) I have referred to this circulation of structured interactional "stuff" as an "institutional circuitry" (Agre, 1995).

This circuitry is often partly professionalized, for example when an industry association sends its members a "manual" of facts, stories, and quotes that they can use when articulating an industry perspective in one site of public debate or another. An institution's circuitry is defined by the genres that circulate within it; stories that photocopier repair people tell among themselves sound different from stories that managers tell among themselves because they serve different purposes—that is, they are located differently in the larger system of institutional relationships.

This discussion of stories should remind us that, in speaking of community "thinking" and "cognition," I have lost sight again of the relational nature of the structural locations that define communities. Everyone lives in a set of institutional locations, and every significant situation that arises is defined (to some degree) in relation to these other locations. This is particularly clear in the case of an industry political voice. The repair technicians, likewise, spend much time discussing how to "fix the customer" as well as how to fix the machine, and this "fixing" is conducted through language—language that nobody could fashion very well on their own, by pure improvisation.

People are often not aware of the extent to which the associational forms of their communities serve the purpose of fashioning a collective voice. They may not even be aware of the crucial role of these associational forms in gathering words for their own individual use back "home" in their interactions with their familiar environment of structurally related others. The associational forms, after all, probably serve other purposes as well, including plain old relaxation, the chance to "talk through" the feelings brought on by troublesome events, the exchange of mutually interesting facts (for example through "gossip"), and so forth. The fact is, though, that we are all members of communities that possess complex mechanisms for the collective construction of a voice. Our voices are not simply our own. This does not imply that we are all puppets who say what we are told—such a system would not work anyway. Nor are we conformists who hide behind the average because it is safe—though some such hiding is often prudent. Nor are we all conspiratists consciously plotting the most expedient utterances to use in manipulating others—though clearly some of this does go on.

Complex as they sound, the mechanisms I am describing require little more than simple, disorganized self-interest: people trying to deal with their own local situations, discovering that others can provide resources that help with this, associating with them for mutual benefit, and then easing into the genres of interaction and the institutional mechanisms that formalize the process and help it scale up. In practice, of course, we inherit these associational forms and institutions from others—in other words, we enter a given community's forms of association by being socialized into them. We may permit ourselves to be socialized because we see the cognitive advantages of it, or we might have other reasons for joining in. The bottom line, though, is that a community's institutional circuitry can grow quite complex without anybody ever understanding it, much less designing it.

It is important to discuss these things for many reasons. I have already mentioned one of them: that mastery of many communities' associational forms is unequally distributed, and this inequality helps reproduce other kinds of inequality in society. But another, more fundamental reason pertains to the nature of democracy. The roots of democracy lie in associational forms: People learn solidarity or division through their associational involvements; communities that can manage to think, speak, and act collectively can defend their interests much better than the ones that cannot; people who define their communities of shared interests in narrow ways will fare differently from people who define their interests in broad ways; communities that can form working alliances with other communities based on shared interests will fare better than those that cannot; and so forth. Too often we think of democracy in formal terms, as something that happens every couple of years at the ballot box. But democracy is something that happens all the time in society; it is the everyday process through which people negotiate their relationships with one another. Such negotiations may appear to our untrained eyes— and the eyes of the law and the economists—as nonhistorical improvisations between isolated individuals, but they are not. Even if it were possible for isolated individuals to negotiate with one another, considerable advantages will accrue to whichever individual then decides to go off and get involved in a community of people who occupy analogous structural locations in society. The reason for this is obvious: By participating in such a community, an individual gets access to the thinking of many other people—people who have probably faced similar negotiations already. As a general rule, any community that preaches against this broadly democratic conception of society will be discovered to practice it with terrific vigor. And anybody who can convince you to abandon your associational forms without abandoning their own will have an enormous negotiating advantage over you forever afterward.

Framework for Media Design

A worthy goal for design for new media, then, is to support the collective cognitive processes of particular communities. The principal *object* of design, I want to suggest, is the genre. I have already indicated some of the role that genres play in the institutional circuitry of a community's collective life. In this section, I propose to formalize the interconnections among these ideas to produce a robust analytical framework that supports the design process.

Let us begin with the concept of a genre—that is, an expectable form that materials in a given medium might take. Here are some examples of genres:

Romance novels

Op-ed articles

IRS tax forms

Scientific research papers

Statistical tables

Romantic poems

"Tagging" graffiti

Classified advertisements

The blues

Business memoranda

Street maps

Page of results from a Web search engine

Conference announcements

Corporate financial reports

Boxing posters

Encyclopedias

Railway timetables

Sales pitches

Action-adventure movies

Legislation

Shoot-'em-up video games

Notice several things about this list:

1. Genres can be defined more or less broadly. One may wish to focus specifically on research papers in biology, or on early blues, or on sales

pitches for condominium time-shares, or on French companies' financial reports. An advertising campaign, for example, might be regarded as a small genre that inserts a range of elements into a recognizable shared frame.

2. Each genre implies a particular sort of audience and a particular sort of activity (Bazerman, 1988). Who the audience actually is and what its members are actually doing are, of course, fairly difficult empirical matters. But romance novels and graffiti and financial reports do fit into people's lives in particular ways. (For romance novels, see Radway, 1984.)

3. Each genre also implies a relationship between the producer(s) and consumer(s) of the materials in question. The relationship may be a one-to-one personal or professional acquaintanceship, or it might be a one-to-many performer-to-audience interaction, or it might be mediated by institutionalized distribution channels. Interests may conflict, matters may be concealed, money may change hands, persuasion may be intended or disavowed, useful information may be conveyed, reputations may be gained or lost, and so forth. All of these aspects of the relationship will shape both the genre and the activities within which it is used.

4. A genre implies not a single document (or other communicative event) but a stream of them. Even if the "rules" of a given genre are never codified, past instances of each genre create precedents and expectations for the interpretation of subsequent instances, and this may create a pressure for future communications to conform to the pattern established by earlier ones. For this reason and others, genres permit people to seek out "more like that one," and they permit the establishment of efficient, familiar, habitual routines for using the materials.

5. The genre does not, however, fully constrain the ways that instances of it might be used. Financial reports might be read as if they were literary texts, IRS forms might be mined for poetic phrases, blues songs might be sampled to make hip-hop songs, video games might be played as if the goal were to *avoid* killing anyone, sales pitches might be solicited for use as sociolinguistic data, research papers might be interpreted as business plans, and romance novels might be read by those who hope that the heroine is going to blow off the guy and get a life.

6. Any given way of life will involve the routine use of several genres. Tourism involves guidebooks, menus, street signs, timetables,

road maps, phrase books, and postcard notes back home. Genres sometimes imply one another, at least in the loose sense that they serve complementary roles in the same kinds of activity.

7. Genres change historically. The changes might be encouraged by regulation, by competition or influence from other genres, from changes in the lives of their users, from shifts to new media, or by the changing purposes of the people who are producing them. The changes might be decided consciously, evolve incrementally, or arise through the "natural selection" of markets and other mechanisms.

I focus on genres because they are the meeting point between the process of producing media materials and the process of using them. Depending on your purposes, be they commercial, political, or personal, you might wish to start your analysis with production or consumption. The point, in either case, is to cultivate an understanding of how the two halves fit together. Building on and summarizing the analysis so far, I want to formalize our understandings of the production and consumption of media materials under five headings: communities, activities, relationships, media, and genres. The abstractions provide a handy schedule of questions to ask in mapping out the relationships between people and media in particular situations. Analysis proceeds by enumerating *all* of the communities, activities, relationships, media, and genres in a given social world and inquiring into their workings.

Communities

A community, once again, is the set of people who occupy a given structural location in an institution or society. A community might have a stronger or weaker sense of itself *as* a community. It might or might not have its own organization and might or might not meet as a group. But most communities engage in some degree of collective cognition—the interactions through which they learn from one another's experiences, set common strategies, develop a shared vocabulary, and evolve a distinctive way of thinking. These interactions might take place through war stories, newsletters, rumors, conference speeches, philosophical tracts, music videos, management consultants, or bards who travel from place to place bearing news.

Activities

The life of every community includes shared forms of activity within a particular institutional logic. The community members do not necessarily follow a rule book, although they might. The point, rather, is that the commonalities of their lives, goals, and surroundings, together with their collective thinking about their situations and futures, tend to lead to similar patterns of activity. These include the activities through which particular kinds of media are used, but they include much more. In particular, it does not suffice to identify such an activity as "reading" without asking how this "reading" is part of some larger pattern of social practice. For example, students studying for an exam may apply procedures of "reading" that chop a book's contents into discrete, memorizable facts according to an economic calculation of which ones are likely to count for how much on the exam. This might be contrasted with the reading engaged in by American men reading the post-Vietnam war fiction that was inspired by characters like Rambo (Gibson, 1994), with the way that Washington insiders read the newspaper to assess how yesterday's action is going to play back home, or with the business people who read the books of business gurus while asking "what concretely does *this* and *this* and *this* mean in the context of my own industry and firm?" Each kind of "reading" reflects a perfectly legitimate way of using a text within a particular system of culturally and institutionally organized practices (Scribner & Cole, 1981). Note that "activities" include both the physical actions (sitting, writing, talking, looking, turning pages, pushing buttons, etc.) and the cognitive and emotional processes (identifying with characters, wondering what the professor thinks is important, catching the allusions, etc). The genre needs to "fit" with the whole complex of "external" and "internal" aspects of the activity.

Relationships

The members of a community share a social location because they share relationships to people in other, adjacent locations. Thus, temporary employees have relationships to temp agency managers, managers of firms that contract for temps, employees of those firms who have permanent status, and so on. Family farmers must contend with bankers, shippers, extension workers, their own family members, and so on. The lives of people in communities are similar largely because of the similarities of their relationships, and much of a community's shared thinking is concerned with these relationships. Farmers chat amongst themselves about their dealings with bankers, managers meet to discuss their dealings with the people they supervise, voters listen to poll numbers about their fellow voters' supposed views on the candidates, sales people read books by other sales people about selling things to buyers, and so on. Many of the characteristic activities of a community either directly involve these relationships (asking for a loan, writing a report, casting a vote, holding a meeting, etc.) or are heavily influenced by them (acquiring skills, gathering ammo, making oneself presentable, thinking about analogous relationships in others' lives, etc.). Relationships among particular individuals or institutions have life cycles: Employment contracts and family relationships, for example, tend to pass through a more or less expectable series of stages within a given society, each with its characteristic issues and forms of activity.

Media

Media are the specific means of communication: telephone, television, CD-ROMs, video tapes, magazines, books, face-to-face conversation, drums, chalkboards, billboards, radio, clothing, and so on. People use media in activities, and the technical affordances of each medium conditions how it can be used. For example, it is difficult to carry a VHS playback system, it is painful to read a long text on a computer screen, radio is more for drivers than television, overhead transparencies can be projected better onto white boards than chalkboards, e-mail requires Net access, face-to-face conversation requires travel, and so on. But media should not be confused with genres: Radio supports both Top 40 programs and call-in talk shows, a magazine usually contains a stable mix of several genres among its contents, and the genres of face-to-face conversation include performance evaluations, party small talk, paranoid harangues, and accounts of one's research interests at a conference.

Genres

A genre, again, is a relatively stable, expectable form of communication. Genres are addressed to particular communities and fit into particular activities in the lives of that community's members. Of course, a given genre might be addressed to several different purposes simultaneously or even to several different communities, but it stands to reason that a genre cannot be too many things to too many communities without diluting its usefulness for any one of them. It is probably best to identify a genre with a particular medium: A folk song goes through important changes in its transition from live performance to audio recording to music video. A novel might not change its words in the transition from paper to CD-ROM, but nobody really knows whether anyone has any use for a novel on a CD-ROM or whether CD-ROMs need new genres that can participate in the activities for which the CD-ROM medium can actually be useful to the members of a particular community. It helps to think of a genre in historical terms as the product of an ongoing process of coevolution between its producers and consumers. Genres are effectively codesigned with forms of activity, even if this codesign process might be unconscious, haphazard, or even the result of conflict between parties with differing interests or worldviews. In particular, every genre implies a distinctive constellation of relationships: It is supposed to be useful to members of a given community, in activities whose forms and purposes are heavily influenced by relationships with the members of particular other communities.

I have sketched, then, an analytical framework consisting of communities, activities, relationships, media, and genres. My purpose is not to give precise abstract definitions to each of these terms. Instead, the framework is supposed to be useful in making sense of particular cases, whether for understanding what people are already doing with genres or for designing new genres. It can be highly illuminating to map out all of the communities, activities, relationships, media, and genres in a given environment. One might start this process anywhere one likes, for example with a community one hopes to assist or a medium for which one hopes to design new materials. I find it useful to start with particular genres. Having conducted an analysis of a community's existing genres and their place in its activities, it becomes possible to reason rationally about what sort of systems might be usefully designed. This approach resembles contextual design (Beyer & Holtzblatt, 1997) and soft systems methodology (Checkland & Scholes, 1990) in its wide-angle institutional analysis. It is relatively distinctive in its focus on collective processes of cognition, but its procedures for translating analysis into concrete design proposals are not as fully developed.

Some Examples

When designing genres for new media, the slogan is, "do more." Pick a community, explore how existing genres fit into existing activities and relationships, and then consider how a new genre might "do more" for the people than the ones they already use. The new genre, for example, might be designed to ease certain functions (like searching, sorting, comparing, or pooling group efforts) that the people now perform laboriously for themselves, or that they rarely perform because it is so difficult. For example, if you are working with reporters who must routinely produce documents that draw together information from several different sources, then you can provide the reporters with documents that draw together as many of those sources as you have access to. These documents would not simply dump the information in a pile but would arrange it in a rational, intelligible form that creates and satisfies a stable set of expectations. I will return to the broader meaning of doing more for communities later on, but here let us consider some examples.

An example that arose during a recent workshop on these issues is the genre of art indexes. These are reference works connecting works of art to the authors who produced them. They are found on paper, but mainly today they are found on CD-ROMs. The communities that employ them consist mostly of students and scholars, and the relationships of these communities include teachers, critics, the artists themselves, the public of art enthusiasts, curators, and scholars in related fields, such as literature. The activities that community members engage in include writing papers (which may be usefully decomposed into a variety of other activities), conducting seminars, and presenting talks. And the other genres produced or consumed in these activities include research papers, scholarly books of art criticism, student term papers, other reference works, class presentations, popular articles, and so on.

Given this background, it is possible to reason about how the art index genre might evolve. More detailed information might be required, for example, what questions someone writing a research paper has in mind when opening an art index, what other questions he or she has in mind at other times, what later uses are typically made of the facts discovered in the index, how particular works of art are employed as examples in classroom teaching and the apprenticeship process of seminars, and so forth. One could spend a lifetime exploring these questions,

but even a little such exploration will quickly provide the raw material
for brainstorms about other applications of the genre or other genres that
might fit into the activities of the relevant communities. For example,
what kinds of reference materials might be invented to support the social
processes of seminars? The media probably would need to be located in
the seminar room itself, though it could have remote connections elsewhere. Perhaps it would be useful to brief specialized librarians ahead
of time on a seminar topic so that relevant materials could be placed in
a menu. Perhaps it would be useful to have a genre of visual presentations to support compare-and-contrast types of reasoning in seminar
settings, and so on.

Evaluating such proposals is obviously not simple. The only real test
of their practicability is to try them, preferably, through iterative prototyping (Bjerknes, Ehn, & Kyng, 1987; Schuler & Namioka, 1993). The
design process itself will presumably lead to fresh discoveries about the
real nature of the relevant communities, activities, and relationships, and
it might even change them. Any such change will not be "caused" by the
new genres, at least not in any simple sense. The changes will express
latent potentials in the local social system, and they will be influenced
heavily by the participants' own (shared or conflicting) understandings
of the situation. The changes might settle into a new equilibrium, with
genres once again fitted to activities that express relationships between
communities. Alternatively the changes might continue, fueled by the
social system's internal dynamics or by exogenous factors, including
further innovations in media and genres of communication.

As another example, let us consider the design process involved in
getting a particular organization "on the Web" by creating some proto-
type Web pages. In my experience, most organizations try to jump
directly to layout and graphics and bullets and hyperlinks, steering by
an unarticulated sense of what they "like" without thinking through the
issues in a strategic way. The relevant questions include

♦ Who are these pages for? What defines their relationship to us?
What goes on in the life of each community? How is each community
changing?

♦ What purpose are these pages supposed to serve in the context of
our relationship with these people? What are the stages in the life cycle
of our relationship with each individual in a given community and what

role (if any) is each medium and genre supposed to play in each stage of the cycle?

♦ What activities are the people going to be engaged in when they call up our Web pages? What are they trying to accomplish? What specific questions do they have in mind? Do they have that kind of question often? What other questions do they have at other times? What other media and genres do they employ in the course of these activities? Are these activities aimed principally at producing materials in other particular genres? Which ones? What is the connection between our materials and theirs?

♦ Are they going to use our pages just once, or whenever a particular problem arises, or on a regular basis? What existing genres, whether on the Web or in other media, are going to shape their expectations when they encounter the new genre of Web pages we are designing?

♦ What are Web pages going to do for these people that cannot be done better on paper memos or brochures, over the telephone, by electronic mail, in meetings, through posters or newspaper advertisements, and so on? What role do these other media already play in our relationship with these people? Do they already use the Web for other things? Do they tend to have a Web client running on their computer at all times? Or do we hope that they will get up to speed on the Web just to use our pages?

♦ How much will our pages change? Will they contain a steady stream of new content? A steady evolution of the existing content? What expectations will the user communities have about these changes, and what expectations would we like to encourage them to have through the design of our genre of Web pages? Through what division of labor will the pages be maintained?

♦ How will the people hear about your Web page and learn your URL? Through a print advertisement? Business card? Electronic mail? News article? Scrap of paper scribbled at a conference? Do your plans effectively require the people to put your URL in their hot list?

♦ How do the practical properties of the Web medium fit with the activities that these people are going to be engaged in? Do the activities take place at a desk with a computer on it? On the move with a Web-connected portable computer? What else can they be doing during the several seconds it takes to boot their computer or launch their Web client or download our page? What else can they be doing during the several

moments it takes to follow each link within our pages? How powerful
are their computers? Do they share their computers with others? What
kind of bandwidth do they have to the Net? Will they be using our pages
at high-load times of day?

    ♦ Is absorbing the futuristic cachet of the Internet going to be a
significant part of the activity of using our Web pages? Will this be the
case next year as well?

    ♦ If we want several different communities to use our pages, are the
answers to these questions similar or different for each? Should we
design separate pages for each group? A separate starting point ("home
page") for each group, perhaps with links to overlapping sets of materials? Do we want to exclude certain communities from access to particular
materials (home phone numbers are a common example) that we wish
to make available to other communities?

These questions will have very different answers for different purposes—
that is the whole point. Some of the answers might be unknown, or they
might be uneven across a given community, or they might change. Having
at least sketched the answers to them, one is in a position to start designing
and prototyping pages. The next step might be to sit down with some
representatives of each user community, show them the pages, and get
them to talk about their activities and the role of various media and genres
within those activities.

Economic Considerations

Discussions of new media are often framed in terms of "where things are
going." The idea is to predict the future and then to accommodate oneself
to it, it is hoped, to maximum advantage. This kind of reasoning leaves
a great deal out. The future is not a deterministic outcome of a mechanical procedure; it is a human choice whose outcome may be constrained
and biased but is not settled in advance. Only when we believe we have
choices do we start articulating our values and figuring out how they
apply to the situation at hand. Economic considerations help in understanding the practicalities of these choices, including the choices that
other people are likely to make. They are only one part of the larger
picture—or at least they ought to be. Nonetheless, the vast range of
potential applications of new media make the choices exceptionally
difficult, and it will be helpful to take a broad range of considerations
routinely into account during the design process. In this section I am

going to describe some economic concepts that can influence the design of genres in new media—or of genres that address new situations using old media.

A genre is a pattern, not a single document or event, and it implies a steady flow of materials that can play a definite role in the activities of some community. The economics of genres are the economics of this flow and these activities. Here are some issues to consider, some of which apply more directly to genres and others of which apply more directly to the media in which they are realized.

Fixed Costs of Distribution. One force for concentration in industry is the overhead involved in creating a network of distribution channels. Because this overhead must be recovered through sales of the stuff that passes through the channels, competition makes it necessary to fill the channels to capacity. Fixed costs of distribution include brand awareness through advertising, creating and updating policies about personnel and customer relationships, facilities and course materials for training personnel, product design costs, capital assets, such as storefronts, vending machines, trucks, and so on. Newspapers have high fixed costs of distribution.

Marginal Cost of Distribution. Once the fixed overhead costs have been paid, what does it then cost to actually sell someone a product? This includes the manufacturing and shipping of a single unit, personnel time, and paperwork to execute the sale; the rate of customer complaints and returns, other transaction problems, and so on. If the total of these costs is low compared to the fixed costs of distribution per customer, then competitive forces will drive the industry toward monopoly until anti-trust enforcement or countervailing diseconomies of scale set in. Information commodities tend to have low marginal costs of distribution because it is so easy to make new copies of an original (Baker, 1997).

Fixed Costs of Consumption. What does it cost to become able to consume a particular kind of product or service? For information commodities, these costs can be usefully classified into machines (to play records you need a record player), skills (to consume sheet music you have to learn to play a musical instrument), and content (to use software 100 times you need to purchase it at least once). Machine costs tend to be associated with media, not genres, and skill costs tend to be associated partly with media and partly with genres (learning to play classical piano gets you halfway toward learning to play jazz piano). These fixed costs must be paid back across the particular occasions of consumption, which, it is hoped, should be numerous. Some genres, like classical CDs and video games, are used in activities that entail using a given package of content repeatedly; others, like novels, are not. When content costs are high, it can make sense to rent (videotapes from Blockbuster) or share (books from the library) the content-bearing artifacts. All types of fixed costs of consumption can raise distributional questions when they are high, as with the case of "equity of access to the NII." This is particularly true when media that have high fixed costs of consumption (e.g., television or network computers) compete against media that have high fixed costs of production (e.g., newspapers or books). As the latter lose their needed economies of scale and are forced to distribute their fixed costs among ever fewer units, they will consolidate among themselves and may ultimately collapse. Those who cannot afford high fixed costs of consumption will be left without any service at all, because they can only consume a limited number of high-fixed-cost commodity streams.

Marginal Costs of Consumption. These include the price of the commodity itself (assuming it has one), but it can include a lot of other costs as well. These can include travel costs, wear and tear on bodies and machines, the risk of accidents, and the opportunity cost of not having done something else instead.

Specialization. Information commodities undergo two powerful economic pressures that push in opposite directions. It is well known, on one hand, that their high fixed costs of production and low marginal costs of production create powerful competitive incentives for distributing them to the largest possible audience. On the other hand, there often exists a pressure for specialization to particular communities, known to marketing people as market segments. This is obviously in part a question of genre: genres often can be tailored to the needs of more specific groups. Both pressures operate at all points in the market at all times. The balance between them can vary wildly, causing markets for particular products and genres to appear or disappear overnight. The emergence of a mass software market, for example, caused some categories of software to drop in price by two orders of magnitude. Content producers are developing a range of strategies to deal with these contending forces. Software can be tailored locally by setting a range of switches or through the purchase of utilities or add-on packages (as with the huge range of packages for use with *Notes*). Printed materials like books and brochures can be tailored locally as well through new technologies for economical printing on demand. This creates a need for genres for specifying a whole grammar of possible documents. Simple versions of this phenomenon include syndicated newspaper columns that include optional paragraphs that can be trimmed to fit space restrictions, as well as professors' "reading packets" assembled from a batch of chapters and articles from various sources. But much more complex versions are possible as well, all the way out to artificial intelligence techniques that design documents (like instruction manuals or advertising brochures) within a set of genre conventions based on elaborate symbolic representations of the uses to which they will be put.

Practicalities of Duplication. Records can be copied to cassette tape and books can be photocopied, but neither process is particularly convenient. Copying software, though, is usually easy. People will be more likely to make illicit copies if their social network includes other members of the relevant community.

Time-Critical Nature of Use. If the value of a commodity decreases rapidly over time, then distribution costs will probably be higher. On the other hand, if an information commodity (like a stock price) loses its value quickly, then illicit copying and sharing probably will be less prevalent.

Third-Party Costs and Benefits of Consumption. Television, radio, and print media advertisers subsidize the publications they advertise in because they expect to profit from your attention having been brought to their advertising. On a more subtle level, companies hire PR firms to "sell" friendly stories to the media because they expect to enjoy benefits if the story gets an audience. Even when no money changes hands, this is effectively a subsidy to the media, because it saves them the trouble of digging up the story themselves, and media firms that do this enjoy a cost advantage, other things being equal, over their competitors (Gandy, 1982). Third parties also can suffer costs from information consumption: Rumors can cause harm to their subjects and trade secrets are worth less to their owners once they leak out. It follows in each case that effort often will be expended to suppress them.

Brand Identity of the Content Stream. One might think about a magazine, for example, as branded content. A brand is a set of expectations and associations that a given community has about a product, and attaching a brand to one's content stream is a way of explaining what it is and enabling satisfied consumers to get "more like that." Newsletter editors, novelists, genre fiction publishers, concert promoters, television networks, record labels, booksellers, trade associations, and think tanks all try to brand the content streams they produce, with varying degrees of success. The ability to extract income from a content brand depends on the audience's ability to predict the qualities of each next unit of content before they buy it. The matter is particularly interesting in the case of brands established by distributors: television networks, booksellers, concert promoters, and so on. In some cases these brands are based on matters that go beyond the "content" narrowly speaking, for example, how well run the concerts are. In other cases, they are based on the selection of materials to suit a particular audience, as in a special-interest bookstore or a magazine. Brands increasingly cross media boundaries; the "Lion King" brand, for example, is generating revenue across dozens of media. A content stream needs a brand whether or not money changes hands; a free Internet newsletter, for example, needs to build an audience over time, consisting of people who have read a few issues and are willing to read further issues on the expectation of getting "more like that." In all cases, the crucial thing (the basis for reckoning "like that") is how the stuff fits into the reader's life (its "use value" in one idiom), and that in turn depends on its relevance to that person's relationships and goals. Libraries and other public sources of information tend to fight against the logic of brands, and reasonably so, because their justification is based on serving the general public's needs, not the summed needs of a series of market segments. Yet it is hard to think about the general public in concrete terms.

Transaction Costs. These are the costs of selling something to someone: finding customers or suppliers, free samples and browsing rights, negotiating the contract, dealing with later problems with the contract, collecting the money, keeping track of the money, getting the money to the bank, and so on. In the case of information commodities, these transaction costs can exceed the marginal cost of producing the commodity itself. As the cost of electronic transactions goes down, the contracts for purchase of information commodities may shift from a fixed per-copy price ($99 for a spreadsheet program) to a per-usage price ($0.001 per command that you type on the spreadsheet).

Compatibility and Standards. As an economic matter, media industries are path-dependent because of effects deriving from the compatibility of different commodities (Arthur, 1996; Farrell & Saloner, 1987; Lemley, 1996). VHS thrived and consigned Beta to a living death, but this was not because VHS was the better format. (Many think it was not.) Rather, each standard had high fixed costs of both consumption (for the player) and distribution (for the stock of the video rental stores), and VHS had a better alliance of content producers and distributors lined up. Microsoft Windows grows and grows but not because it is the better operating system. In each case, an initial market advantage permitted a de facto standard to become embedded in the economy. People buy Windows because a lot of software exists for Windows; a lot of companies write software for Windows because a lot of people have bought Windows; people generally use just one operating system because of the high costs and low benefits of using more. Telecommunications industries in particular exhibit powerful critical mass phenomena. Everything needs to work the same way because everyone's equipment needs to be compatible with that of everyone they call; it is hard to introduce new categories of equipment if the equipment is not useful unless most everyone you call is also using it.

All of these considerations should influence anybody who is considering the introduction of a new medium or genre. The really harsh effects operate more strongly on the media than on the genres, but in each case it is not sufficient for one's product to be "better" as measured in a vacuum. In particular, the considerations just listed include three arguments for believing that media industries tend toward monopoly:

1. Information commodities, to an even great extent than classical monopolies based on physical infrastructures, like utilities and railroads, have high fixed costs and low marginal costs of production. A company is rewarded heavily for having a large customer base because it can distribute its costs more widely, thereby creating huge barriers to entry.

2. When consumers make frequent choices among commodities whose qualities are hard to assess in advance, as with books and videos, brand identity counts for a great deal. A great advantage thereby goes to the organization that can amortize the high fixed costs of establishing a

brand identity across a higher number of customers. (An advantage also derives from generating a higher number of media products under the same brand umbrella, but this can be accomplished through licensing once the brand has been established in the first place.)

3. Once proprietary standards become entrenched in the marketplace, so that compatibility effects create ever higher barriers to entry for potential competitors, their owners can start to extract rent from a variety of other parties. Moreover, network externalities (benefits to individuals that derive from everyone else's choices) mean that dominance over a market tends to expand once it is established. Microsoft Windows is perhaps the worst possible case of these effects. Such situations can be prevented if a critical mass of customers (or, in some cases, other such interested parties as content producers for a prospective new medium) can exert bargaining power by acting in a coordinated way early enough to influence vendors' choices in the direction of nonproprietary standards and open architectures. This can happen if the customers are few and large, are able to cooperate, have a high degree of understanding of the issues, and are thinking ahead—conditions that are rarely all met.

Political Considerations

Economic reasoning about the media easily gives the impression of an impenetrable logic that neither requires nor permits dialog with political concerns. Yet the most significant questions surrounding the emergence of new media pertain precisely to their role in encouraging or discouraging democratic values. To be sure, technologies do not straightforwardly determine political cultures. A given technology can be appropriated in a variety of different ways, and technologies always coevolve to a certain extent with the institutional structures around them. In the past it has seemed sufficient to inquire about such things one medium at a time—"what is the effect of television on democracy?," "need radio have evolved into a centralized medium driven principally by advertiser sponsorship?," and so on—or else to pose the issues in terms of an orderly whole called "the media" or "the press."

The rapid proliferation of new media, however, may call for a new type of analysis. Digital networks, such as the Internet, are so flexible that it is practically impossible to imagine the range of architectural choices that lie ahead. Indeed, the Internet is capable of simultaneously supporting a considerable range of facilities, each of which would count in normal times as a separate medium. These media might in turn support a wide range of genres, which might fit into people's lives in a wide variety of ways. To reason about the political values that such technological developments might support or inhibit, we must return to basics and pose the general question of the role that communications genres as such play in the life of a democracy.

It is useful to pose this question specifically in terms of genres because, as I have suggested, genres tend to imply and be implied by forms of activity within communities. Of course, communities engage in numerous forms of activity, some of which have greater significance for democratic values than others. Perhaps the most democratically signifi- cant activities are the ones I sketched at the outset, the forms of associa- tion through which communities conduct the collective cognitive pro- cesses of sharing experiences, maintaining memories, conducting conflicts, and building solidarity with regard to the other communities to which they are structurally related. It is obvious that, in society as we know it, some communities have more effective means for engaging in these kinds of group thinking than others. A core democratic value, I would suggest, is broad access to the means of collective cognition.

What are the conditions of collective cognition? In some cases, they might include physical meeting spaces, and it may be important for these spaces to serve a range of other functions in addition to formally orga- nized discussions. In other cases, they might include the existence of a viable community publication, such as a newsletter or newspaper. It probably matters whether the community is dispersed geographically and whether its members can travel. It probably matters whether other communities, such as employers, derive benefits from the shared think- ing of the community's members, as in the case of many professional associations. It probably matters whether the community's members have some way of accumulating capital by serving as thought leaders. All of these considerations, in turn, depend on the economics of genres, travel, careers, professions, real estate, and much else. It follows that someone who wishes to design genres of communication that support democratic values must assess a larger and probably quite complicated picture. No single solution will fit all purposes.

Nonetheless, some general considerations do apply broadly. Much attention has been focused on one of these: the relationship between producers and consumers of content within a given genre and medium. Broadcast television and the Internet are frequently held out as opposite extremes in this regard, in the sense that anybody with a computer and some basic skills (admittedly with significant fixed costs of both production and consumption) can create content for the Internet, but hardly anybody can create content for television (and only under a great mass of constraints). But the degree of symmetry in the producer-consumer relationship is not wholly determined by the technology. Marketing considerations are significant as well: The power to create a coherent brand image across a coherent segment of the population is also the power to concentrate enough capital to gather facts, pay writers, support travel to the places where news can be gathered, maintain the most attractive production values, and so on. Whether the future brings 500 channels or 50 or 5,000 may depend as much on the market logic of segmentation as on the physical capacity of the medium.

At the same time, the experience of fanzines teaches different and more appealing lessons. The 1980s fanzine genre was adapted to numerous aspects of the music-centered youth culture from which it emerged. Because the genre created a stable set of expectations, people could decide that they were interested in 'zines as a category, and this enabled such mechanisms as Factsheet 5 to arise to spread knowledge of them to a definite audience. Broad access to desktop publishing and photocopying provided basic production methods, and the genre incorporated the properties and limitations of these methods as part of its visual language. But fanzines did not operate in isolation from other genres; to the contrary, they coevolved with the genres of popular music on which they were explicitly predicated. A fan who found something of value in a particular band, whether on the radio or through clubs and cassette circulation, could employ the fanzine network to join a community with a common language and common concerns. Mainstream elite discourse may reduce bands like Metallica or Hole to stereotypes, not least because the arbiters of this discourse do not participate in the relevant communities' activities and thus cannot comprehend the genres that are adapted to them. But such bands do sometimes provide occasions for serious social discourse among their adherents, largely through fan publications and the other spaces where fans find one another.

Another broadly relevant issue, already mentioned in my enumeration of economic factors above, is the role of third-party costs and benefits in a community's collective cognition. The problem is not that a community might be influenced by outside voices and opinions and pleas. The problem, rather, is the practice of simulation among practitioners of public relations. Many of the magazines that serve as the primary forums for interest communities, such as car and sports enthusiasts, for example, are thoroughly corrupted by the influence of advertisers and other interested parties on the editorial copy. Even general interest publications, such as newspapers, rely on information subsidies from a wide range of interested parties. In each case, the journalistic voice of the publication is shaped in covert ways by the interventions of interested parties whose messages would not have the same credibility if openly owned up to. These effects continually throw into question the notion of an authentic community voice. How can the channels of a community's collective cognition be designed to be immune to these types of corruption? One straightforward solution is to make them cheap so that outside subsidies are not necessary. And the rapidly decreasing cost of communications bandwidth ought to contribute to the emergence of inexpensive channels of group thinking, such as Internet mailing lists. But the bandwidth for distributing digital material is not the only cost of producing a publication.

One final set of broadly applicable issues concerns the infrastructure of a political organization. A modern organization, such as the ACLU, Planned Parenthood, or the Christian Coalition, employs a broad range of genres of communication for its internal operations, chapter and member relations, campaign mobilizations, networking with related organizations, recruiting, training, and so on. These genres might include fact books, pitch letters, member newsletter articles, op-eds contributed to newspapers, legislative briefings, support materials for lobbyists, meeting announcements, and many recurring types of phone calls. One of the innovations of GOPAC under Newt Gingrich was the development of a range of additional genres, such as issue-focused conference calls and training videotapes sent to candidates for use while on the road between campaign stops. Likewise, electronic mail can permit an organization to hold fewer meetings (particularly of committees) by doing much of the work on-line. The point is not that e-mail substitutes for meetings by any fixed proportionality but, rather, that groups can explore which parts of their collective work can be performed in which medium, postponing until the physical meeting those interactions that must be conducted face-to-face. This exploration is precisely the evolution of genres of communication. As usual, each genre fits into the broader patterns of activity in the individuals' lives and the life of the organization, and participation in the genres is a skill that is acquired and in some way transmitted to others. To consciously design these genres of communication is precisely to design the social relationships of the organization and the values that these relationships reflect.

It is hard to generalize any further about these matters. Few fixed rules or lessons may exist. The important thing is to use the proliferation of new media as an opportunity to completely rethink the place of communication in our lives. We are all designers in our daily practice of communicating—in the small ways in which we innovate and evolve the relatively stable genres of our mediated interactions with others. But we are equally dependent on the professional designers who have the resources and skills to map out the broad systems of community relationships within which genres of communication live. This is why it is so important for the broadest public in a democracy to become conscious of, and choose, the values that inform professionalized design, for this design work provides some of the central conditions for the extension of democracy in the future or else its decline.

References

Agre, P. E. (1995). Institutional circuitry: Thinking about the forms and uses of information. *Information Technology and Libraries, 14*(4), 225-230.

Arthur, W. B. (1996). Increasing returns and the new world of business. *Harvard Business Review, 74*(4), 100-109.

Baker, C. E. (1997). Giving the audience what it wants. *Ohio State Law Journal, 58*(2), 311-417.

Bakhtin, M. (1981). *The dialogic imagination: Four essays* (C. Emerson & M. Holquist, Trans.). Austin: University of Texas Press. (Original work published 1975)

Bazerman, C. (1988). *Shaping written knowledge: The genre and activity of the experimental article in science.* Madison: University of Wisconsin Press.

Beyer, H., & Holtzblatt, K. (1997). *Contextual design: A customer-centered approach to systems designs.* Los Altos, CA: Morgan Kaufman.

Bjerknes, G., Ehn, P., & Kyng, M. (Eds.). (1987). *Computers and democracy: A Scandinavian challenge.* Aldershot, UK: Avebury.

Checkland, P., & Scholes, J. (1990). *Soft systems methodology in action.* Chichester, UK: Wiley.

Farrell, J., & Saloner, G. (1987). Competition, compatibility and standards: The economics of horses, penguins and lemmings. In H. L. Gabel (Ed.), *Product standardization and competitive strategy* (pp. 1-22). Amsterdam: North-Holland.

Gandy, O. H., Jr. (1982). *Beyond agenda setting: Information subsidies and public policy.* Norwood, NJ: Ablex.

Gibson, J. W. (1994). *Warrior dreams: Paramilitary culture in post-Vietnam America.* New York: Hill & Wang.

Hayek, F. (1945). The use of knowledge in society. *American Economic Review, 35*(4), 519-530.

Hutchins, E. (1995). *Cognition in the wild.* Cambridge: MIT Press.

Jackall, R. (1988). *Moral mazes: The world of corporate managers.* New York: Oxford University Press.

Lave, J., & Wenger, E. (1991). *Situated learning: Legitimate peripheral participation.* New York: Cambridge University Press.

Lemley, M. A. (1996). Antitrust and the Internet standardization problem. *Connecticut Law Review, 28,* 1041-1094.

Orr, J. E. (1996). *Talking about machines: An ethnography of a modern job.* Ithaca, NY: ILR Press.

Radway, J. A. (1984). *Reading the romance: Women, patriarchy, and popular literature.* Chapel Hill: University of North Carolina Press.

Schuler, D., & Namioka, A. (Eds.). (1993). *Participatory design: Principles and practices.* Hillsdale, NJ: Lawrence Erlbaum.

Scribner, S., & Cole, M. (1981). *The psychology of literacy.* Cambridge, MA: Harvard University Press.

4

Feminist Fictions of Future Technology

Cheris Kramarae

When we look at what we can't see, what we do see is the stuff inside our heads.

—Le Guin (1989, p. 143)

The claims for what the Internet has done or will do to change our lives for much the better are widely available in the media, in news stories, advertisements, and editorials. Clearly many people in many countries are going about their work, their communication, and their relationships in somewhat different ways because of their use of the Net. Much of the reporting either portrays or assumes that computer technology is a major technical and social innovation, equally desirable to almost everyone, capable of solving numerous problems, and worthy of our time and money because it is progress—or the reporting describes individualized, sensational, usually sexual-based stories about the trouble primarily a few women and children experience.

AUTHOR'S NOTE: I have followed the APA style except that I have included first names of authors in the list of references. Given my subject material, this is a valuable addition.

To see what other worlds of possibilities are being imagined, I will describe and critique some of the proposed futures of cyber interaction, contrasting the futures as depicted by a number of experts writing in the popular press, with the possibilities suggested by a number of feminists, alternative plans that could benefit all participants. Women are increasingly using the Internet, in a variety of ways. Nonetheless, many of those women are expressing a great deal of concern about the materials and conventions of Internet interaction. I will consider just a few, but key, topics of concern along with suggestions provided by feminist critiques, especially those of feminist science fiction (SF).

Revolution

So much of the speculation about the future involving cyberspace assumes a continuation, expansion, or acceleration of features of our present civilization, even as many write about the revolutionary changes that are coming. About revolution: There *are*, of course, technologically based communication innovations that are being used in the United States and many other places to change the way many of us communicate, entertain, and work. Nonetheless people in other decades during the past two centuries and more also have experienced many changes— perhaps more swiftly and dramatically—as, for example, the uses of inventions that encouraged people to move from farm to cities and from horses to cars (Lohr, 1997). The technological changes did not, of course, benefit everyone equally. The people most likely to benefit in the innovations were the least likely to listen to the critiques of those most likely to suffer, the long term or short term, as the result of the innovations.

These days, the media and the corporations who spend the most in advertising in the media determine to a large extent what we come to call revolutionary. Many computers have been sold because we have been told they are the very latest in a process that everyone must join in on or lose out altogether. Many of us have been caught up in and contribute to the hype created by capitalism.

Of course computers *are* changing many of our lives in important ways. Many of us are corresponding and working with people in ways we didn't dream of just 20 years ago. But 20 years ago I thought that I was in a revolution that would have more lasting and more critical implications than the computers are having. Women in many countries had revived the women's movement for social, political, economic equality. In some countries they had pressed for and won the legal means for more personal control of reproductive actions. Many of us thought that the relationships and lives of women and men around the world soon would be fundamentally and quickly changed. That revolution, although having a great impact on millions and millions of people and on the institutions of our lives, has not been as dramatic or as all-encompassing as we imagined it would be. And the predictions being made for uses of the Net make me realize that the women's revolution, although promoting major improvements, has not yet brought about fundamental changes in the relationships between women and men.

Feminist critics do share some of the same preoccupations as other critics of the new technologies, but our critiques often are different, because they are more likely to focus on women's material practices in the world and the kinds of knowledge and concerns resulting from these practices; they are more ready to trust the experiences and viewpoints of the subjugated than the dominant; they are more likely to be wary of talk about progress unless the discussions are open to women's arguments about what problems need to be solved and what factors need to be considered in any planned changes. Increasingly in feminist critiques these factors include ecological connections and the work of women in all parts of the world (including the caring labor too often omitted from definitions of work).

Feminists are not, of course, speaking with one voice. Our knowledge, experiences, politics, goals, and privileges (including access to various public platforms) are vastly varied, as is made obvious even by just the past 30 years of feminist debates and feminist science fiction, which is not only fantasy about what might be but is often composed from what Haraway (1997) called "personal and collective yearning for just barely possible worlds" (p. 129; she used bell hooks's term "yearns," which can take us beyond pragmatic, potential politics to a lust for new stories involving more people and better lives). What are the plots and outcomes we are most interested in? What are the narratives that tie together our various dreams and our various actions? That tie together our individual human needs and wishes and our concerns for the rest of the earth, through time?

There is a very large gap between the immediate future and the imaginative agendas described by feminist science fiction. Nevertheless, it seems to me particularly important to consider our long-range dreams and goals, our yearnings, at a time we are convinced there are major changes in the wind, sweeping through many of our lives.

Why science fiction? This source of feminist ideas initially might seem strange because the SF genre is generally thought of as male, with plots and rockets often blasting men into new difficult territories and adventures, encountering some women on the way or at least on the cover. And indeed, there is much horrific science fiction. However, SF includes a rich variety of imaginative thinking, and throughout SF history there have been women writers whose interests create new possibilities, often involving technology. In Western SF, a long history of women writers, from Mary Shelley and her *Frankenstein* in 1818 through 19th-century Gothic fiction, through "out of this world" explorations in the 20th century, has helped construct the genre. The feminist utopian writings, which also have roots in the 19th century, have focused on critiques of male-dominated social and political structures and have offered visions of something different. In each period, the writers have, of course, written from their own ideology, which often has been more directly revealed in the case of the feminist fiction. As Sarah Lafanu (1988) pointed out, most SF has been mute about social development in general, and on the personal and political relationships between women and men in particular, a lack that Joanna Russ called a failure of imagination (cited in Lafanu, 1988, pp. 3-5). Feminist science fiction has been, in part, a critique of what is called mainstream (or menstream) science fiction. It's an expanding genre that, although often marginalized in academe and literary circles, requires thinking anew, even imagining the everyday unimaginable.

In the past two decades an increasing number of readers are finding feminist science fiction a place that combines (implicit or explicit) discussion of the horrors of the present with experimentation of very different futures, which include many women's aims, aspirations, expressions, worries, contradictions, differences, ideas, characters, and plots. Even the feminist dystopias are often healthier, in their insightful ugliness and criticism, than the Brothers Grimm types of tales that have been so prominent in the education of girls and women for so many years in so many different forms.[1] We need women's ideas about possible futures and understandings of the past even more than we need men's at the moment, because so much already has been made of men's and it's not looking all that good for men or women. We need some additional destabilizers and some positive features concerning the vision, sound, feel, and taste of possible worlds.

A Few Words
About A Few Words

For years, through our U.S. educational system, we have learned to judge the current knowledge and smartness of an individual by his or her use and control of the jargon of fields of expertise. Increasingly, the way a person talks authoritatively about the Internet and computers is now a common way of evaluating their knowledge, power, and adaptability for many fields of study and many jobs. Many people who cannot talk knowingly about whatever is, at the moment, called computer technology are apologetic about their "ignorance" even if they do not have the resources or the incentives to use these technologies.

Any words I use here to symbolize the processes and articulation of machines and humans will likely quickly become dated. Old words about technology become historical artifacts in a commercial system of continuous economic growth that thrives on replacement, change, and waste, often called progress. Donna Haraway (1997) pointed out that "computers" is the word frequently used for the joining actions of humans and nonhumans "through which potent 'things' like freedom, justice, well-being, skill, wealth, and knowledge are variously reconstituted" (p. 126). She continued, " 'The computer' is a trope, a part-for-whole figure, for a world of actors and actants, and not a Thing Acting Alone. . . . Computers are not the cause of anything, but the human and nonhuman hybrids remake words" (p. 126). As shorthand, I will use *computers* and *technology* in these senses, as symbols for the processes in which humans and computers or software make connections and take actions that have many social implications.

Reviews of works of fiction that explore change and possibilities often distinguish among science fiction, myths of technology, speculative fiction, magic realism, fantasy, cyberpunk, utopia, and dystopia. In practice, the lines often blur. The discussions about the terminology are very useful in sorting out some of the narrative strategies authors use in writing about ecology, relationships among women and men and between humans and machines. Some of these discussions are in Wolmark (1994) and Laura Quilter's WWW page (http://www.uic.edu/laluramd/femsf/). As with any lively, evolving genre, the writers and readers do not agree on definitions. Writing about the phrase "speculative fiction written by women," Marleen Barr (1987) pointed out that efforts to find new, more convenient, telling terms should not be considered "mere textual facades" but, rather, suggest that we are working with a language ill prepared to receive the women's ideas and writings (pp. 156-157). I'll use the terms rather casually, recognizing that if my focus were on the fiction rather than on the technology these categories would deserve more attention.

A chapter is a short and too static a space to make many of the numerous useful links on the issues of feminism, technology, and predictions. In the first edition of this book, my chapter used feminist science fiction to evaluate virtual reality (VR) and to suggest some alternatives. Since that publication, the boundaries between the dreams or nightmares of VR and current computer practices and predictions have become even more blurred, and so here I write more about some of the general predictions about computers and communication. Quickly the specifics will become dated, if U.S. consumerism continues. However, the questions and visions regarding equality, knowledge, and justice in technological changes are likely to remain only too timely. In order to imagine how computers can best work to relieve problems and bring us new possibilities, we best start with a look at what many women in many situations state are current problems, needs for the present, and predictions for a better future.

Report From the Present

Futurists work from their places in the present, of course. The women who are single mothers employed in difficult, tiring jobs, women who are homeless, women who are working double time to get a formal education and keep families fed have quite different wishes and dreams and speculations than those who are employed in jobs that, for example, leave them some space for voluntary computer use. In a telling account, workers in a computer learning center free to users, with special invitations to the homeless and women who otherwise would not have access to the Internet, found that most of those who used the service were middle-class white males (Whitcomb, 1997). When the women did arrive, it was usually with the specific objective of preparing for work by learning basic office applications or job searching. Few came into the center even on Women's Night, when children under 12 were made welcome and all the volunteer instructors were women. Those who visited on Women's Night came because of the all-women environment rather than because of the chance to surf the Net. In fact, the women almost never casually surfed the Net (Whitcomb, 1997).

One set of predictions is included in *The Futurist* (May/June 1997) in a section titled "Women's Preferred Futures." While the responses included in the feature come from women in a variety of jobs, most have some resources that come from "higher" education. Still, their preferred future considered benefits for many women and men. We can note that their suggestions, which included implied criticism of present conditions, have little to do with specific features of new technologies, and a lot to do with sustainable relationships, economies, and ecology. Very briefly, they suggest the following for a better future:

The concept of self is no longer a gender identity. Health centers emphasize health rather than sickness. Entertainment is active and expressed through community-scaled sports, musical groups, and theatricals. While most day-to-day interaction and business is at the level of the neighborhood or village, women and men are equally represented at all levels of government. Social institutions have a commitment to knowledge sharing, spiritual growth, and tolerance for change; new laws give tax benefits to companies that promote equality among workers and provide environmentally sane modes of production. Families are functional relationships valued in part for apprenticeships, service learning, and, in some homes, sharing of child care. Children are valued for what they can teach adults; villages are committed to raising the children in many collaborative ways. Mentors work with teenagers as they learn community work and careers. All women have access to natural herbal birth control methods that have no side effects. Interactions with the environment are based on principles of sustainability. Education is a task and pleasure provided by work places as well as schools, and literacy programs are available to all. Warring and other violence are considered unacceptable behavior.

Faster modems aren't needed for these kinds of changes. Super technology is not stressed (in fact not even mentioned by most of the women), although one writer proposed that prospective parents could screen child care givers via the World Wide Web, and one of the writers, enrolled in a "Studies of the Future" graduate program, wrote about not only a multiphone that operates a technowave but also a new way of contact called Inner Communication Patterns, based on advanced telepathy, a training and a practice that causes no environmental messes.

We will all benefit from listening to these and other alternatives from other women who know about the present and thus are very concerned that unless central dominant values and practices are wildly and widely changed, the future might be as dangerous to women and others.

Looking through speculative fiction seems a particularly good way of looking at how people relate to their environment, because creating stories requires that the writers not only create creatures and features and situations of potential interest to readers but also apply these elements to new relationships.

Women and Cyberspace

Computer technology often is advertised as equally applicable, desirable, and valuable to everyone. The uses of computers are often presented as a major, valuable innovation, solving numerous problems, including social problems. We are encouraged to invest in it—with our time, money, interest—because it is progress; it is the inevitable future. Computer technology is sometimes portrayed as most helpful to those with past economic and political problems related to gender, education, class, age, and race discrimination.

Looking at the programs and the discussions of computer technologies, we see that women are in this cyberspace but in the same basic ways they have been in the rest of men's technology creations, not as primary decision makers but primarily as tools or concepts to be used in the creations of men.

What I'm concerned about here is the place of girls and women in the designing and analyzing of our futures. Given the supposed concern of educational administrators about the past gender, race, and class inequities in our school systems, and given the stated goals of providing meaningful education to students from a variety of backgrounds, we would think that those administrators might be encouraging all manner of studies and providing support to those who are studying the genderizing of the computer studies and programs inside and outside the classrooms. They are not.

We can define the problems of access to common electronic programs as occurring at two levels. The first is at the hardware and software level. As anyone who looks with even semi keen eyes can see, girls and women do not have the access that boys and men have. Studies that indicate that many little boys quickly learn that they can and may push girls off classroom computers should be of great concern to all of us, as should be the assumptions on campuses about the people who most need the new equipment. The distribution of hardware and software seems to have a direct relationship to the distribution of women and men teachers across the campus. We are seeing that science professors are assumed to need the most and the newest of computer equipment but those teaching nursing classes don't.

Second is the problem of access to relevant databases, equipment, programs, bulletin boards and newsgroups. Whereas there are thousands of on-line discussion groups to be found via electronic searches, only a very few of the electronic forums are germane to the feminist student and scholar (Ebben & Kramarae, 1993).[2]

Our own research and our experience in organizing a working colloquium—Women, Information Technology, and Scholarship (WITS)—at the University of Illinois at Urbana-Champaign, in 1990 make clear to us that girls and women will have to work, often under difficult circumstances, to alter the trends, to find or create funding for computer equipment and programs and other relevant and useful resources. Judging from what is and is not going on in cyberspace these days, it is vital to all of us that women do this finding and creating. The WITS women have been very interested in the new technologies and talk about potentials for increasing communication among women, of making child care easier and better for all, of making their professional lives better rather than more difficult and dangerous. We talk about the importance of being active participants in the learning process, the value of multiple learning modes (rather than assuming that everyone enjoys learning by waiting for the program to crash). We talk about easy access to a broad array of information (including such basics as telephone numbers and household information) and information retrieval customized to one's personal history (see Banich & Wilson, 1993, p. 67). Taking our cues from Marge Piercy's SF account in *He, She, It,* we are writing and reading essays that deal with the poor working conditions and wages of women in other countries who are producing the computer parts that have allowed the rapid increased buying of personal computers in the United States. We are asking questions about the impact of technological change for rural women in the United States and elsewhere and questions about social and health issues that come with the new technologies. We are outlining the future we'd like to experience. For example, we drew pictures of what we'd like the computerized universities of our future to contain. In addition to the electronic networks, we also included such desirable features as child care facilities, health centers complete with aromatherapy, campus woods, streams, colorful and U-shaped classrooms for better interaction. We are discussing the masculinity of science and what that means for all our work in all disciplines.

Information

Of course, as many have pointed out, the current structure of the Net allows sending and receiving a lot of material uncensored by any government or corporation. But who is reading and listening to whom? Many of us are aware of what has been called "information poverty." But because of the very centrality of host computers in the United States, the predominance of English on the Net, and the control of the telecommunication companies in the North, those of us in the United States can all too easily forget some of the problems this has created for others not in the rich North. The great majority of the world's peoples still are without basic telecommunication, and Internet access time and computer equipment are relatively much more expensive for those in South Asia and Africa than for those living in most Northern countries. A survey of the U.S. on-line population in 1997 indicated that women were 47% of the users (NUA Internet Survey, 1997). Yet, if we consider amount of time spent on computers, the type of equipment, and the influence on programming, everywhere the technologically elite overwhelmingly are men, a condition that perpetuates and exacerbates long-term, large-scale economic and educational gaps. Most of the glorification of "global communication" and the "free flow of information" comes from those who are in the position to determine what that will cost and in which language it will be said. For others, these terms often mask the loss of cultural integrity, national values, and an increase in the homogenization of electronic and print media (Holderness, 1996-1997, pp. 41-42). Unfortunately, Global often means *Centralized*—a centralization by those who have less interest in receiving ideas from others than in exporting and selling ideas.

Throughout the 1980s and early 1990s when computers were discussed, there was often reference to the information revolution, to the ways that computers can spread information across class and national boundaries. The stress on information has been unfortunate, as if there were shared ideas about what constitutes information and as if this information or knowledge (the two words were often used as synonyms) could be transferred via computers or any other way in a manner and form beneficial to everyone. The *Encyclopedia Britannica* often has been given as an example of information or knowledge that can be digitized and made more accessible to many. That encyclopedia and most other encyclopedias are, of course, very limited works containing not the knowledge of people around the world but, rather, some of the beliefs and interests of a relatively small number of people. Yet the encyclopedias are heavily used in education settings and are taught as knowledge—containing the kinds of things one has to know if one is to be considered educated. In the first wave of justification of selling and investing in computers, encyclopedias were there, ready to be converted into a new form to help distribute the Information Revolution everywhere—for a price.

Suzette Haden Elgin is writing an SF novel in which the status of sight and touch in the United States are reversed so that most valued information comes through touch. Another SF author, Ursula K. Le Guin (1985), told us about the Atheasheans, a forest people for whom touch was a main channel of communication. The Atheasheans were puzzled by the very limited language of the invading Terrans whose touch "is always likely to imply threat aggression, and so for them there is often nothing between the formal handshake and the sexual caress." Because touch is part of their language, it is "therefore patterned, codified, yet infinitely modifiable" (p. 543). The Terrans, however, were unable to see in the touch exchanges anything but their own eroticism that, focused on sex and then repressed and frustrated, "invades and poisons every sensual pleasure, every humane response" (p. 543). Will our (Terran) language become even more limited with increased on-line communication? Could we usefully think more critically about what we consider information and what resources we have, and want to use, to express our experiences, feelings, and ideas?

Education in These New, Better Worlds

In the United States, most formal education systems have stressed competition and conformity rather than creativity. New uses of computers allow for some major changes.

Many people have commented on the difficulty of sorting out real from unreal, authenticated from rumored. They ask: Who will maintain the standards that we have used to determine truth in this new system that allows anyone with access to computers and modems to post almost anything, even if they haven't done a proper job of checking their information? Of course for women trying to figure out what is real has been a lifelong project. We haven't been the knowledge makers. We have learned to be skeptical of the "truths" we've been told. Now we have to be even more careful perhaps, but this is not a new problem for us. Getting access to computers and literacy will be the more immediate problem for most.

Supposedly everyone can share knowledge, a situation that can help the poorer people and countries. As Harlan Cleveland (1997), President of the World Academy of Art and Science, declared, as a result of information creating wealth in poor countries, we are

> living at a very special moment in humankind's long ascent toward civilized behavior. It is the consequence of the enormous advances of science and technology, sparked by information science and informa- tion technology, which have now made the human species, for the first time, the lead actor in its own evolution. (p. 18)

An administrator for the International Space University wrote that "since the time of ancient Greece, the accumulated information of our world has increased by an estimated 10 million times," adding that in the next century it will likely increase another 10 million times (Pelton, 1996, p. 18). Others argue that the new computer technologies will enable everyone to learn at their own pace, beginning when they are still in their cribs. Teachers, mentors, or peers won't be vital to the process. Of course this means that each student needs his or her own computer. Bill Gates (1997) said, "The idea is that each student feels in control of what they're doing, that they don't have to stand in line to wait to use the resource" (p. 9).

But wait. In general, the communication, information, and sensation revolutions and industries have not been designed with women in mind. Whereas many teachers may wonder what will happen to the printed word as words and people become electronic, many of us also wonder just what exclusion will look like with the new changes. Dale Spender (1995) pointed out that the era of books was not one that included women as writers:

> Given our history, it's not possible to assume that women will automat- ically share equally in all gains that come from the present information

revolution. Women were excluded from the process of knowledge-making when the printing press was invented; and there's plenty of evidence today to suggest that women are again being kept out of the production of information as we move to the electronic networks. (p. 161)

It's been men and their technologies; women as their tools. Remember the typewriter? Initially, the typists were men. Then, as it became a common machine in offices used mainly to print the words of men, the typewriter, as the operator was called, became a woman. The telephone was designed and made for men and their businesses (in some places "social calls" initially cost more than "business calls"), but women were employed to do the switching until new technology took care of most of that (Rakow, 1992). Eventually computers will be constructed to print the words spoken to them, but for now, many women work in many computer centers tapping away, typing businessmen's words. In general, women are employed to do what the men don't want to do and the machines can't do yet.

Teaching writing with the use of computers breaks the tradition somewhat, because both men and women are learning to type their compositions. Nonetheless, if we track the students through universities and into their workplace, we find that women and men have very different dealings with computers and other machinery. And if we look at the activities of the middle-class girls and boys who eventually will come into the composition classes, we see very different modes of dealing with computers. We all know this, of course. We know that it's primarily the middle-class boys who are spending long hours playing "games" on computers. I think that if we are concerned about our students and what they are learning from us and the rest of the culture, we need to look closely at these differences. We need to consider the changing definitions of sex, gender, intimacy, privacy, and identity, and also the remaining gender hierarchy that continues to construct the basis of sex, gender, intimacy, privacy, and identity. I think analysis of the gendered work and play with these technologies makes clear that non-traditional forms of expression contain much of the same old ideas about gender roles.

Assuming that we think the gender splits and hierarchies of the past, current, and (unless there are major changes) the future are destructive, what can we do? First, we need to pay mind to what's going on with the activities of millions of young boys and girls. Many working-class children have little access to computers in or out of classroom; for many children here and in other countries, life is about just trying to live. Many middle-class boys are becoming electronic demons on the Net and all the computer games they can get their hands on; the girls are not. The reasons for the very different experiences that girls and boys have with the new technologies are many but all involve the very present gender, race, and class divisions that remain in our culture, because those who have the most power to do something basic to alter this situation don't want to or really don't know how to. We need to continue to watch, listen, analyze, and make interventions when we can, particularly in times of change. Cyberspace can provide freedoms of various sorts, but they are designed and constrained by powerful structured forces of assumptions and goals; they are not equally friendly environments or opportunities for everyone.

Ecology and Environment

Frank Biocca argued that virtual reality "will allow all kinds of protean forms of visual and physical expression without transforming physical reality. . . . [I]t is suggested that virtual reality is a green technology." Jaron Lanier agreed that "Media technology is a minor contributor to the ecological malaise of our planet. . . . To the degree that it might encourage telecommuting that is probably more important than anything else" (Lanier & Biocca, 1992, p. 169).

We'll leave aside the mention of telecommuting, at once a very promising and a very problematic concept these days, especially for the women who try to work two jobs—working for a company while watching the children, without benefit of union support or day care. What about the argument that VR and other computer activity takes little fossil energy and avoids trampling on the grass? In general, computer work uses a lot of electricity and a lot of paper. For example, the world's personal computers used 115 billion sheets of paper in 1994. Steve Anzovin, author of *The Green PC*, claimed that the expanding structure of the World Wide Web is the main reason that paper use has been increasing by more than 25% each year (cited in ebb & flow, 1996-1997, p. 3) Computer equipment quickly becomes antiquated and junked, when newer models become available. Sally Gearhart (1985), author of the feminist speculative fiction *Wanderground: Stories of the Hill Women* has called for an end to technology development, writing that we are growing more and more dependent on Western science and technology with the result we are virtually helpless when it fails, as in the nuclear meltdown at Three Mile Island and in the many failures of computers that leave consumers stranded in airports and library patrons without a catalogue. More important, in our dependency on technology we stand in an adversarial relationship to our environment. To study and control our environment we alienate ourselves from it, she wrote. Technology as it is being used leads to power domination, control—in a failed relationships to our planet. Gearhart (1991) wrote, "An extraterrestrial observing our polluted and diseased planet would have to conclude that homo sapiens, the inventor of technology, was an evolutionary blunder and should now silently . . . steal away" (pp. 83-85). She suggested that if we knew we were to have no more of us, we might change our character pretty quickly and quit poisoning, killing, and beating up on each other (actions that haven't shown much interest in species preservation any-way), and become more appreciative of our environment. If we can't or don't want a voluntary cessation of reproduction, we have another option offered by her *Wanderground*—the training of our senses so, for example, we hear and see with more sensitivity, and we learn to live much more cooperatively with other animals in order to bring some harmony to all. I'm watching to see what earthly creatures we'll see in VR programs. In the VR literature, I see references to some creatures called "interstellar pukoids" and "nasty phlegm throwers," but except for some few discussions about rain forest plants and animals, there seems to be little interest in rethinking our relationship with our envi-ronment. In fact, the interest seems to be in distancing humans from it, away from the dirt and also away from the pollution we have caused.

There *are* other scenarios. For example, in her writing, Starhawk (1993) took us to a community in the mid-21st century California where, in the midst of a nightmare world, a community had established a culture that honors diversity of races, languages, and religions, and promotes the Sacred Things that sustain life. At council meetings, masked repre-sentations sit in trance in the corners of the room, deeply conscious and channeling The Voices of wind, fire, water, and earth; every decision the people made needed to take them into account (pp. 45-46). Imagine the initial confusion if the other animals, the plants, the water, and the air had privileged voices in management meetings at Microsoft and other computer companies. A work of speculative fiction indeed.

Intimacy and Sex

A fond prediction of many futurists is that cybersex systems or sexbots will provide personally designed sex models that can be traded in, redesigned, and available at any time. As an author (Maxwell, 1997) of a book on "cybersex" wrote, "People will be able to pick out a good-looking virtual partner from an electronic catalog and engage in a completely safe and fulfilling encounter" (p. 33). Robotic sex will, some futurists predict, eliminate adultery, teen pregnancy, sexually transmitted diseases, abortions, and sex crimes, and may result in "an entire class of humans" who not only will never have sex with other humans but won't desire it (Snell, 1997, p. 32). For them, sex will not require any conversation, health care, or reciprocal attention. "Advanced devices" will be able to "stimulate the specific pleasure centers of the brain to enhance sensations beyond anything experienced naturally" (Maxwell, 1997, p. 33).

Male interest in sex-with-machines already has been played out in the movies for many years. Early on there was the female robot of Fritz Lang's *Metropolis,* followed more recently by sexual mechanisms in *The Stepford Wives,* as well as in *Westworld* and *Futureworld* (in which the sexual robots are preponderantly female). And then there's Ilia-probe of *Star Trek.* Donald Palumbo (1982) argued that most science fiction films have at the least an underlying metaphor of a human sperm-figure going through a vaginal tunnel, emerging victorious.

Howard Rheingold (1991) wrote,

> The secondary social effects of technosex are potentially revolutionary. If technology enables you to experience erotic frissons or deep physical, social, emotional communication with another person with no possibility of pregnancy or sexually transmitted disease, what then of conventional morality, and what of the social rituals and cultural codes that exist solely to enforce that morality? Is disembodiment the ultimate sexual revolution and/or the first step toward abandoning our bodies? ... perhaps cyberspace is a better place to keep most of the population relatively happy, most of the time.
>
> Privacy and identity and intimacy will become tightly coupled into something we don't have a name for yet. (pp. 352-353)

For many men in particular, heterosexual intimacy means primarily sex, while women more often talk about intimacy in terms of general closeness including sharing thoughts and discussing problems. This conflict of interests is clearly going to be played out once again in the New Media. The alt.sex.news groups and related pages on the Web have very high traffic, with mostly men exchanging messages. In France the national fiber-optic Minitel system has in the past been largely funded by phone sex (Stefanac, 1993).

Mike Saenz, who created his idea of playmates—Virtual Valerie and MacPlaymate —stated that he wanted to create something new:

> Most games are performance tests—violent performance tests. Most look as if they've been programmed by sadistic nerds—this is largely because they were. I wanted to create a nonviolent interactive simulation that a user could enjoy simply for the experience. . . . Virtual Valerie . . . she's your cybernetic fantasy!. . . . This is our chance to create a whole new form of erotic art. . . . When I explain virtual reality to the uninitiated, they just don't get it. But they warm immediately to the idea of virtual sex. . . . I have a silly idea for a product called Strip Teacher. She goes, "Tell me the name of the thirteenth president of the United States and I'll show you my tits." (Saenz, quoted in *Mondo 2000*, 1992, pp. 272, 274)

I'll venture that he was not thinking of this product as primarily an educational experience. He continued, "I think lust motivates technology. The first personal robots, let's face it, are not going to be bought to bring people drinks" (quoted in *Mondo 2000*, 1992, p. 275).

These forms of intimacy come without any necessity or even desirability of giving to another. In her fictional but serious warning of the future, Marge Piercy (1991) wrote of the simulations of the 21th century: "You watch or rent a stimmie and you enter that actor or actress. You feel what they feel. They're yours. But you don't belong to them. You are freed from the demands of reciprocity" (p. 382).

Another writer (Mort, 1992) wrote about this freedom from worries of responsibilities for others:

> Imagine a cyberspace mate whom you see only when you want to—one designed to your specifications, who doesn't argue, doesn't require medical care, never goes away. For some, such a virtual world might be addictive and debilitating. For others, it might be kind. (p. 191)

Another writer called virtual reality "the emotional condom of the 21st century" (Ulrich, 1992).

We could, however, talk about some differing ways of expressing intimacy and closeness. You've heard the feminist critiques of men's ways of expressing intimacy. Men disclose less and mostly about current events, sports, and money; they think sex is primarily doing rather than being; they have more, but less intimate, same-sex friends, and their friendships are based more on activities rather than talking things over.

Recently, some communication researchers have pointed out that the research on men's and women's friendships has been female-biased.[3] In focusing on differences we have often overlooked that girls and boys, women and men all want relationships that are validating and satisfying. Men, the argument continues, have taken a different, rather than less meaningful, path to closeness. They do things for those about whom they care. Also, they show friendship by sharing activities rather than expressing feelings through talk. Sharing joint activities (rather than the sharing of information, feelings, and secrets) is also an active way of cultivating closeness, these critics point out. Through the sharing of activities men have reported that they create feelings of interdependence, affinity, and experience personal development (Swain, 1989). Other critics have suggested that men's relative unwillingness or disinterest in talking about personal matters means that in intimate interactions with women it becomes very difficult to have discussions about problems. (Maybe one of the reasons that women are, in general, better at reading nonverbal cues is that they have to learn that when the best man in a woman's life washes the car he is really saying things like "I understand that you are feeling bad about the death of your cat and the fact that you have a unexplained lump on your elbow and I'm doing my best to tell you that I am also concerned, that I think that the lump might be caused by the stress that you and I have been under at work; I really care about you and your mental and physical health and I'm showing it the only way I know how. I'm saying all this and the car is clean. What more would you want?") We should talk more about this, however difficult it might be for some. Electronic sex and intimacy, as illustrated and planned in most computer programming, is very limited and limiting.

The SF thought experiments can be useful in giving us quite other ways of thinking about female, male, gender, and sex. For example, in *The Left Hand of Darkness*, Le Guin (1969) offered the story of the Gethenians, who were neither men nor women but individuals who shared the biological and emotional makeup of both. They could not have sexual intercourse unless both partners were willing, because they could not rape or be raped. In an essay about the book, Le Guin (1989) wrote that she was trying to open up an alternative viewpoint to suggest, "if we were socially ambisexual, if men and women were completely and genuinely equal in their social roles, equal legally and economically, equal in freedom, in responsibility, and in self-esteem, then society would be a very different thing" (p. 16). Might our new computer "stories" try for some spectacular new ways of experiencing sex in ways that work not on dominance and duality but sensuous sensibility?

Community and Shared
Dreams and Possibilities

"Community" is one of four themes that have been prevalent in U.S. discussions of activities on the Internet. While the others, anarchy, frontier, and democracy, have become less mentioned as the Internet becomes increasingly commercialized, the concept of community is used frequently and rather loosely in discussions of the Internet. It often seems to mean any group of people with one common characteristic, or (especially, on the Net) any group of people that shares an interest in at least one topic. If, however, we define community as including interpersonal interaction, economic interdependency, sharing of social life, including sickness, health, spiritual concerns, we see we don't have many of these in cyberspace. And it's an impoverished community that knowingly allows large numbers of people to be excluded from the Internet (Kramer & Kramarae, 1997). Of course, many people without a sense of a neighborhood or a web of friendships may have not experienced a sense of community and, in fact, might find more connections with others in cyberspace. And many women are certainly using the Internet to organize in many ways. But often cyberspace hype includes more discussion of democracy and lack of power structures in cyberspace than discussion of the fact that, for the near future at least, unchecked majority rule on the Internet will almost always exclude women's interests.

Many women would argue that if we are interested in Internet community, we need to be concerned about how to consider the importance and distinctiveness of parenting and caring, about establishing nonviolent connections, about showing respect for life and life giving, about reaching out to help others, about the special needs that some members of the community have.

Octavia Butler (1993) wrote of a California society several decades from now in which the street poor (squatters, jobless, homeless) are numerous, desperate, and make life for all others also dangerous. "Progress" and "growth" are no longer goals. Staying fed and alive are the major concerns of everyone. Large television screens are going dark, people can no longer afford to subscribe to multisensory broadcasts, and there were no more "reality vests, no touch-rings, and no headsets," and very few computers. Many people, children and adults, are illiterate, with many learning instead to rob to survive and to terrorize to scare off or kill those who appear to be ready to rob or kill. We read about someone who once worked with computers, but when his company went out of business he got a job driving slaves (people owned by others or heavily in debt to others), pushing them to work faster. Guns and radios have become more important to people than are computers networks. In this speculative fiction work, hope for a better life comes from the possibility, encouraged by a young girl, an empath (who experiences the pain of others), that many people could come together to form new collaborative communities—Earthseed communities—that take root in the earth, with the needs of all the people involved, and with action that is only useful "if it steadies you, focuses your efforts, eases your mind" (p. 197).

Collective, decentralized administration is a feature in many feminist speculative fiction novels. However, as Margrit Eichler pointed out, while the speculative societies in many feminist novels place a greater value on beautifying and equipping public rather than private space, this is the opposite of the real situation we have today (Eichler, 1981).

Given that our U.S. society is highly focused on individual "freedom," and is bringing about a rapidly deteriorating environment, we need some new scenarios badly. As we try to foresee and plan the future, we might usefully look at our past as well. The predictions of radically better communication or universal community for "everyone" were made for the uses of telephone, ham radio, community cable TV, CB radio. In actuality, in each case the costs of "belonging" remained substantial for many, and those without the expensive equipment and knowledge to use it were usually omitted from the many decision-making processes that determine what can be done and at what expense by whom. In considering the predictions made for most communication technologies, we might do better to think of these primarily as businesses rather than as communication channels. Certainly the Net is becoming more business-like every day.

Global Communication

One foreseer, Jessica Lipnack (1997), wrote of a 2020 meeting of the Network of Regions Nations, Provinces, Cultures, and Indigenous People. Most of the 5,000 delegates are women, a dramatic reversal of the representation of the old (i.e., present) United Nations. The Network grew out of small-affinity groups formed by young women around the world, corresponding through e-mail. Wherever there were Internet connections, women participated in conversations, in honor of the new millennium. Whereas men weren't excluded, the driving force "was female, feminine, and feminist, meaning that listening, creating, exploring, and nurturing were the binding values" (p. 3). The on-line conversations lead to face-to-face meetings, linked by video conferencing. Instead of one-time events, there were continuous convocations "mirroring the way women live their lives—activities flowing into events leading to celebrations" (p. 3). Within a decade, women had been elected president, premier, or prime minister in every nation. Meeting in Iceland, they agreed to restructure the United Nations to be more representative of the natural groups of people and of the issues in the women's discussions.

On a smaller scale, some of this work already has begun. I was fortunate to work with an international group of women, meeting at the UN, to plan the most cost-effective ways women throughout the world can use computer networks to continue the work of the Fourth World Conference on Women. (See WomenWatch http://www.un.org/womenwatch, which was launched on International Women's Day, March 8, 1997.) At the planning meeting in 1996, all the participants, including those who saw no immediate way many women in their countries would access WomenWatch, agreed on the importance of women being involved in the development of communication technologies that can be used primarily to increase cooperation, interaction, and equality. However, all the women were aware that the present or planned electronic links would not quickly bring about better connected lives for women around the world.

As one critic (Iyer, 1997) has written, "In fact, the world could be said to be growing less and less connected, if only because the gap between the few of us who babble about the wiring of the planet and the billions who do not grows ever more alarming" (p. 28). Pico Iyer went on to point out that in Haiti, for example, 70% of the people have no jobs and 60%

of those over the age of 25 have never had a day of formal schooling; in such a situation to talk of glories of a virtual workplace and communities seems, Iyer suggests, "almost obscene" (p. 28). And yet the future of Haiti will be tied in various ways to the behavior of those in other countries with these other concerns. We are wise to note that the increased reliance on technologies that are created and produced in industrialized nations may have quite unexpected implications for the political, economic, and cultural lives of individuals and nations (Hanson & Narula, 1990, pp. 2-3).

Given that the Internet was initially developed for U.S. defense research and communication purposes, we should not surprised that English was the assumed language of initial Internet communication. However, the 1980s, when the National Science Foundation promoted the technology as a universal educational aide, would have been a good time to discuss what language structures and norms would best serve the education of the greatest number of people.

In addition to English, there are approximately 6,000 other languages, with estimates that, without special efforts, a century from now half of them may be extinct, a threat that is as much a concern to many people as the continuing extinction of animals. The Internet may actually provide a means of fostering interest in some of these languages. (See the Web site of the Summer Institute of Linguistics.) And some would argue that having something as close to a world language as English is becoming international and on the Internet will eventually promote clear communication and peace. However, a shared language is not a guarantee of either. And the more fluent speakers of the language have a major advantage over other speakers, particularly in chat rooms. Further, if one of the benefits of the Internet interaction is learning about other cultures, we need to be concerned about all the languages and voices that are seldom heard on the Internet.

As David Crystal (1997) wrote,

> To lose a language is to lose a unique view of the world that is shared by no other. Each has its own figures of speech, its own narrative style, its own proverbs . . . we can learn from the way in which different languages structure reality. . . . And there is no reason to believe that the differing accounts of the human condition presented by the peoples of, say, Irian Jaya will be any less insightful than those presented by writers in French, English, Russian and Sanskrit. (p. 44)

Some writers point out that English itself is used in quite different ways in various cultures throughout the world (Kachru, 1991). We could develop ways of encouraging discussions and appreciations of these differences.

In *Native Tongue*, Suzette Haden Elgin (1984) wrote about a future when interplanetary trade has made language study a necessity and the creation of a new women's language a reality. (Elgin actually created the language, Láadan, in the process of working on this novel.) She encouraged us to think about what we would wish for a language. Not only what kinds of sounds and what kinds of words and concepts but what we would like our language to do for us. Would it be useful for our writings and conversations to have language norms that include prefixes or suffixes that simply and quickly tell, for example, whether what is said is based on one's own experiences, comes from someone the writer or speaker respects, or is from an unknown source? Is it too late to have international, cooperative, inclusive discussions about how we'd like our new communication to work?

Given that Internet communication is based on text and graphics and not on the nonverbal communication, including intonation, of the people providing messages, it would be wise to hold international planning conferences about the language systems to be used internationally to make connections most effective for everyone. Inevitably some new symbols develop with new uses of a language. (We can think of the emoticons and abbreviations for frequently used phrases employed, for example, in many chat rooms.) However, the primary users in the early days of the Internet seem to have determined, without much discussion, the basic linguistic conventions all the rest of us are expected to follow if we are to participate in meaningful ways on the Internet. And this process continues. As writers in one forecasting journal stated, "The needs of scientists brought about the age of intra-computer communication and the age of the Internet . . . but it's the needs of gamers that are taking the Internet to a new generation . . . virtual reality environments" (WKC, 1995, p. 24). The SF creation of Láadan, by Elgin's fictional women several hundred years hence, suggests that even the process of collaborative thinking about how a language might work more usefully to more people is beneficial.

Those who don't assume that English should be the only language of the Internet frequently propose the development of a translator to enable transcultural communication. This is a huge task that has engaged and discouraged many linguists, translators, and computer scientists for years. Noting one nonmechanical problem of such a project, Elgin (1996) pointed out that in English, for example, most emotional information is conveyed through intonation and body language, not by the words. Languages are so critical to our understanding of our cultures and so complex, she suggested that linguistics ought to be a subject taught from the earliest schooling years (p. 7).

Computer communication while still considered quite a feat, is in many ways pretty pathetic. When I talk face-to-face with a colleague we establish eye contact, look away, grimace at bad news, laugh together at good news, use varying intonation, gestures, raised eyebrow, frown, gasp, blink, sigh, eyes open wide, and in other ways use our intelligence, feelings, cultural knowledge and conventions, and bodies to converse. On the computer I have printed words, black and white displays, a little punctuation, capital letters, some smiley faces, and little else. This is changing, of course. Already some of the World Wide Web pages are visually involving, and some even sound interesting. Additional specific attention to the languages of the Internet might bring new engaging possibilities for more global communication.

Limiting Danger and Hostilities

> "If you really want an idea of what computers could become, don't think of typewriters, think of cruise missiles." (Rawlins 1996, p. 111)

Writing science fiction provides writers who have radical ideas about what our culture could be with a forum for introducing into our language and culture some alternatives, some of which are incompatible with the survival of the present culture. That kind of introduction is certainly the mission of linguist and science fiction writer Suzette Haden Elgin (1990) who, believing that it is violence that keeps patriarchy alive, writes more about blessings than curses, more about healing than wounding.

Another futurist, Gregory J.E. Rawlins (1996) disagreed with the possibility of a more blessed society, arguing that while "the future is always more peculiarly strange than any of our tidy imaginings," one thing seems sure: "We'll always need soldiers" (p. 111). He continued to argue that without war practice, "peacetime military forces turn to mush"; fortunately, Rawlins argued, we can produce and use computer simulators that are cheaper, in financial costs and human lives, than real war (pp. 33-34). He pointed out, further, that using telepresence—linking a robot's senses to some of our own—we can mine ore from above ground, or perform surgery on a patient on another continent, play a game of tennis with a partner who's a mile or 1,000 miles away. We can look in on the Himalayas (p. 36). But, I argue, until we have some major changes in our relationships, including those of child care, most women will have to be here, not the Himalayas. He doesn't deal with what should be basic questions of any discussions of our future: Who looks after the children in any contemplated brave new world? What's in the best interest of the children and their caretakers? Can we use our new technologies to challenge and change the many violent practices that damage us and the entire world?

Women have been dealing with security problems for many years, even if they live in a home with locks. Men with homes are more likely to have had things under control. They could lock up their money and records in files and safes in homes, hospitals, banks, police departments, and other government offices. Women have worried about their personal security; they have worried about harassment and terrorism on the streets, in their homes, on the telephone. Now, with all the computer files in danger, men have to figure out new ways of keeping their information and money secure. Women have to add computers as a new way of receiving threats. The teen hackers are often called the revolutionaries of cybersociety. Nonetheless, the revolutionary purpose often is not clear. The goal appears to be unimpeded access to information, but it is not clear for what cause (Critical Art Ensemble, 1996, p. 15). The hackers' work often appears to be electronic trespassing for the sake of trespassing, or the capturing or destroying of electronic files as a personal skills challenge, rather than from a principled effort to keep cyberspace as a free space.

Rather, Caruso, a critic of the technology, asked might we work together to coexist on this planet "whether that be in business, in our personal lives, or in our spiritual practices?" She pointed out that "setting up competitors, enemies, fall guys— that's not a long-term win" (quoted in Spayde, 1996, p. 67). Everyone is going to feel a lot safer if we work from the goal of there being enough room and resources for everyone.

We will likely continue to want to transcend or at least improve our own experiences, our own realities. Most current Net planning, with its roots in male science fiction, television and movie scripting, and consumerism, is one way to go. The feminist science fiction writers, ready to experiment and free to do so in this genre, show us other ways to play serious games with history and gender assumptions, encouraging us to imagine, in culturally rich ways, present alternative ways of thinking about the future.

Our ideas about what our futures could be come from our under-standings of the world we live in and from our dream wishes and fears. If we consider the understandings and the speculative and fantastic ideas of many women, perhaps our futures will be more life-ful. We should not have it any other way.

Notes

1. Feminist science fiction or speculative fiction has been accused by some critics of presenting a nostalgia for a never-never time with an emphasis on matriarchal relationships, a oneness with the earth, and a resistance to technology. Such criticism is simplistic and inaccurate inasmuch as feminist speculative fiction deals with many issues in a rich variety of methods. Yet even the feminist "cyberpunk" novels have received relatively little popular, commercial, and academic interest. (See, for example, Stephanie A. Smith, 1993, for a discussion of Olivia Butler's Xenogenesis.) This is, in part, because the feminist speculative fiction authors do challenge, through utopias and dystopias, the prevailing conceptions of bodies, genders, relationships (including to the earth), and sexual violence.

2. Margie, researching a story on "cyberspace" for Sassy (Margie, 1993), checked out the Women On-Line forum, where the posts were overwhelmingly from males. (Eighty-five percent or more while she was looking.) Margie reported that, "Someone guessed that 'less than one percent of the people on line are actual females, and only one-tenth of those I would actually describe as women. The rest are feminazis and bored obese trashbag-wearing housewives.' Very nice" (p. 80).

The percentages may change depending on the time and the on-line forum, but women on many lists are reporting similar observations about the behavior of many of the participants in the cyberspaces created by women for their discussions.

3. See the critical review offered by Julia Wood and Christopher Inman (1993).

References

Banich, Marie, & Wilson, Betsy (1993). Imagining the ideal information technology. In H. Jeannie Taylor, Cheris Kramarae, & Maureen Ebben (Eds.), *Women, information technology, and scholarship* (p. 67). Urbana-Champaign: Center for Advanced Study at University of Illinois.

Barr, Marleen S. (1987). *Alien to feminity: Speculative fiction and feminist theory.* Westport, CT: Greenwood.

Butler, Octavia E. (1993). *Parable of the sower.* New York: Warner Books.

Cleveland, Harlan. (1997, January-February). Information is the critical resource of the future. *The Futurist: A Magazine of Forecasts, Trends, and Ideas About the Future, 31*(1), 13.

Critical Art Ensemble. (1996). *Electronic civil disobedience and other unpopular ideas.* New York: Autonomedia.

Crystal, David. (1997, Feb./March). Vanishing languages. *Civilization,* pp. 40-45.

ebb & flow. (1996-1997, Winter). *Earth Island Journal: International Environmental News,* p. 3.

Ebben, Maureen, & Kramarae, Cheris. (1993). Women and information technologies: Creating a cyberspace of our own. In H. Jeannie Taylor, Cheris Kramarae, & Maureen Ebben (Eds.), *Women, information technology, and scholarship* (pp. 15-27). Urbana-Champaign: Center for Advanced Study at University of Illinois.

Eichler, Margarit. (1981). Science fiction as desirable feminist scenarios. *Women's Studies International Quarterly, 4*(1), 51-64.

Elgin, Suzette Haden. (1984). *Native tongue.* New York: DAW.

Elgin, Suzette Haden. (1990, March 3). *The feminist pragmatics of applied fantasy.* Paper presented at Texas A&M University, College Station.

Elgin, Suzette Haden. (1996, Jan./Feb.). *Linguistics & Science Fiction, 15*(3), 7.

Gates, Bill. (1997, August, 9). Keynote. *T.H.E. Journal, 24,* 9.

Gearhart, Sally M. (1985). *The wanderground: Stories of the hill women.* London, UK: The Women's Press.

Gearhart, Sally M. (1991). An end to technology. In John Zerzan & Alice Carnes (Eds.), *Questioning technology: Tool, toy, or tyrant?* (pp. 83-85). Philadelphia: New Society Publishers.

Hanson, Jarice & Narula, Uma. (1990). *New communication technologies in developing countries.* Hillsdale, N.J.: Lawrence Erlbaum.

Haraway, Donna. (1997). *Modest Witness@Second Millennium.FemaleMan Meets OncoMouse*™ Feminism and Technoscience. New York: Routledge.

Holderness, Mike. (1996-97, Winter). The Internet and the South. *Earth Island Journal: International Environmental News,* pp. 40-42.

Iyer, Pico. (1997, October 6). The Haiti test: Proving the world *isn't* small—except in our minds. *The Nation, 28,* 30-31.

Kachru, Braj B. (1991). *Alchemy of English: The spread, functions, and models of non-native Englishes (English in the global context).* Urbana: University of Illinois Press.

Kramer, Jana, & Kramarae, Cheris. (1997). Gendered ethics on the Internet. In Josina Makau & Ronald Arnett (Eds.), *Communication ethics in an age of diversity* (pp. 226-243). Urbana: University of Illinois Press.

Lafanu, Sarah. (1988). *Feminism and science fiction.* Bloomington: Indiana University Press.

Lanier, Jaron, & Biocca, Frank. (1992). An insider's view of the future of virtual reality. *Journal of Communication, 42,* 150-172.

Le Guin, Ursula K. (1969). *The left hand of darkness.* New York: Ace.

Le Guin, Ursula K. (1985). The word for world is forest. In Ursula K. Le Guin (Ed.), *Five complete novels.* New York: Avenel.

Le Guin, Ursula K. (1989). Science fiction and the future. In Ursula Le Guin (Ed.), *Dancing at the edge of the world: Thoughts on words, women, places.* New York: Grove Press.

Lipnack, Jessica. (1997, May/June). Global network coordinator named. *The Futurist: A Magazine of Forecasts, Trends, and Ideas About the Future, 31*(3), 3.

Lohr, Steve. (1997, October 5). The future came faster in the old days. *New York Times,* Sec 4, 1.

Margie. (1993, May). Hi Girlz, See You in Cyberspace! *Sassy,* pp. 72, 73, 80.

Maxwell, Kenneth. (1997, July/August). Sex in the future: Virtuous and virtual. *The Futurist: A Magazine of Forecasts, Trends, and Ideas About the Future, 31*(4), 29-31, 33-34.

Mondo 2000. (1992). New York: HarperCollins.

Mort, John. (1992, September 22). Electronic concept, still in its infancy, both a promise and a threat. *Kansas City Star,* p. 19.

NUA Internet Survey. (1997, September 9). Available: http://www.nua.ie/surveys

Palumbo, Donald. (1982). Loving that machine; or, the mechanical egg: Sexual mechanisms and metaphors in science fiction films. In Thomas P. Dunn & Richard D. Erlich (Eds.), *The mechanical god: Machines in science fiction* (pp. 117-128). Westport, CT: Greenwood.

Pelton, Joseph N. (1996, Nov.-Dec.), Cyberlearning vs. the university: An irresistible force meets an immovable object. *The Futurist: A Magazine of Forecasts, Trends, and Ideas About the Future, 30*(6), 17-20.

Piercy, Marge. (1991). *He, she, and it.* New York: Fawcett Crest.

Rakow, Lana F. (1992).*Gender on the line: Women, the telephone and community.* Urbana: University of Illinois Press.

Rawlins, Gregory J. E. (1996). *Moths to the flame: The seductions of computer technology.* Cambridge: MIT Press.

Rheingold, Howard. (1991). *Virtual reality.* New York: Summit Books.

Smith, Stephanie A. (1993). Morphing, materialism, and the marketing of Xenogenesis. *Genders,* pp. 67-86.

Snell, Joel C. (1997, July/August). Impacts of robotic sex. *The Futurist, 31*(4), 32.

Spayde, Jon. (1996, March/April). What the world needs now. *Utne Reader, 94,* 62-77.

Spender, Dale. (1995). *Nattering on the Net.* Melbourne: Spinfex Press.

Starhawk. (1993). *The fifth sacred thing.* New York: Bantam Books.

Stefanac, Suzanne. (1993, April). Sex & the new media. *NewMedia, 3*(4), 38-45.

Swain, S. (1989). Covert intimacy in men's friendships: Closeness in men's friendships. In B. J. Risman & P. Schwartz (Eds.), *Gender in intimate relationships: A microstructural approach* (pp. 71-86). Belmont, CA: Wadsworth.

Ulrich, Allen. (1992, March 7). Here's reality: "Mower" is less. *San Francisco Examiner.*

Whitcomb, Coralee. (1997, Spring). Report from a den mother. *Women'space, 2*(4), 6-7.

WKC. (1995, August). Pioneers of the next generation of online. *The Net, 3,* 24.

Wolmark, Jenny. (1994). *Aliens and others.* Iowa City: University of Iowa Press.

Wood, Julia, & Inman, Christopher. (1993). In a different mode: Masculine styles of communicating closeness. *Journal of Applied Communication Research, 21,* 279-295.

5

Text as Mask: Gender, Play, and Performance on the Internet[1]

Brenda Danet

The mystique of the mask is powerful. One immediately feels different behind it. When an actor is responding to the commands of the mask, he experiences a sense of wholeness, relaxation, and well-being. There is a calm sensation of being taken over by it. If he is improvising he finds himself doing unexpected things, feeling impelled to obey the choices suggested by the mask.

—Bari Rolfe (1977, p. 14)

Part I: Gender, Mask, and Masquerade in Virtual Culture

It is a remarkable fact that many people who have never before been interested in cross-dressing as a member of the opposite gender are experimenting with gender identity in typed encounters on the Internet. Males are masquerading as females, and females are masquerading as males.[2] In cyberspace, *the typed text provides the mask.* Motivations for doing so are varied. Men are curious about what it is like to be a woman or seek the attention that female-presenting individuals typically receive. Women want to avoid being harassed sexually or to feel free to be more assertive. For still others, women and men, textual masquerade may be a source of titillation or a way to experiment with their sexuality.

The experimentation discussed in this chapter is just one of the new forms of virtual culture now developing in cyberspace. Virtual culture is a "culture of simulation" (Baudrillard, 1983; Jameson, 1984; Poster, 1990; Turkle, 1995, p. 10), of images with no necessary physical reality behind them, and of copies without originals (Baudrillard, 1983; Benjamin, 1969; Pinchbeck, 1994). Sherry Turkle suggested that it "is affecting our ideas about mind, body, self, and machine" (p. 10). It is also changing our ideas about social relations, conviviality, and the forms of human communication we will consider "real," and "meaningful" in the 21st century.

Some people are leading double or multiple lives in cyberspace, even with different gender identities. Others are trying out what it might mean to be gender-free, neither male nor female. Like Sherry Turkle (1995) and M. H. Dickel (1995), I believe that masquerading in this fashion promotes consciousness-raising about gender issues and might contribute to the long-term destabilization of the way we currently construct gender.

This chapter develops a research agenda for studies of textual masquerade—the performance of gender, textual cross-dressing, and gender-neutrality—in synchronous chat modes. These topics are of interest to students of gender, cross-dressing, and transgenderism (e.g., Bem, 1993; Bornstein, 1994; Bullough & Bullough, 1993; Butler, 1990; Ekins & King, 1996; Garber, 1992; Herdt, 1994; Kessler & McKenna, 1978; Senft & Hom, 1996; Tseelon, 1995), masquerade and carnival (e.g., Bakhtin, 1984; Burke, 1978; Castle, 1986; Craft-Child, 1993; Docker, 1994, Part III; Turner, 1982), and the new virtual culture (e.g., Danet, Wachenhauser, Bechar-Israeli, Cividalli, & Rosenbaum-Tamari, 1995; Dickel, 1995; Jones, 1997; Porter, 1997; Stone, 1996; Turkle, 1995).

Writing, Play, and Performance
in Synchronous Chat Modes

Experimentation with the performance of gender is just one of a number of forms of playful expressivity in cyberspace, a domain in which many activities, of hackers, young people, and grown-ups, are subversive or even carnivalesque (Barlow, 1996; Danet, Ruedenberg, &

Rosenbaum-Tamari, 1997; Danet, Wachenhauser et al., 1995; Meyer & Thomas, 1990; Ruedenberg, Danet, & Rosenbaum-Tamari, 1995; Stone, 1996). In cyberspace it is always "night." Because communication is mainly text-based, people cannot see one another. Even basic characteristics such as age and gender are invisible. The anonymity and dynamic, playful quality of the medium have a powerful, disinhibiting effect on behavior. People allow themselves to behave in ways very different from ordinary everyday life, to express previously unexplored aspects of their personalities, much as they do when wearing masks and costumes at a carnival or a masked ball.

Synchronous chat modes (e.g., IRC [Internet Relay Chat], MUDs) challenge our past assumptions about community, conviviality, and communication. Research is demonstrating that artful, stylized improvisation and wordplay flourish not only in face-to-face encounters but also among persons communicating remotely via computers (Danet, in press; Danet, Ruedenberg et al., 1997; Danet, Wachenhauser et al., 1995; Kendall, 1996; Marvin, 1995; Ruedenberg et al., 1995; Werry, 1996). Experiences in typed on-line chat can be powerfully "real," whether very exciting or very upsetting, despite the invisibility of the bodies of players (Dibbell, 1996; Ito, 1997; Jacobson, 1996; McRae, 1996, 1997; Turkle, 1995).

Part II: The Tyranny of Gender in the Real World

In this chapter, I adopt Erving Goffman's definition of gender: "the culturally established correlates of sex" (Goffman, 1979, p. 1, cited in Ekins & King, 1996, p. 1). "We make a gender *attribution* . . . every time we see a new person" (Kessler & McKenna, 1978, p. 2). Our decision is based not on inspection of the sexual organs of individuals but on judgments about their performance in relation to culturally constructed gender categories. From early childhood, individuals learn to signal their gender identity in accord with gender stereotypes. They learn to *perform* "maleness" or "femaleness," "masculinity" or "femininity." So salient have gender and the perception of gender been to our consciousness that we may speak of *the tyranny of gender*. In modern Western culture we have been prisoners of an all-pervasive, two-category system. Thus, physicians "correct" children born with ambiguous sexual organs to fit one or the other of the two reigning categories (Bullough & Bullough, 1993, chap. 9; Ekins & King, 1996, Part III; Kessler, 1990).

The obsession with just two sexes and two genders is not universal. There is strong historical and anthropological evidence that some societies recognize a third and perhaps even a fourth gender (Ekins & King, 1996; Herdt, 1994; Kessler & McKenna, 1978, chap. 2; Ramet, 1996; Wikan, 1982), for example, the *hijra* in India (Jaffrey, 1996; Nanda, 1994).

The idea of a third (and perhaps even a fourth) gender is also relevant for our own times. Whether or not one chooses to view gay men and lesbian women as third and fourth genders, perhaps transsexuals should be viewed as such (Bornstein, 1994; Connell 1987, p. 6, cited in Ekins & King, 1996, p. 2; Senft & Davis, 1996; Whittle, 1996).

The Pervasiveness of Gender Stereotypes

The pervasiveness of gender stereotypes in contemporary life is easily documented. In one study, adults interacted with a 3-month-old infant in a yellow jumpsuit. When the infant was labeled a "girl," subjects chose a doll for it, rather than a football or teething ring (Seavey, Katz, & Zalk, 1975). By age one, children shown pictures of adults of both genders and asked "Where is Mummy?" and "Where is Daddy?" already choose a picture of the "correct" gender (Belotti, 1976, p. 51). In another study, people were asked to describe the person who had sold them subway tokens. Gender was the first or second characteristic mentioned 100% of the time (Beall, 1993, p. 135, cited in Unger & Crawford, 1992).

Gender, Gender Ambiguity, and Fashion

Many prominent components of 20th-century fashion, for example, jeans, T-shirts, short hair cuts, and the preference for a slim, boyish figure for women, and longer hairstyles and earrings for men, have promoted an androgynous look. Think of Michael Jackson—with his light skin color, makeup, long hair, and costumes, he is neither black nor white, neither male nor female. At the same time, heterosexual individuals of both biological sexes, if not homosexual ones, rarely wish to be perceived as truly neither male nor female, as unequivocally neuter. Notwithstanding fashion's frequent encouragement of women to borrow items and modes of men's dress, "[i]t is characteristic for cross-gender clothing signals . . . to be accompanied by some symbolic qualification, contradiction, jibe, irony, exaggeration, etc., that advises the viewer not to take the cross-gender representation at face value" (Davis, 1992, p. 42).

Thus, in a photograph of Marlene Dietrich wearing a man's suit, shirt, tie, and beret, other features besides her face give her away as a woman: her makeup, hourglass figure and protruding breasts (Lurie, 1981, p. 244). In Davis's (1992, p. 42) own example, a woman wearing otherwise "male" clothing softens her look with a scarf headband. Women trying to "dress for success" in business are told to wear suits but to add secondary "feminine" details (Davis, 1992; Molloy, 1977).

As Goffman (1976) showed, advertisements encode gender in a host of subtle ways, constantly reinforcing our internalization of these cultural categories. This may be changing in the postmodern period. Some advertisements, for example, those of Calvin Klein, have been promoting a more genuinely androgynous look. On the face of it, the unisex look seems to be evidence of a softening of gender boundaries. This look peaked in the 1960s and 1970s. Nonetheless, although unisex fashion continues to be popular, by the late 1970s male fashion had returned to a more masculine look. Unisex is today primarily an option for women, thereby reinforcing inequality (Gottdeiner, 1992).

Gender and Gender Ambiguity in Film

Film after film plays on our curiosity about others' gender. In *Victor/Victoria*, a woman, played by Julie Andrews, plays a man impersonating a woman; the audience knows of the impersonation and is invited to ask, "Does she really look like a man?" In *M. Butterfly* a man impersonates a woman, "taking in" both the audience and the person's lover—the high point of the play is the astonishing revelation that the "man" is "really" a woman. The play was based on the true story of a Chinese opera dancer and spy who had an affair with a French diplomat in the 1920s (Bullough & Bullough, 1993, p. 243; Garber, 1992, chap. 10). There is a similar shock effect in *The Crying Game*—the character Dil is a female-presenting person, an attractive "female" who happens to have a penis. The film confronts us with the fact that Dil herself is not bothered by her "condition," which conventional society cannot tolerate (van Lenning & Maas, 1996).

When male actors play women, as in *Some Like It Hot, Tootsie,* and *Mrs. Doubtfire,* we scrutinize them to see how well they carry off their role. As in the case of *Victor/Victoria*, these films are less challenging to the social order than *The Crying Game*, because we never have any doubt as to the ascribed biological classification or sexual orientation of the "real" character, the real actor, or both (van Lenning & Maas, 1996).

Transsexuals and the Social Construction of Gender

Real-world (RL) transsexuals—who have undergone sex-change operations—are a source of endless fascination. Do former males "really" now look female, or do they still look male? Thus, the photographs in Kate Bornstein's book on her transformation from a married, biological male to a transsexual lesbian invites readers to ask: Can that dashing male marine officer really be the same person as the attractive woman with the long, luxuriant hair, plunging neckline, and earrings? The cover of the autobiography of Mark Rees (1996), a female-to-male transsexual, teases us too, displaying both a photograph of a young person, ambiguously either a boy or girl, and the obviously masculine adult Rees, with a light mustache and beard. Autobiographical accounts of transsexuals document that hormonal intervention and surgical changes alone are not enough. These individuals work very hard to learn to perform their desired gender.[3]

Gender Ambiguity and Cross-Dressing as an Art Form

There *are* certain exceptions to the usual distaste for gender ambiguity and cross-dressing, notably, in contexts having to do with art, theater, and performance. The traditional theaters of both China and Japan cultivated the arts of the female impersonator (Garber, 1992, p. 245; Scott, 1966, p. 181). In traditional Japanese theater—*Kabuki*—actors specializing in *onnagata* (female impersonator) roles were cherished as artists who exquisitely mime femininity (Inoura & Kawatake, 1981, p. 142). To this day, *onnagata* actors are still the most famous stars of Kabuki (Inoura & Kawatake, 1981, p. 189). In the past they wore feminine dress offstage as well as on; today they live as men (Scott, 1966, p. 173). As for Western tradition, the film *Farinelli, il Castrato* reminds us that in Baroque opera, *castrati*, including Farinelli himself, were objects of worship like rock stars today. Castration at the age of 12 preserved the pure tone of the boy soprano. At first castrati sang mainly male roles but increasingly appeared in female roles; some lived as men, others as women (Garber, 1992, p. 254). The real Farinelli had an astonishing range, from middle baritone to very high soprano (Hirshfeld, 1996a) and was able to perform vocal feats beyond the reach of conventional female or male singers (Hirshfeld, 1996b).

Another recent film that presents the idea of a third gender in the context of performance is *Priscilla, Queen of the Desert,* a vibrant, hilarious celebration of the *joie de vivre* and performing skills of three itinerant drag performers. At the same time, we learn of the sadness in these men-women's lives because they don't fit conventional gender categories.

Part III: Gender Games in Cyberspace

Until the advent of the digital era, the idea of a gender-free existence was conceivable only in science fiction. Feminist science fiction writers have experimented with this possibility. Ursula Le Guin's (1969) novel *The Left Hand of Darkness* is a "thought experiment" about the possibility of genuine cultural, as well as biological androgyny. In his "field notes," an observer of this imaginary society who came from Earth wrote,

> Our entire pattern of socio-sexual interaction is non-existent here. The Gethenians do not see one another as men or women. This is almost impossible for our imaginations to accept. After all, what is the first question we ask about a newborn baby? Yet you cannot think of a Gethenian as an "it." They are not neuters. They are potentials . . . One is respected and judged only as human being. (pp. 94-95)

In this society, Bassnett (1991) noted,

> People exist in a state of non-gender until they come into "kemmer" when they develop sexually for a brief period randomly as either males or females, and consequently the absence of sexuality is a "continuous social factor" for most of the time. (p. 56)[4]

The Possibilities for Playing With
Gender in Cyberspace

As I pointed out earlier, in text-based, digital communication, conventional signals of gender, such as intonation and voice pitch, facial features, body image, nonverbal cues, dress, and demeanor, are absent. Thus, the idea of gender-free communication becomes conceivable for the first time. A well-known New Yorker cartoon brought this point home: Its caption is "On the Internet no one knows you're a dog."

Play with gender and with identity flourishes in chat modes, in the *nom de plume* that players adopt and in their contributions. Individuals' real names may not be known. Until recently, at least, most of the participants on IRC and MUDs were young people, typically students, and more often than not, male. Players play with language, the software, cultural content of all kinds, as well as with aspects of their identity (Bechar-Israeli, 1995; Danet, 1995; Danet, Ruedenberg, et al., 1997; Danet, Wachenhauser, et al., 1995; Marvin, 1995; Ruedenberg, et al., 1995; Stivale, 1997; Turkle, 1995). Because people can type in their pajamas in the middle of the night, it is easy for them to pretend to be someone else. According to Turkle (1995),

> You can be whoever you want to be. You can completely redefine yourself if you want. You can be the opposite sex. You can be more talkative. You can be less talkative . . . you can just be whoever you want, really. . . . You don't have to worry about the slots other people put you in as much. It's easier to change the way people perceive you, because all they've got is what you show them. They don't look at your body and make assumptions. They don't hear your accent and make assumptions. All they see are your words. (p. 184)

Although there are social and cultural constraints on individuals' behavior, for women in particular, this medium is potentially very liberating. Not only is appearance neutralized, but the software generally guarantees to those who type that they will be "heard" without having to compete for the floor. At the same time, a growing literature claims that the subordinate status of women is being reproduced in cyberspace (Dickel, 1995; Hall, 1996; Herring, 1993, 1994b; Kramarae, 1995; Schmeiser, 1996; Wu, 1993). There is only an apparent contradiction here: Synchronous chat modes may offer possibilities for undermining the social arrangements

Nick	Userid and Address	Additional Material
<Lucia>	soulr@vm1.huji.ac.il	
<Thunder>	root@xxxxxxxxxxxxxxxxx	(-: Raam/ Chundeung :-)
<Kang>	GENGHISCON@xxxxxxx	(<Drax the D>)
<Rikitiki>	rpa3@xxxxxxxxxxxxxxxxxx	
<BlueAdept>	dlahti@xxxxxxxxxxxxxx	
<Jah>	miksma3@xxxxxxxxxx	(Baba)
<Lizardo>	lizardo@xxxxxxxxxxxxx	(Doctor Lizardo)
<Teevie>	ssac@xxxxxxxxxxxxxxx	

Figure 5.1. The players at a virtual party on IRC.
SOURCE: Reproduced from Danet, Ruedenberg, and Tamari, 1997.

and perceptions that asynchronous modes—discussion lists and news-groups—merely reproduce.

Playing With Gender on IRC

On IRC many people are "regulars" in one or more channels. Most people adopt a "nick," or nickname. To create a nick, one types, for example, "/nick topsy," and hits the enter key. Immediately, one's nick is registered for all to see as "topsy." Although players can change their nick at any moment, they generally choose one nick carefully and use it continuously. Players respect each others' rights over their nicks (Bechar-Israeli, 1995). Like RL masks, nicks (as well as personas on MUDs) echo the two great principles in nature: the *principle of camouflage* and the *principle of conspicuous marking* (Gombrich, 1984, p. 6). They both hide players' RL identity *and* call attention to the players in their virtual guise.

Reexamining a corpus of 260 nicks gathered from four IRC channels (Bechar-Israeli, 1995), I find that *less than one-fifth* invite an inference with respect to gender. Thus, <Arafat>, <dutchman>, and <madman> are all obviously male, either by cultural association (<Arafat>) or they are explicitly marked as male (the others ending in -*man*). Similarly, <Sylvie>, <pcWoman>, and <Darkgirl> are female. <Emigrant>, <meat>, and <surfer>, on the other hand, are gender-neutral. There is no reliable way to find out whether the ostensible gender matches the RL one.

In a study of a virtual party on IRC in which the participants simulated "smoking dope" with typographic symbols, most of the nicks were unidentifiable with respect to gender (see Figure 5.1). Using her real

>> @gender male Your pronouns: Example:	Gender set to male. he,him,his,his,himself, He,Him,His,His,Himself He reads his book himself.
>> @gender female Your pronouns: Example:	Gender set to female. she,her,her,hers,herself,She,Her,Her,Hers,Herself She reads her book herself.
>> @gender neuter Your pronouns: Example:	Gender set to neuter. it,it,its,its,itself,It,It,Its,Its,Itself It reads its book itself
>> @gender either Your pronouns: Example:	Gender set to either. s/he,him/her,his/her,his/hers,(him/her)self,S/He Him/Her,His/Her,His/Hers, (Him/Her)self S/he reads his/her book him/herself.
>> @gender spivak Your pronouns: Example:	Gender set to Spivak. e,em,eir,eirs,eirself,E,Em,Eir,Eirs,Eirself E reads eir book eirself.
>> @gender splat Your pronouns: Example:	Gender set to splat. *e,h*,h*,h*s,h*self,*E,H*,H*,H*s,H*self *e reads h* book h*self.
>> @gender plural Your pronouns: Example:	Gender set to plural. they,them,their,theirs,themselves,They,Them, Their,Theirs,Themselves They read their book themselves.
>> @gender egotistical Your pronouns: Example:	Gender set to egotistical. I,me,my,mine,myself,I, Me,My,Mine,Myself I read my book myself.
>> @gender royal Your pronouns: Example:	Gender set to royal. we,us,our,ours,ourselves,We,Us,Our,Ours,Ourselves We read our book ourselves.
>> @gender 2nd Your pronouns: Example:	Gender set to 2nd. you,you,your,yours,yourself,You,You,Your,Yours,Yourself You read your book yourself.
@gender set to person. Your pronouns: Example: *MediaMOO only	 per,per,per,pers,perself,Per,Per,Per,Pers,Perself Per reads per book perself.

Figure 5.2. Available Genders on MediaMOO and LambdaMOO

name as her nick—<*Lucia*>—Lucia Ruedenberg, my collaborator, was the only obviously gendered player. One player used the nick <*Kang*>— the name of a male character in *Star Trek*. From extended interaction with

<Thunder>, the main player in this sequence, both on-line and off, we knew that he was male (Danet, Ruedenberg, et al., 1997; Ruedenberg et al., 1995).

These findings suggest that IRC players can successfully camouflage their gender identity, even over long periods of time. Of course, many players with gender-ambiguous nicks may later reveal their gender. Thus, a person nicknamed *<MeatLoaf>* might flirt with players having clearly female nicks, inviting the inference that this person is male.

It is interesting to compare these results with Susan Kalcik's (1985) study of the "handles" chosen by female CB radio activists. In Kalcik's corpus, most women chose conventional female-marked handles, such as *"Sweet Sue," "Cinderella,"* or *"Queen Bee."* Some women whose husbands were also involved in CB chose a handle reflecting their relationship to them, for example, *"North Star's Lady,"* or *"Comanche's Angel."* By and large, women chose handles reflecting the two classic female stereotypes, the sex kitten (e.g., *"Hot Pants," "Bouncing Boobs"*), and the sweet, gentle woman (*"Sweet Pea," "Sugar Cookie," "Sweet Angel"*). Whereas some gender-neutral handles were chosen (e.g., *"Bookworm," "Stargazer"*), and there are even a few instances of male-sounding ones (*"Lucky Louie," "Samurai"*), these women did not play much with gender in the ways discussed in this chapter.

Playing With Gender on MUDS

Play with gender is much more elaborate and probably much more far-reaching in its consequences on MUDs than on IRC. The first, and most famous, social MUD, LambdaMOO, was created by Pavel Curtis and others in 1990 (Curtis, 1996),[5] and now has about 8,000 characters; it has become the virtual equivalent of a small town (Coe, 1995). MediaMOO was created by Amy Bruckman while a doctoral student at MIT, for researchers of new media. Despite its professional goals, it is also very social, running a "happy hour" at the end of the work week. On LambdaMOO, the RL identity of the players behind the characters is not revealed, whereas on MediaMOO, in keeping with its partially professional nature, the RL names of players are known.[6] Thus, players are freer on LambdaMOO to experiment with role playing.

When they join a MUD, individuals create an elaborate "persona" or "character," whose description can be read by anyone logged on to it

(Bruckman, 1992, 1996; Turkle, 1995). Whereas IRC does not explicitly require players to attend to the matter of gender, MUDs do so.[7] After registering their character, players role play in this guise for months if not years. Thus, a male college student might create "Samantha, a gorgeous blonde with a fabulous figure," who conducts love affairs with males, has virtual sex, and even "gets married"—all on-line. Players may even play different fantasy characters, of different genders, in different MUDs *simultaneously*. Turkle tells of a male player who played four different characters in three different MUDs, including a seductive woman, a macho cowboy type, and a rabbit of unspecified gender. He told Turkle that reality "is just one more window" (Turkle, 1995, p. 13). The following account (Leslie, 1993) illustrates aspects of the impersonation of females by males on MUDs:

> Christian Sykes is no nerd: he's 23, married, a religious studies major at the University of Kansas . . . he decided to find out whether he could portray a woman convincingly. Many males who impersonate females on MUDs are easy to detect, for they behave not as real women do but rather as late-adolescent males wish they would, responding with enthusiasm to all sexual advances, sometimes in quite explicit terms; . . . he kept the description of his character simple and as consistent with his own appearance as possible. Women on the MUD spoke among themselves about boyfriends, menstruation, or even gynecological problems, he drew upon lore gleaned from his wife and female friends.
>
> Sykes' major revelation . . . was the extent of sexual harassment of women. Though not one person suspected Sykes' prank, he abandoned it after four months because he could not write programs without being constantly interrupted by male advances. Revealing the hoax didn't even end Sykes' problems, for one male player who apparently had a crush on Eris [his character's name] became so irate that he tried to get Sykes banished from the MUD.

The software of MUDs offers an amazing variety of genders. Figure 5.2 lists the genders available on MediaMOO and LambdaMOO. Besides "male" and "female" one can choose *"neuter," "either," "spivak," "splat," "plural," "egotistical," "royal"* (as in the royal "we"), "2nd," and "person." Each gender has its own set of pronouns. Some are familiar from ordinary usage—for "neuter," the pronouns are "it, its, itself." In the case of "either," the player will be represented consistently with "s/he, him/her, his/her, his/hers/ (him/her)self," and so on. To make the unfamiliar ones comprehensible, I have added permutations of the simple sentence "I read my book myself," in each of the genders. Thus, in the "royal we" choice, the sentence becomes "We are reading our book" (Figure 5.2).

MediaMOO recently added an additional choice not available on LambdaMOO: "person." Players can say "Per reads per book perself." Such seemingly bizarre sentences are comprehensible when we recall that on MUDs action is rendered in the third person: chatting resembles writing collective fiction more than dramatic dialogue.

Origins of Gender Options

To learn the origins of these gender options, I contacted Pavel Curtis, the main developer of LambdaMOO. Curtis referred me to Roger Crew, who had personally added the category "spivak" to the program in May, 1991:

> I wrote some code and then introduced several extra "genders" (pronoun sets) to test it out, including, as something of a joke, various gender-neutral "genders" and, as even more of a joke, sets of pronouns that were in fact plural and/or non-3rd-person, thus totally violating the actual grammatical notion of gender. Nevertheless, some of these caught on, including—much to my dismay, actually—the Spivak "gender."[8]

He had named the "Spivak gender" for Michael Spivak, a mathematics professor who used gender-neutral pronouns in his textbooks.[9] Crew never dreamed that "spivak" would catch on, attributing its success to its intensive use by several particularly active individuals. As he puts it, "In a milieu where people were routinely being brown Labradors, space aliens, and fractal dragons, alternative pronoun sets seemed pretty ordinary"[10] When making his choices, Crew was quite conscious of the public debate about English grammatical gender and the issue of sexism in language in the United States.

As for "per," evidently, the inspiration came from science fiction. In Marge Piercy's (1979) novel *Woman on the Edge of Time*, persons in 21st-century society use it as the sole third-person pronoun when referring to others, thus obscuring the gender of those persons.[11] Finally, I learned that "splat" is the vocalization of the asterisk * in mathematics and computing.[12]

TABLE 5.1. Conventional and Unconventional Genders Actually Chosen on MediaMoo and LambdaMOO.

Gender	MediaMOO*	LambdaMOO**
male	495	3651
female	197	2069
neuter	280	1162
spivak	10	74
either	9	15
plural	7	26
royal	6	30
splat	5	17
egotistical	2	16
2nd	2	5
person	2	—
Total	1015	7065
Percentage male	48.8	51.7
Percentage female	19.4	29.2
Percentage unconventional	31.8	19.1
	100.0%	100.0%
	(1015)	(7065)

*Breakdown as of January 17, 1996
**Breakdown as of February 9, 1996

Actual Gender Choices on LambdaMOO and MediaMOO

Data on the distribution of actual gender choices on LambdaMOO and MediaMOO[13] are fascinating: Many players on both MUDs are choosing unconventional genders. The relative proportions choosing each gender are remarkably similar in the two MUDs (upper half of Table 5.1). The single most common choice is "male," followed by "female," but the biggest surprise is the substantial proportion choosing a category other than these two. To sharpen the contrast between categories, I collapsed them into just three (lower half of Table 5.1). On both MUDs, about half the players choose "male" gender, with the proportions choosing "female" and "unconventional" or "neuter" reversed on the two MUDs. *On MediaMOO nearly a third chose an unconventional gender; on LambdaMOO it drops to about a fifth.* My 1996 figures for LambdaMOO jibe with Lori Kendall's (1996, p. 217) 1994 figures: 25.5% were unconventional; 23% were female and 53% male, suggesting that the general pattern is consistent over time.[14]

Sherry Turkle (1995) cited data that on a Japanese MUD with 1.5 million users, there is a ratio of four RL men to one RL woman, whereas among characters registered, the ratio is only 3 to 1. She concluded that "a significant number of players, many tens of thousands of them, are virtually cross-dressing" (p. 212). In short, this is not a rare phenomenon.

"Spivak" and Other Unconventional Pronoun Usage at a MUD Wedding

Although its use is still relatively rare, "spivak" appears to have become a salient part of MUD culture, as is indicated by the following hilarious text from a virtual wedding (Jacobson, 1996):

> Dearly belagged, we are connected here today, to join this [bride and groom] in wholly mootrimony. If there be any character here, who has any reason why this [couple] should not be joined together, let h^{**} speak now, or forever hold h^{**} peace. Do you, [groom's name], take this moowoman, [bride's name], to be your moofully wedded significant other, to connect with and to send hug-verbs, in lag and in line-noise-less-conditions, from this CST Time forward, until character reaping do you part?. . . . Do you, [groom's name and bride's name] promise to love, cherish, and support each other, for paid phone-bills or unpaid, in gloom and in sunshine, for agreement or disagreement, from this moment unto forever, as long as the Internet shall last?. . . . [After receiving confirmatory answers, he intones] May the blessings of the Bovine Illuminati fall upon this couple. May the Internet guide and never disconnect on them. May the curse of line-noise never intrude upon their passionate emotings. May they always page each other with kind and loving words, and may their RL phone calls be as wonderful as their VR existence. . . . [Finally, he concludes the ceremony] *Ladies, Gentlemen, and Spivaks,* [italics added] under the authority of my position as Master of Ceremonies, I present to you, [names of groom and bride], Man, and wife, Woman, and husband. May they connect in harmony, forever!!! (p. 470)

Note also the use of h^{**} to blend "him" and "her," as provided by the "splat" option (see Figure 5.2).[15]

Additional Evidence of Play With Gender

Besides the fixed gender options on MUDs, players also can create their own idiosyncratic gender, though few players do so. Thus, on LambdaMOO, in addition to the 7,065 persons choosing a fixed gender category, another 243 persons, not shown in Table 5.1, created their own. On MediaMOO, in addition to the 1,015 choosing one of the fixed genders, another 40 tailored their own.

Choices jibe with the patterns already discussed. On both MUDs, the large majority of nonstandard choices are clearly neutral, for example, "Chaos," "salty," "neutral," "opus," and "none" on MediaMOO, or "lover," "me," "Ghost," "wood," and " married" on LambdaMOO. Thus, the proportions choosing neutral genders are actually slightly higher than those shown in the lower half of Table 5.1. But surely the significance of these data lies not only in percentages. If we combine the numbers for MediaMOO and LambdaMOO, between 1,500 and 2,000 persons are playing a neutral character![16] Also worth noting are choices like "whatever I feel at the time" ("Tanya") or "mood-dependent, usually neuter" ("The-Prisoner") "s-he" ("Natalia") for three characters on LambdaMOO.

The majority of players on MUDs and in cyberspace generally are known to be male. Until recently, a figure of 80% male and 20% female was widely quoted for persons active on the Internet; a recent survey indicates that the proportion of women is still low but now has risen to 30%.[17] Thus, we can be quite sure that many males on both MUDs are choosing either "female" or some unconventional gender. Unfortunately, data are not available on the match or lack of match between RL and MUD gender identity for LambdaMOO. In the case of MediaMOO, because RL names are known, in principle one might be able to figure out the actual gender of players from their first names—except, of course, in cases where the RL person has a gender-ambiguous name, such as "Lee."

Textual Cross-Dressing and Getting Into Trouble

As the account from the Leslie (1993) article indicated, players who cross-dress textually sometimes get into trouble (Stone, 1991, 1996, chap. 3; van Gelder, 1986). For instance, a New York Jewish male psychiatrist in his 50s played a female called "Talkin' Lady" on Compuserve; he created an elaborate persona of a woman who had been in a car accident in which her fiance had been killed. At first "depressed," "she" gradually became more outgoing and made many friends. Eventually the subterfuge was discovered, much to the chagrin of those who had been taken in (van Gelder, 1986).[18]

A couple called "Mik" and "Sue" met and fell in love on MUD1. For a very long stretch "Sue" was able to pass as a woman because she presented a coherent and consistent image. One person (Reid, 1994) who had interacted extensively with "Sue" reported,

> it had occurred to me several times that Sue might have been male, but every "test" I set was passed with flying colours. We'd even get little unsolicited details, like when she didn't reply to a message immediately because she'd just snagged a nail. It was little details like this which made her so convincing.[19]

Part IV: Questions for Research

In the final portion of this chapter, I propose a set of research questions that integrate the study of gender experimentation on-line with literature on RL gender, language and gender, carnival and masquerade, and interactive writing as playful performance. At least on the face of it, textual cross-dressing should be much easier than the RL variety. Nonetheless, it may be much more difficult than appears at first glance.

"Once [males] are on-line as female, they soon find that maintaining this fiction is difficult. To pass as a woman for any length of time requires understanding how gender inflects speech, manner, the interpretation of experience" (Turkle, 1995, p. 212). Elizabeth Reid's (1994) experience while doing on-line ethnography for her MA thesis on MUDs confirms these difficulties:

> It is indeed a truly disorienting experience the first time one finds oneself being treated as a member of the opposite sex. My own forays into the realm of virtual masculinity were at first frightening experiences. Once deprived of the social tools which I, as female, was used to deploying and relying on, *I felt rudderless, unable to negotiate the most simple of social interactions. I did not know how to speak, whether to women or to "other" men, and I was thrown off balance by the ways in which other people spoke to me. It took much practice to learn to navigate these unfamiliar channels, an experience that gave me a greater understanding of the mechanics of sexual politics than any other I have ever had* [italics added]. (chap. 3)

I propose to problematize these linguistic and textual aspects of masquerade and the performance of gender on-line. Here are some questions for future investigation:

1. *What types of personae do players create? What are the cultural sources of these personae, for example, science fiction, fairy tales, myths? What types of personae are mapped onto the various gender choices offered by the software? In particular, what personae are invented for gender-neutral characters?*

2. *What is the textual equivalent of visual éclat in RL masquerades?* Terry Castle (1986) has written of 18th-century English masquerades:

> The overriding object of costume, obviously, was to gratify, horrify, or seduce others. It was the masquerader's duty to be beautiful or uncanny, but never insipid. Several anti-conventions defined how such a visual éclat was to be achieved.
>
> The costume's object was radical festivity, a violent transformation of everyday appearance . . . one was obliged to appear . . . as one's opposite . . . masqueraders exploited a host of symbolic oppositions . . . sexual, economic, and racial incongruities; the oppositions between human and animal, natural and supernatural, past and present, the living and the dead. (pp. 75-76)

How is éclat accomplished when the only resources at one's disposal are words?

3. *What are the similarities and differences between the games played at RL carnivals and masked balls and those on MUDs and in IRC channels? What RL carnival tradition or period, if any, is comparable and why? In particular, what is the significance of the reduced presence of the body in on-line masquerades, and how does this relate to the performance of gender, gender games and sexuality?* The evidence thus far suggests, paradoxically, that the atmosphere in on-line masquerades can be nearly as eroticized as in RL ones and in some cases perhaps even more so (McRae, 1996, 1997). To "wear text as mask" is potentially as much of a tease as to wear a "domino," the all-encompassing, neutering black cloak and mask worn by many men and women, in carnivals all over 18th-century Europe. As Castle (1986) pointed out,

> Certainly, for those without the imagination or the exhibitionistic elan needed to wear more spectacular costume, the domino was a conven-

ient choice. At the same time, its somewhat sinister power of efface-
ment, its utter incommunicativeness, was in its own way compelling.
What Caillois has written of the archtypal black mask, "the mask
reduced to its essentials, elegant and abstract," also applies to the
domino . . . the quintessential sign of erotic and political cabal, the mark
of intrigue itself. (p. 59)

One thing is clear: the preoccupation with class reversals so characteristic
of RL European carnivals over the centuries is absent; at present, on-line
masqueraders are a relatively homogeneous elite of fairly affluent, educated, computer-literate individuals.

4. *How are gender and gender-bending performed?* What linguistic and
substantive features characterize on-line performance? How are cross-
dressing and gender-neutrality performed, in both substance and style?
For ideas one could turn to the research literature on language, discourse
and gender in the real world (Buckholz & Hall, 1995; Coates, 1986;
Graddol & Swann, 1989; Herring, 1993; Lakoff, 1975; Philips, Steele, &
Tanz, 1987; Smith, 1985; Tannen, 1990, 1993, 1994; Thorne & Henley,
1975), and on the Net (Cherny, 1994; Hall, 1996; Herring, 1993, 1994a,
1994b; Herring, Johnson, & DiBenedetto, 1995; Kendall, 1996, in press;
McRae, 1996, 1997; Senft & Hom, 1996; Wu, 1993), feminist stylistics
(Cameron, 1992; Mills, 1995), and the scripts of films in which men play
women and vice versa. Because films originate as words—scripts—
scriptwriters probably assign stereotypical, even caricatured female
style to these characters.[20]

In particular, what differences are there between the communication
styles of genuine and pretend males and between genuine and pretend
females? Do cross-dressed males caricature textual femininity, just as RL
drag queens parody embodied femininity? Do people pretending to be
gay men simulate a stereotype of gay speech? (Hall, 1996).

5. *What can the availability and use of gender-free pronouns on MUDs
contribute to the debate about sexism in RL language ?* This issue has a long
history of debate (e.g., Baron, 1986; Cameron, 1992; MacKay, 1983;
Martyna, 1980; Smith, 1985, chap. 3). Can extended use of neutral pronouns change perceptions about one's own and others' gender, for
children, if not for adults? Roger Crew, of LambdaMOO, has suggested
that, in addition to players being able to experiment with choice of
gender themselves, one might also configure the computer program so
as to make the gender of messages *received* optional. Thus, a person could
choose to experience the virtual world as all-male, all-female, or all-

neuter! Might this not also offer a mode of fostering gender-free perceptions in children—an hour or two every day in a fully gender-neutral
environment, while they are still quite young?[21]

6. *When does textual cross-dressing succeed, and when does it break down
and why?* The beginning of an answer to this question lies, apparently, in
Goffman's (1974) concepts of coherence and consistency. Successful
"passers" present a coherent, self-consistent image; but how is this
constructed textually? Is "passing" mainly a matter of supplying consistent, coherent substantive cues, as the examples from Leslie (1993) and
Reid (1994), discussed above, suggest, or is it also a matter of packaging
one's contributions linguistically in stereotypical ways?

7. *How is gender experimentation different on IRC and on MUDs?* Is
experimentation more extensive and more profound in its consequences
on MUDs (and therefore more interesting as a site for research), as I
suspect?[22] Earlier, I suggested that in choosing to call oneself <meatloaf>
or <pentium> on IRC, one is opting for a gender-neutral nick. It is also
possible that individuals are playing primarily with *other* categories:
with the animal or vegetable or mineral distinction, or with the animate
or inanimate distinction, and not with gender.

8. *Why is there so much interest in gender-bending on the Net right now?*
Is it merely an extension of the obsession with cross-dressing in contemporary (and past) culture generally (Garber, 1992), in films, and in a
veritable flood of print publications, or are there other cultural forces at
work too? Is it a temporary response to the novelty of new technology,
or will it persist as cyberspace evolves? As more and more people
develop personal Web sites and increasingly want to become known on
the Internet, the potential for extended masquerade may decline, unless
chat modes continue to guarantee anonymity.

9. *What is the wider cultural significance of experimentation with gender
on-line? Can it truly destabilize our current gender categories?* Will research
strengthen Sherry Turkle's (1995) claim that in this postmodern era,
identity has become a fluid, floating thing—where the "virtual" is as real
as the "real," and where, multiple identities of differing genders can be
maintained simultaneously, even over long periods of time?

Terry Castle (1986, p. 72 ff.) rightly argued that we must distinguish
between individual experience, highlighted in Sherry Turkle's (1995)
research, and a broader anthropological view. Some analysts of carnival
argue that it offers only temporary respite from the tyranny of hierarchy

and even reinforces it, whereas others see it as promoting genuine social and cultural change. Of course this would vary with the particular context and historical era. Castle (1986, pp. 90-91) distinguished between imitation of the powerless by the powerful (men impersonating women) and imitation of the powerful by the powerless (women impersonating men): downward impersonation is generally merely comic, vulgar, not really provocative. Because men currently dominate the design and use of technology in cyberspace, and because the numbers of individuals now engaging in textual masquerades are still fairly small, the prospects for genuine change seem very limited, at least until women become equal participants in cyberspace (Kramarae, 1995).

After a year of fieldwork on MUDs, Lori Kendall expressed considerable pessimism about the possibility of change; in the MUD she studied, whatever gender people chose for their characters, they often were pressed to reveal their RL gender (Kendall, 1996, pp. 217-218). Moreover, when attempting to role-play the opposite gender, players often resort to gender stereotypes, thereby, perhaps, actually reinforcing conventional gender thinking, rather than destabilizing it (Kendall, 1996; McRae, 1996, pp. 249-250). One thing is sure: these phenomena are much too new to generate facile generalizations. Every virtual environment is its own little world, with a unique subculture. Thus, what characterizes a fairly stable group of people interacting on one particular IRC channel or one MUD may not be characteristic of others.

10. *How will the advent of video conferencing alter these experiments with gender identity?* There is already much speculation about whether video conferencing will replace textual communication in cyberspace. Technologies such as CU-SeeME can be used together with programs like IRC; more sophisticated video conferencing equipment is already in use among corporations. When full video possibilities become widespread, will the current spate of gender-bending disappear?

Perhaps not: Some argue that text will continue to be the preferred medium even when video is available, not only because it is cheaper but because its limited technical possibilities offer a creative challenge to users and because the anonymity of text will continue to have its charms. Another recent development offers additional resources for fantasy and experimentation. Software such as "The Palace" enables players to adopt an avatar—a graphic, virtual embodiment of their virtual selves that they can move around in a three-dimensional environment, "dress" and "accessorize." The image may be of a person, an object, or a living thing such as a butterfly. Individuals continue to type their words; thus the masking of identity is preserved.

If and when full video does arrive and becomes widely available, it will be harder to pass as a member of the opposite gender or to pretend to be gender-free than in the text-based virtual environments I have discussed in this chapter. On the other hand, video could offer marvelous new opportunities for dressing up!

Notes

1. Earlier versions of this chapter were presented at a conference on "Masquerade and Gendered Identity," Venice, February 21-24, 1996 and at a conference in honor of Elihu Katz's 70th birthday, at the Van Leer Institute and Institute for Democracy, Jerusalem, May, 1996. Special thanks to Lee-Ellen Marvin and Keith Wilson for material on gender options on MediaMOO and LambdaMOO. Amia Lieblich led me to the "Baby X" study. Thanks to Pavel Curtis, Roger Crew, and other subscribers to MOO-Cows@xerox.com for information on gender options on MOOs. Discussions with Barbara Kirshenblatt-Gimblett and Lori Kendall have greatly benefited this chapter. Tsameret Wachenhauser provided technical help. For another treatment of themes of this chapter, discovered only after it was first drafted, see Dickel (1995).

2. The growing literature on this topic includes Curtis (1996); Dickel (1995); Kendall (1996, in press); McRae (1996, 1997); Reid (1991, 1995, 1996); Stone (1991, 1996: chap. 3); Turkle (1995); van Gelder (1986).

3. Resources for transsexuals learning to pass are available on the World Wide Web. See URL http://www.pond/com/~julie/general/gper10.html (*A Cross-Dresser's Guide to Stepping Out*), and URL http://julie.pond.com/~julie (*The Gender Home Page*).

4. Radical though her thought experiment was, Le Guin was attacked for not being radical enough. See Bassnett (1991, p. 56) and Le Guin (1989).

5. Roger Crew supplied the information about the year in which LambdaMOO was created.

6. Personal electronic communication from Lee-Ellen Marvin. In MUDs, such as "BlueSky," in which many participants also know each other in real life, Kendall (1996, in press) reports that despite the use of on-line personas, there is relatively little role playing or cross-dressing.

7. Benny Shanon called the importance of this difference to my attention.

8. Personal e-mail communication from Roger Crew, March 15, 1996.

9. The "spivak" gender category first appeared in Spivak (1990; McRae, 1996, footnote 6).

10. Personal communication from Roger Crew, March 16, 1996.

11. See "The Gender-free Pronoun" FAQ at URL http://www.eecis.udel.edu/~chao/gfp/. Pavel Curtis referred me to this source.

12. See the Cyberlore Central Website at URL http://pass.wayne.edu/~twk/compfolk.html#play, the information for "Pronunciation Guide."

13. These data were supplied to me by Lee-Ellen Marvin and Keith Weston, known on MUDs as "Luna" and "Lemper," respectively. Such data are available directly from the software at these sites.

14. Kendall cautions that many guest characters are listed as neuter because they haven't chosen their gender classification. Thus, a better question is: what is the distribution of "regulars" by chosen gender?

15. For further discussion of the use of spivaks on MUDs, see McRae (1996, 1997).

16. A word of caution: some characters may be inactive; personal communication from Lee-Ellen Marvin.

17. See URL http://www.cc.gatech.edu/gvu/user_surveys/survey-10-1995/#exec.

18. There are many versions of this story; for some variations, see Stone (1996, chap. 3) and Turkle (1995, pp. 228-230).

19. The full text of this case is available in an earlier version of this chapter, at URL http://atar.mscc.huji.ac.il/~msdanet/mask.html, or in Reid's (1994) thesis. "Sue" turned out to be a man arrested for financial fraud in real life.

20. I am thinking for example, of "Mrs. Doubtfire's" habit of concluding utterances to her "employer" with "dear," as in "That's a lovely blouse, dear."

21. Personal communication from Roger Crew, March 16, 1996. Of course, very young children do not know how to type, and if we wait till they *can* type, gender stereotypes already will be deeply entrenched.

22. Kendall's (1996, in press) portrayal of interaction on "BlueSky" suggested that this MUD is more like IRC channels such as #*gb* ("Great Britain"), in which individuals have strong RL ties and do not engage in much role play. Clearly, one should avoid generalizing about all IRC channels versus all MUDs. There are also IRC channels with rich role playing and fantasy.

References

Bahktin, M .(1984). *Rabelais and his world* (H. Iswolsky, Trans.) Bloomington: Indiana University Press.

Barlow, J. P. (1996). Crime and puzzlement. In P. Ludlow (Ed.), *High noon on the electronic frontier: Conceptual issues in cyberspace* (pp. 459-486). Cambridge: MIT Press.

Baron, D. (1986). *Grammar and gender*. New Haven, CT: Yale University Press.

Bassnett, S. (1991). Remaking the old world: Ursula Le Guin and the American tradition. In L. Armitt (Ed.), *Where no man has gone before: Women and science fiction* (pp. 50-66). New York: Routledge.

Baudrillard, J. (1983). *Simulations*. New York: Semiotext(e).

Bechar-Israeli, H. (1995). From <Bonehead> to <cLoNehEAd>: Nicknames, play and identity on Internet Relay Chat. In B. Danet (Ed.), *Play and performance in computer-mediated communication* [Special issue]. *Journal of Computer-Mediated Communication, 1*(2). Available: URL http://jcmc.huji.ac.il/vol1/issue2/ or URL http://www.usc.edu/dept/annenberg/vol1/issue2/.

Belotti, E. G. (1976). *What are little girls made of? The roots of feminine stereotypes*. New York: Schocken.

Bem, S. L. (1993). *The lenses of gender: Transforming the debate on sexual inequality*. New Haven, CT: Yale University Press.

Benjamin, W. (1969). The work of art in the age of mechanical reproduction (H. Zohn, Trans.). In H. Arendt (Ed.), *Illuminations* (pp. 219-253). New York: Schocken.

Bornstein, K. (1994). *Gender outlaw: On men, women, and the rest of us*. New York: Routledge.

Bruckman, A. (1992). *Identity-workshop: Emergent social and psychological phenomena in text-based virtual reality*. Available: URL http://www.cc.gatech.edu/fac/Amy.Bruckman/papers/index.html

Bruckman, A. (1996). Gender swapping on the Internet. In P. Ludlow (Ed.), *High noon on the electronic frontier: Conceptual issues in cyberspace* (pp. 317-325). Cambridge: MIT Press. Also available: URL http://www.cc.gatech.edu/fac/Amy.Bruckman/papers/index.html

Bucholz, M., & Hall, K. (Eds.). (1995) *Gender articulated: Language and the socially constructed self*. New York: Routledge.

Bullough, V. L., & Bullough. B. (1993). *Cross dressing, sex, and gender*. Philadelphia: University of Pennsylvania Press.

Burke, P. (1978). *Popular culture in early modern Europe*. London: Temple Smith.

Butler, J. P. (1990). *Gender trouble: Feminism and the subversion of identity*. New York: Routledge.

Cameron, D. (1992). *Feminism and linguistic theory*. New York: Macmillan.

Castle, T. (1986). *Masquerade and civilization: The carnivalesque in 18th-century English culture and fiction*. Stanford, CA: Stanford University Press.

Cherny, L. (1994, April). Gender differences in text-based virtual reality. *Proceedings of the Berkeley conference on women and language*. Available: URL http://bhasha.stanford.edu/~cherny/genderMOO.html

Coates, J. (1986). *Women, men, and language*. New York: Longman.

Coe, C. (1995, November). *Difference and utopia in an electronic community.* Paper presented at the Annual Meeting of the American Anthropological Association, Washington, DC.

Connell, R. W. (1987). *Gender and power.* Oxford, UK: Basil Blackwell.

Craft-Child, C. (1993). *Masquerade and gender: Disguise and female identity in 18th century fiction by women.* University Park: Pennsylvania State University Press..

Curtis, P. (1996). MUDding: Social phenomena in text-based virtual realities. In P. Ludlow, (Ed.), *High noon on the electronic frontier: Conceptual issues in cyberspace* (pp. 347-374). Cambridge: MIT Press.

Danet, B. (Ed.). (1995). *Play and performance in computer-mediated communication* [Special issue]. *Journal of Computer-Mediated Communication, 1*(2). Available: URL http://jcmc.huji.ac.il/vol1/issue2/ or URL http://www.asc.edu/dept/annenberg/vol1/issue2/

Danet, B. (in press). *Keybo@rd K@perz: Studies of digital communication.*

Danet, B., Ruedenberg, L., & Rosenbaum-Tamari, Y. (1997). 'Hmmm . . . where's that smoke coming from?' Writing, play and performance on Internet Relay Chat. In F. Sudweeks, M. McLaughlin, & S. Rafaeli (Eds.), Network and netplay: Virtual groups on the Internet [Special issue]. *Journal of Computer-Mediated Communication, 4*(2). Available: URL http://jcmc.huji.ac.il/vol2/issue4/ or URL http://www.usc.edu/dept/annenberg/vol2/issue4/. Abridged version. Full version in book of same title, Cambridge, MA: AAAI/MIT Press, 1998, pp. 41-76.

Danet, B., Wachenhauser, T., Bechar-Israeli, T., Cividalli, A., & Rosenbaum-Tamari, Y. (1995). Curtain time 20:00 GMT: Experiments in virtual theater on Internet Relay Chat. In B. Danet (Ed.), *Play and performance in computer-mediated communication* [Special issue]. *Journal of Computer-Mediated Communication, 1*(2). Available: URL http://jcmc.huji.ac.il/vol1/issue2/ or URL http:// www. usc.edu/dept/annenberg/vol1/issue2/

Davis, F. (1992). *Fashion, culture, and identity.* Chicago: University of Chicago Press.

Dibbell, J. (1996). A rape in cyberspace; or how an evil clown, a Haitian trickster spirit, two wizards, and a cast of dozens turned a database into a society. In P. Ludlow (Ed.), *High noon on the electronic frontier: Conceptual issues in cyberspace* (pp. 375-396). Cambridge: MIT Press.

Dickel, M. H. (1995). Bent gender: Virtual disruptions of gender and sexual identity. In S. Doheny-Farina (Ed.), *Networked virtual realities* [Special issue]. *EJC: Electronic Journal of Communication, 5*(4). Available to members from Comserve at URL http://www.cios.org.

Docker, J. (1994). *Postmodernism and popular culture: A cultural history.* Cambridge, UK: Cambridge University Press.

Ekins, R., & King, D. (Eds.). (1996). *Blending genders: Social aspects of cross-dressing and sex-changing.* New York: Routledge.

Garber, M. (1992). *Vested interests: Cross-dressing and cultural anxiety.* New York: Penguin.

Goffman, E. (1974). *Frame analysis. An essay on the organization of experience.* Cambridge, MA: Harvard University Press.

Goffman, E. (1976). *Gender advertisements.* London: Macmillan.

Gombrich, E. H. (1984). *The sense of order: A study of the psychology of decorative art.* London: Phaidon.

Gottdeiner, M. (1992). Fashion and gender role change. In M. Gottdeiner (Ed.), *Postmodern semiotics: Material culture and the forms of postmodern life* (pp. 209-232). Oxford, UK: Basil Blackwell.

Graddol, D., & Swann, J. (1989). *Gender voices.* Oxford, UK: Basil Blackwell.

Hall, K. (1996). Cyberfeminism. In S. C. Herring (Ed.), *Computer-mediated communication: Linguistic, social, and cross-cultural perspectives* (pp.147-170). Philadelphia: John Benjamins.

Herdt, G. (Ed.). (1994). *Third sex, third gender: Beyond sexual dimorphism in culture and history.* New York: Zone Books.

Herring, S. C. (1993). Gender and democracy in computer-mediated communication. *EJC: Electronic Journal of Communication, 3*(2). Available to members from Comserve at URL http://www.cios.org.

Herring, S. C. (1994a, June). *Gender differences in computer-mediated communication: Bringing familiar baggage to the new frontier.* Keynote talk at panel, *Making the Net*Work*: Is there a Z39.50 in Gender Communication?* Paper presented at the annual meeting of the American Library Association, Miami, Florida.

Herring, S. C. (1994b). Politeness in computer culture: Why women thank and men flame. In M. Bucholtz, A. Liang, & L. Sutton (Eds.), *Communication in, through, and across cultures: Proceedings of the third Berkeley women and language conference.* Berkeley, CA: Berkeley Women and Language Group.

Herring, S. C., Johnson, D., & DiBenedetto, T. (1995). "This discussion is going too far!" Male resistance to female participation on the Internet. In M. Bucholtz & K. Hall (Eds.), *Gender articulated: Language and the socially constructed self.* New York: Routledge.

Hirshfeld, A. (1996a, April 5). He was more than a woman, he was a work of art: A meditation on castration, homosexuality, and harnessed voices. *Ha'aretz,* (Hebrew).

Hirshfeld, A. (1996b, April 12). The operatic voice is blood. *Ha'aretz,* (Hebrew).

Inoura, Y., & Kawatake, T. (1981). *The traditional theater of Japan.* New York: Weatherhill.

Ito, M. (1997). Virtually embodied: The reality of fantasy in a Multi-User Dungeon. In D. Porter (Ed.), *Internet culture* (pp. 87-110). New York: Routledge.

Jacobson, D. (1996). Contexts and cues in cyberspace: The pragmatics of naming in text-based virtual realities, *Journal of Anthropological Research, 52,* 461-479.

Jaffrey, Z. (1996). *The invisibles: A tale of the eunuchs of India.* New York: Pantheon.

Jameson, F. (1984). Postmodernism, or the cultural logic of late capitalism. *New Left Review, 146,* 53-92.

Jones, S. G. (Ed.). (1997). *Virtual culture: Identity and communication in cybersociety.* London: Sage.

Kalcik, S. (1985). Women's handles and the performance of identity in the CB community. In R. Jordan & S. Kalcik (Eds.), *Women's folklore, women's culture.* Philadelphia: University of Pennsylvania Press.

Kendall, L. (1996). MUDder? I Hardly Know 'Er! Adventures of a Feminist MUDder. In L.Cherny & E. R.Weise (Eds.), *Wired_women: Gender and new realities in cyberspace* (pp. 207-223). Seattle, WA: Seal Press.

Kendall, L. (in press). Meaning and identity in "cyberspace": The performance of gender, class, and race on-line. *Symbolic Interaction.*

Kessler, S. J. (1990). The medical construction of gender: Case management of intersexed infants, *Signs: Journal of Women in Culture & Society, 16*(1), 5-25.

Kessler, S. J., & McKenna, W. (1978). *Gender: An ethnomethodological approach.* New York: Wiley.

Kramarae, C. (1995). A backstage critique of virtual reality. In S. G. Jones (Ed.), *CyberSociety: Computer-mediated communication and community* (pp. 36-56). Thousand Oaks, CA: Sage.

Lakoff, R. (1975). *Language and woman's place.* New York: Harper & Row.

Le Guin, U. K. (1969). *The left hand of darkness.* New York: Ace.

Le Guin, U. K. (1989). Is gender necessary? In U. K. Le Guin (Ed.), *The language of the night.* London: Women's Press.

Leslie, J. (1993, Sept.). Technology: MUDroom. *Atlantic Monthly, 272,* 28-34. Also available as electronic ms. from Leslie at jacques@well.sf.ca.us.

Lurie, A. (1981). *The language of clothes.* New York: Vintage.

MacKay, D. G. (1983). Prescriptive grammar and the pronoun problem. In B. Thorne, C. Kramarae, & N. Henley (Eds.), *Language, gender, and society* (pp. 38-53). Rowley, MA: Newbury House.

Martyna, W. (1980). Beyond the he/man approach. *Signs: Journal of Women in Culture & Society, 5,* 131-138.

Marvin, L. (1995). Spoof, spam, lurk, and lag: Aesthetics of text-based virtual realities. In B. Danet (Ed.), *Play and performance in computer-mediated communication* [Special issue]. *Journal of Computer-Mediated Communication, 1*(2). Available: URL http://jcmc.huji.ac.il/vol1/issue2/ or URL http://www.asc. edu/dept/annenberg/vol1/issue2/

McRae, S. (1996). Coming apart at the seams: Sex, text and the virtual body. In L. Cherny & E. R.Weise (Eds.), *Wired_women: Gender and new realities in cyberspace* (pp. 242-264). Seattle, WA: Seal Press.

McRae, S. (1997). Flesh made word: Sex, text and the virtual body. In D. Porter (Ed.), *Internet culture* (pp. 73-86). New York: Routledge.

Meyer, G., & Thomas. J. (1990). The baudy world of the byte bandit: A postmodernist interpretation of the computer underground. In F. Schmalleger (Ed.), *Computers in criminal justice* (pp 31-67). Bristol, IN: Wyndham Hall. Also available: URL www.soci.niu.edu/~gmeyer/baudy.html

Mills, S. (1995). *Feminist stylistics*. New York: Routledge.

Molloy, J. (1977). *The woman's dress for success book*. New York: Warner.

Nanda, H. (1994). Hijras: An alternative sex and gender role in India. In G. Herdt (Ed.), *Third sex, third gender: Beyond sexual dimorphism in culture and history* (pp. 373-418). New York: Zone Books.

Philips, S. U., Steele, S., & Tanz, C. (Eds.). (1987). *Language, gender, and sex in comparative perspective*. Cambridge, UK: Cambridge University Press.

Piercy, M. (1979). *Woman on the edge of time*. London: The Women's Press.

Pinchbeck, D. (1994). State of the art. *Wired, 2*, 157-158, 206-208.

Porter, D. (Ed.). (1997). *Internet culture*. New York: Routledge.

Poster, M. (1990). *The mode of information: Poststructuralisms and contexts*. Chicago: University of Chicago Press.

Ramet, S. P. (Ed.). (1996). *Gender reversals & gender cultures*. New York: Routledge.

Rees, M. (1996). *Dear sir or madam: The autobiography of a female-to-male transsexual*. London: Cassell.

Reid, E. (1991). Electropolis: Communication and community on Internet Relay Chat. Available: URL http://members.xoom.com/elizrs/ Excerpted as Communication and community on Internet Relay Chat: Constructing communities (pp. 397-412). In P. Ludlow (Ed.), *High noon on the electronic frontier: Conceptual issues in cyberspace*, 1996, 397-412. Cambridge: MIT Press.

Reid, E. (1994). *Cultural formations in text-based virtual realities*. Unpublished Masters' thesis, University of Melbourne, Australia. Available: URL www.crl.com/~emr/cult-form.html

Reid, E. (1995). Virtual worlds: Culture and imagination. In S. G. Jones (Ed.), *CyberSociety: Computer-mediated communication and community* (pp. 164-183). Thousand Oaks, CA: Sage.

Reid, E. (1996). Text-based virtual realities: Identity and the cyborg body. In P. Ludlow (Ed.), *High noon on the electronic frontier: Conceptual issues in cyberspace* (pp. 327-345). Cambridge: MIT Press.

Rolfe, B. (1977). *Behind the mask*. Oakland, CA: Persona Books.

Ruedenberg, L., Danet, B., & Rosenbaum-Tamari, Y. (1995). Virtual virtuosos: Play and performance at the computer keyboard. *EJC: Electronic Journal of Communication, 5*(4). Available to members from Comserve at URL http://www.cios.org, or at URL http://atar.mscc.huji.ac.il/7Emsdanet/virt.htm

Schmeiser, L. (Ed.). (1996, March). Women and gender on-line [Special issue]. *Computer-Mediated Communication Magazine*. Available: URL http://www.december. com/cmc/mag/1996/mar/ed.html

Scott, A. C. (1966). *The kabuki theatre of Japan*. New York: Macmillan.

Seavey, C. A., Katz, P.A., & Zalk, S. R. (1975). Baby X: The effects of gender labels on adult responses to infants. *Sex Roles, 9*, 103-110.

Senft, T. M., & Davis, K. (1996). Modem butterfly reconsidered. In T. M Senft & S. Hom (Eds.), Sexuality and cyberspace: Performing the digital body (pp. 69-104) [Special issue]. *Women and performance, 17*(1). Also available: URL http://www.echonyc.com/~women/Issue17/senftmodem.html

Senft, T. M., & Hom, S. (Eds.) (1996). Sexuality and cyberspace: Performing the digital body [Special issue]. *Women and Performance, 17*(1), 69-104.

Shaw, D. F. (1997). Gay men and computer communication: A discourse of sex and identity in cyberspace. In S. G. Jones (Ed.), *Virtual culture: Identity and communication in cybersociety* (pp. 133-145). London: Sage.

Smith, P. M. (1985). *Language, the sexes and society.* Oxford, UK: Basil Blackwell.

Spivak, M. (1990). *The joy of TEX: A gourmet guide to typesetting with the AMS-TEX macro package.* Providence, RI: American Mathematical Society.

Stivale, C. J. (1997). Spam: Heteroglossia and Harassment in cyberspace. In D. Porter (Ed.), *Internet culture* (pp.133-144). New York: Routledge.

Stone, A. R. (1991). Will the real body please stand up? Boundary stories about virtual cultures. In M. Benedikt (Ed.), *Cyberspace: First steps* (pp. 81-118). Cambridge: MIT Press.

Stone, A. R. (1996). *The war of desire and technology.* Cambridge: MIT Press.

Tannen, D. (1990). *You just don't understand: Women and men in conversation.* New York: Ballantine.

Tannen, D. (Ed.). (1993). *Gender and conversational interaction.* Oxford, UK: Oxford University Press.

Tannen, D. (1994). *Gender and discourse.* Oxford, UK: Oxford University Press.

Thorne, B., & Henley, N. (Eds.). (1975). *Language and sex: Difference and dominance.* Rowley, MA: Newbury House.

Tseelon, E. (1995). *The masque of femininity.* London: Sage.

Turkle, S. (1995). *Life on the screen: Identity in the age of the Internet.* New York: Simon & Schuster.

Turner, V. (1982). *From ritual to theatre.* New York: Performing Arts Journal Publications.

Unger, R. K., & Crawford, M. (1992). *Women and gender: A feminist psychology.* Philadelphia: Temple University Press.

van Gelder, L. (1986). The strange case of the electronic lover. In G. Gumpert & S. L. Fish (Eds.), *Talking to strangers: Mediated therapeutic communication* (pp. 128-142). Norwood, NJ: Ablex.

van Lenning, A., & Maas, S. (1996, February). *Is womanliness nothing but a masquerade?* Paper presented at the Conference on Masquerade and Gendered Identity, Venice, Italy.

Werry, C. C. (1996). Linguistic and interactional features of Internet Relay Chat. In S. C. Herring (Ed.), *Computer-mediated communication: Linguistic, social, and cross-cultural perspectives* (pp. 47-64). Philadelphia: John Benjamins.

Whittle, S. (1996). Gender fucking or fucking gender: Current cultural contributions to theories of gender blending. In R. Ekin & D. King (Eds.), *Blending genders: Social aspects of cross-dressing and sex-changing* (pp. 196-214). New York: Routledge.

Wikan, U. (1982). The Xanith: A third gender role? In U. Wikan (Ed.), *Behind the veil in Arabia: Women in Oman* (pp. 168-186). Chicago: University of Chicago Press.

Wu, G. (1993). *Cross-gender communication in cyberspace.* Unpublished manuscript, Simon Fraser University, Canada. Available: URL gopher:// english.hss.cmu.edu/

6

Dating on the Net: Teens and the Rise of "Pure" Relationships

Lynn Schofield Clark

At the end of the 16th century, Marianne Dashwood, the fictional teenaged character in Jane Austen's novel *Sense and Sensibility*, committed an impropriety of great consequence to her own reputation: She wrote letters conveying her affection to John Willoughby, despite the fact that they were not engaged to be married (Austen, 1795/1989). Teenaged males and females, at least of the class and stature of which Austen wrote in the 18th century, did not interact except in suitably supervised situations or within the bounds of engagement to be married. Times certainly have changed.

Using qualitative interviews, participant observation, and teen-led focus groups, this chapter explores the emergent practice of teenage dating on the Internet. I consider these practices in the context of dating patterns throughout this century to develop an understanding of the possible cultural significance of the current practice. Net relationships provide many routes to emotional satisfaction among their participants, and Internet dating affords teen girls in particular the opportunity to experiment with and claim power within heterosexual relationships. Yet, are the resultant relationships more emancipatory than those found in the "real-life" experiences of teens as a result? Are new teen communities constituted as these seemingly egalitarian relationships are formed? And by extension, do these Net relationships foster change in the lived social relations of the teens' local context? I argue here that the practice of Internet dating shares many characteristics with the "pure" relationship, Anthony Giddens's (1991) term for those relationships, characteristic of modernity, which are engaged in primarily for the gratifications they offer through interpersonal intimacy. Internet dating provides an illustration of the "pure" relationship in its contemporary form. Yet Internet dating relationships among teens also challenge Giddens's analysis, suggesting that our cultural understandings of the nature of relationships, and how they are evaluated in relation to issues of trust, commitment, and longevity, may be changing in subtle and not fully emancipatory ways.

Studying Teens and the Internet

This study on dating and the Internet emerged out of a broader qualitative study on the role of media technologies in the domestic context of the household.[1] Over the course of a year, I conducted a series of interviews and observations with 15 families and two focus groups, devoting between 4 and much more than 30 hours of conversation, observation, or both to each family. A total of 47 teens and 26 of their family members were included in the interviews, groups, and observations. An additional six families (14 teens) were interviewed by an associate researcher on the project, who has corroborated my findings.

From the families interviewed, three teenagers were selected for the further study of Internet use: Elizabeth, a 15-year-old white female from a lower-income single parent household; Jake, a 17-year-old white male from a middle-income blended (two-parent, second marriage) household; and Michael, a 15-year-old African American male from a lower-income single parent household. These individuals were chosen because they represented "information-rich cases," in that I expected that they would yield findings that would contrast from expectations and from each other due to their differing social, economic, and political positions within the wider culture (Yin, 1994, pp. 45-46). As one example, Elizabeth, whose family is on a very limited income and is of course female, has been very active in on-line chat rooms, whereas Jake, the middle-class male in a well-educated family, has been the least active. Michael falls somewhere in between in chat room use, but he is noteworthy as an underprivileged youth who has developed competence in Web design through opportunities in a community center and through his own initiative. I also selected them for their ability to be thoughtful, articulate, and responsible, as I wanted to train them to serve as leaders of what I have called *peer-led discussion groups*, focus groups that were led and participated in solely by teens. This format was adopted as a means to more closely observe how teenagers "really" talk about these issues when an adult is not present. The method follows the suggestion of qualitative methodology expert Elizabeth Bird (personal communication, 1995). In addition to training each of the teens to serve as a discussion group leader, I also worked with each of them to modify an interview guide I had constructed, making it appropriate and comfortable for each leader. Each of these teens recruited six friends of the same gender to participate in their discussion group, which the leader arranged, conducted, and tape recorded. Once the group had met, I transcribed the audiotapes and then met with the leaders once again to discuss the process and their responses to it. They listened to the tapes and checked to be sure that the statements were properly attributed. They also provided information about the group's dynamics, giving me insight into why some individuals may have answered (or declined to answer) as they did.[2]

Whereas my research primarily is based on these interviews and observations in "real life," I supplemented the knowledge gained through these methods by "lurking" in teen chat rooms. Elizabeth also allowed me to read many of the e-mail exchanges she had had with her on-line male friends.

Although many of the teens discussed using the Net for school-related research, the teens in my study primarily used the Net to communicate with other young people in the teen chat rooms of Microsoft Network, America Online, and the teen lobby of Yahoo! These "socially produced spaces" constitute a form of "synchronistic communication," in that the posts are ephemeral and immediate (Baym, 1995; Jones, 1995). They are seen by all those in the chat room at the same time, and answers to various queries posted to the chat room often overlap, creating a cacophony of conversation. Most of the teens with whom I spoke had experienced similar periods of intense experimentation in the chat rooms, sometimes devoting more than 4 hours a day to on-line chats for a period of several weeks or even months. In most cases, however, this period was followed by parent sanctioning, which either severely limited or discontinued the teen's chat room participation altogether. Despite the frequent warnings concerning the dangers facing teens on the Internet, parents were largely unaware of the content of the chat rooms; the limits were set based on what in some cases were alarmingly high bills from their service providers.[3]

Much like the adults on the Net discussed by Rheingold (1991) and others, teens seemed to be drawn to Internet chat rooms by the promise of fantasy and fun. As Kramarae (1995) noted in her critique of the overwhelmingly male population in cyberspace, the males far outnumbered the females in teen chat rooms as well. Yet there were also differences between the communications between teens and those I witnessed on the adult chat lines. Perhaps most obvious was the "age and sex check," the frequent request that resulted in the sharing of ages and genders among participants, often serving as a precursor for those of similar ages to break off into a separate chat room of only two persons, which the girls, at least, agreed constituted an "Internet 'date' " (the boys were less comfortable with the term "dating" to describe the interaction between males and females on the Net, as I will discuss more fully at a later point). As Elizabeth explained:

> What would usually happen is that we would meet for the first time in a chat room, and then if I decide I want to talk to them more personally, I would get a chat room for only like two or three people, so we wouldn't get people coming in and out all the time. And we'd talk for a little while, until one of us had to leave or something. We'd exchange e-mail addresses, and we'd like write every once in a while. And like, we could get together at a certain time. I'd say, "I'm gonna be on the 'Net' at this time, if you can meet me at this chat room at this time, then I'll see you there." And if they can't, then that's okay.

Sometimes these initial conversations between two teens would last for several hours. The topics of conversation mirrored those one might hear at a teen party. Internet dating, much like the practice's counterpart in "real life," exists within a specific environment that in many ways, not surprisingly, shares similarities with the other social contexts in which teens find themselves. Thus, we turn to a discussion of the environment of teen chat rooms within which (or out of which) Internet dating occurs, beginning with a review of the practice in its historical context.

Teenagers and Dating:
A Brief History

Teenage "dating"—the casual romantic interactions between males and females (or, even more recently, between persons of the same gender)—is a relatively recent phenomenon. Historians argue that it emerged among middle-class teens in the 1920s during a time of gender role upheaval (Bailey, 1988). With the rise of both compulsory education and restrictive child labor laws during this era, teens of immigrant and farm families who once had been expected to work, as well as teens from more privileged classes, were now sent to school. Education was cemented into the American teen experience, affording increased public opportunities for young people to interact with one another under minimal supervision by their parents.

The rise of the "dance craze" in the 1920s also has been linked to the emergence of the practice of "dating" (Modell, 1989). Whereas some teens in the decade before had attended community dances that were sponsored by neighborhoods or other social clubs (and hence had fairly strict social restraints that limited the "tendency to overstep moral rules"), it was the opening of a dance "palace" in New York City in 1911 that ushered in new practices surrounding dancing and dating (Modell, 1989, p. 71). The large dance halls that subsequently sprang up in urban areas made dancing with relative strangers an accessible and intriguing new option for teens. The dance style of the period, as it moved away from formal steps and toward increased free expression and physical contact, encouraged the establishment of casual heterosexual relationships in a way not previously seen.

During the same era, film houses multiplied throughout urban as well as rural areas, and weekly attendance at motion pictures increased dramatically. The darkened theater and the heightened emotions film evoked offered further opportunities for physical closeness. Whereas films often were attended by groups of teens, they quickly became vehicles for the exploration of exclusive intergender relations as well (Blumer, 1933).

Modell (1989) credited middle-class girls of this era with actually initiating the practice of dating, as they had the most to gain from the establishment of the practice. He wrote, "Before dating, parents had tended to construe strictly girls' obligation to enter marriage untainted by even a hint of scandal, and they supervised courting accordingly, limiting both its occasion and the set of eligibles." As parents were more concerned with their daughters' reputations than their sons', "girls were far more constrained by parental oversight" (Modell, 1989, p. 95). Whereas dating in the early part of the century still required the male to take initiative, it shifted control over the girls' interactions—and by extension, her sexuality—from her parents to her peers. It thus served as a potent aspect of youth rebellion against parents and their traditional ways. Whereas girls of this generation would not be considered sexually liberated by today's standards, dating enabled girls to play a more active role in constructing and maintaining heterosexual interaction through informal rules of conduct. Dating required teen boys to negotiate with teen girls and their peers directly, rather than through their families. To a significant extent, dating shifted the approval and sanctioning of romantic relationships from parents to peers.

Dating then, as now, consisted of going to movies, dances, or restaurants. As such, dating, and by extension romance, quickly came to be linked with leisure and consumption, as Illouz argued (Illouz, 1997). Moreover, as the rising consumerism of this era encouraged immediate gratification, young people began to think of self-denial for its own sake as old-fashioned, seeking in dancing and dating some fulfillment of the sexual tensions of adolescence (Fass, 1977). Whereas chaperoning and "calling" were steadily replaced among middle-class teens by the practice of dating, however, those teens of all races with less means were less likely to date. Part of this is due to the fact that these teens were usually encouraged to lighten the family's financial obligations either by seeking employment or marrying. By the middle of the century, however, in part due to the popular romanticized narratives of the practice in film, television, and magazines, "dating" became an integral part of the teen experience in the United States.

Since the cultural shifts and sexual revolutions of the 1960s, however, dating as a teenage institution has been in decline. Ironically, as Modell (1989) pointed out, dating, which originally caught on as a form of rebellion from establishment and traditional values, "had moved from a 'thrill'-based innovation half a century before to a somewhat fading bastion of essentially 'traditional' marriage values" by the 1960s (p. 303). Today, teens use the term "dating" in a somewhat bemused way, often with self-conscious ironic reference to the 1950s version of the practice. Whereas they still go out on dates, these occasions are less fraught with specific expectations. They are less frequently planned in advance, for example, and there is also less compulsion to report on the experience to one's peers. "Dating" has become much more idiosyncratic, with less reference to the external peer group and more relation to the self-gratifications and pleasures of the individuals involved. This is part of a larger turn toward issues of self-reflexivity and identity as central aspects of relationships, as I will show.

Cyberdating Relationship as Emancipatory

Cyberdating's potential to limit emotional pain in relationships seems particularly appealing for teen girls. Indeed, the girls in my study were, on the whole, much more enthusiastic about the possibilities afforded to Net dating than the boys of the same age. "I'm not too popular with the guys," 15-year-old Elizabeth explained to me, noting that Net relationships held less potential for the pain of rejection. On the Internet, employing her excellent skills in verbal articulation and humor, she seemed to have no difficulty meeting and developing relationships with boys and was even "dating four guys at once." "Usually I act a lot more aggressive when I'm on the Internet," she stated. "I just express my feelings a lot more in the chat rooms and stuff, so if somebody talks about something that I don't like, then I'll say it. And I would probably never do that in class, in school and everything." As Reid has written of the Net experience in general, "Users are able to express and experiment with aspects of their personality that social inhibition would generally encourage them to suppress" (Reid, 1991, cited in Baym, 1995, p. 143). This suggests that girls may use the verbal skills they might otherwise suppress to parlay themselves into a stronger position in relationship to their male counterparts, thereby assuming more authority in the construction of the heterosexual relationship. This was illustrated in one of the peer-led discussion group's conversations about sexual behaviors on the Net:

— Elizabeth: The only thing I didn't like about those guys [two "brothers" she was dating simultaneously] was that they liked sex just a little bit too much.
— Vickie: Cybersex?
— Lisa: Kinky?
— Elizabeth: They liked sex, it was scary. They e-mailed me a message that like, had a lot to do with sex, and you know, we

didn't—I didn't have my own screen name or e-mail address, so it was like, oh my God! [Either her mother or brother, who share her account, could have read it] So I like deleted it before I even read it. And when I was talking with them later, they're all, "did you get my message?" And I'm all, "uh, no. Yes, I did, but I didn't have a chance to read it. My brother tried to read it, so I deleted it before I could read it, I'm sorry." Yeah—right! [the girls all laugh]. But you know I never even told those guys I was getting off the Internet when I did. So I just kinda like, disappeared.

— Betsi: How long do you think they were talking, thinking you were there?

— Vickie: They're like, sitting there writing all these messages to you, and you're gone.

— Elizabeth: Well, I got off the Internet, my mom canceled the thing [the AOL account], and I never told them that I was gonna cancel.

In this situation, unwanted sexual advances were not only rebuffed but resulted in Elizabeth's creation of a potentially embarrassing situation for the boys as they may have found themselves talking (or masturbating?) without an audience. Further, the boys were objectified as the story became a shared experience of female triumph among the girlfriends.

To further strengthen their position in the dating interaction, several teen girls reported that they adopt new physical personae, describing their looks in such a way as to appear more attractive to the males. This not only fulfills the function of avoiding potential pain and rejection but also neutralizes some of the power aspects of the heterosexist system in which beautiful girls are given more attention and more social opportunities (Brown & Gilligan, 1992). If everyone constructs their appearance in accord with the imagined "ideal," after all, no one can be judged more or less desirable based solely on appearances. Thus in effect, boys lose some of their power as one of the primary tools of the evaluation of desirability is removed from the equation. It would appear that in these relationships, it is no longer wholly a matter of the men as consumers and women as consumed, as has been argued in less interactive contexts (see, e.g., Kramarae, 1995). Girls feel empowered through the power of self-presentation.

Interestingly, both Michael and Jake state that they dislike it when girls lie about their looks in the chat rooms. As Jake said,

— Jake: You can kinda like tell [if they're lying, because of] how they're putting it and all. Sometimes they get too extreme with their lying. You're like, "whatever."

— Interviewer: So that's kind of a turnoff, then, when you can tell that they're lying?

— Jake: Yeah. "Bye." And then go back into the chat room.

Michael noted that looks are less important on the Net than they are in real life.

— Interviewer: So what is the difference, do you think, between meeting someone in the chat room and dating somebody in person?

— Michael: Well, when you're dating somebody and it seems like, you're more looking at them, but when you're like, chatting to them, you can't see them, but you can get that trust going with the person, and you can really get to know them before you see them. And if you know 'em before you see them, you'll like, even if they don't look physically attractive to you, you'll still like them because you know them and you have a lot in common.

When he learned that one of the girls with whom he was chatting had lied about her looks, Michael noted that he did not abandon the relationship because he had not entered it with romantic intent based on looks:

— Michael: Okay, I ask them [girls he's met in chat rooms] to describe themselves, and some of them, they lie. Like one girl, she said she was 5'5," 130 some pounds, I forgot, and I went on her Web page, and she was pretty big. [laughs.] So I asked her why she lied, she was like, "I was scared you wouldn't like me." But I talk to her still, though . . .

— Interviewer: Have you ever, when people have said what they looked like, decided that you didn't like them?

— Michael: No. Mostly, when I go on the Web, I'm looking for friends, so it really doesn't matter what they look like.

Thus, even though boys may dislike the changing of looks, they are still able to find on-line relationships with girls satisfying. Instead of being under pressure by their peers to pair with the "right" girls whose looks approximate the ideal, the Internet allows for more egalitarian exchange freed from most of the restraint of peer approval. Indeed, several of the teens noted that what begins as somewhat romantic or titillating Internet exchanges often grows into positive, ongoing relationships with members of the opposite sex. This suggests some hope for the Net's ability to contribute to positive teen communities both in cyberspace and beyond. Also, because physical contact is (usually) impossible in a Net relationship, young people may find that they are able to communicate with one another free from the social and peer pressures toward expressed sexuality.

Yet, whereas this might suggest a depth of relationship is possible, my research actually affirmed that the opposite is much more common. This is not surprising, as the environment of teen chat rooms in many ways mirrors the social restraints teens experience in "real life." For example, let us return to the consideration of the fact that girls change their appearances to achieve more social power. In this action, teen girls are not redefining standards of acceptability based on beauty but are using the Net to actively construct what they believe is a more socially acceptable version of themselves. Each of the teen discussion groups expressed agreement in the fact that "on the Internet, they [persons of the opposite sex] cannot see you." Whereas the lack of physical presence undoubtedly lowers inhibitions as Kiesler and colleagues argued, the fact that each group mentioned this when contrasting dating on the Internet to dating in "real life" demonstrates the importance of visual appearance in the currency of popularity and hence one's desirability as a "date" (Kiesler, Siegel, & McGuire, 1984). Not surprisingly, given the opportunities afforded on the Net, girls are very conscious of the on-line presentations of themselves. Elizabeth notes, for example, "Usually I describe myself skinnier or taller. Skinnier and taller, with longer hair, and a lighter color blond, usually." In this way, Elizabeth's employment of the technology is in keeping with social conventions concerning gender roles. She was not interested in meeting the boys with whom she conversed, as this might undermine her attractive and aggressive on-line persona. In fact, when one of the male friends suggested that they talk on the phone, she deliberately kept her phone line busy during the appointed time so that he would not be able to get through. She said that they did not "talk" again on-line after that, something she seemed to have no regrets about, even though she reported that the relationship had been fairly intimate before that time. She also noted that although she had never "met" anyone on-line from her own school, she had decided to terminate one relationship owing to the fact that the boy attended a neighboring school:

> We started comparing notes about who we knew in each others' schools. But I didn't want to meet him, or someone from my own school, because then what if I knew who he was in person and he said something mean about me, I'd be like, hurt.

"Dates" with faceless and voiceless boys from faraway places held no such possible consequences. The fact that Elizabeth avoided rejection in "real" relationships and still sensed a need to censure her ideas when not on-line further demonstrates that the power afforded through self-construction on the Net does not translate into changed gender roles and expectations in the social world beyond cyberspace. Consistent with the findings of Rakow and Navarro in their study of the introduction of cellular phones, therefore, we must conclude that the possibility that new communication technologies might subvert social systems is limited (Rakow & Navarro, 1993; see also Rakow, 1988). Indeed, there is evidence of much more that is socially reproduced into the chat rooms from the environment of "real life."

Border Patrol: The Policing of Gender and Taboo Relationships

The content of teen chat rooms on the whole appears to be much tamer than many of the adult chat rooms.[4] Whereas adults are explicit about their desires, as Seabrook (1997) has illustrated, teens are much more reserved and, not surprisingly, less creative verbally. Much like the furtive illicit activities of the proverbial backseat, teens were reluctant to speak of their sexual experimentation, and what happened in the "private" two-person chat sessions was not up for discussion in the more public chat rooms.

Sex was an exciting but also heavily policed topic in the teen chat rooms. On several occasions in teen chat rooms, in fact, persons who issued explicit invitations for cybersex were sanctioned through prolonged "silences" (in which the on-screen dialogue was halted) followed by statements such as, "Whoa" or even "watch the language." There were also comments of mockery directed at the overzealous pursuer, such as the comment following an age and sex check: "ha ha RYAN, all 2 young 4 you!" On the whole, the teens seemed much less comfortable expressing their sexual desires and fantasies in the larger group of a teen chat room than the adults did in their counterpart rooms, although there were suggestive screen names adopted by the teens, such as "Tiger-lover," or the more explicit "Rydher69her."

Just as in "real life," teens in chat rooms seem to be more vocal than their adult counterparts in policing the boundaries of race and sex. In the following exchange, a racist remark was "policed" by calling on homophobic language, thus substituting gender for race in the goal of "policing" what is "normal":

— Rydher69er: What the fuck was up with that racist remark earlier
— Rydher69er: That was gay ass shit!!!!!!
— Kandi1998: 17/f/cali
— UziKlown: gay, eh?
— UziKlown: Are you saying you like gay ass?
— Brocky8638: Right back where I started
— UziKlown: or just "gay ass shit"?
— Hhoneycutt: Nahh, I ain't racist
— UziKlown: Pretty messed up, I say

This exchange illustrates another difference between adult and teen chat rooms: Teens are more overtly critical of homosexuality and use derogatory terms to police the boundaries of heterosexuality and to place themselves safely within its realm. In his analysis of the heterosexist culture of adolescent schooling, Friend (1993) has observed, "a systematic set of institutional and cultural arrangements exist that reward and privilege people for being or appearing to be heterosexual, and establish potential punishments or lack of privilege for being or appearing to be homosexual" (p. 210). Friend pointed to textbooks that assume a heterosexual norm and teachers reluctant to discuss homosexuality altogether as ways in which heterosexism is reinforced through silencing. Heterosexist ideas extend beyond the classroom to the adolescents' homes and are reinforced in the media through texts that assume the norm of heterosexuality. Being labeled a homosexual or lesbian by one's peers, regardless of the reason, then, has real material consequences: Loss of friendships, marginalization, and physical violence may result. Thus teens, both heterosexual and homosexual, have a great investment in maintaining a "straight" identity in the context of public schools and constantly seek to assert their heterosexuality. Teen chat rooms, along with other locations in which teen discussions occur, serve as platforms on which young people may assert their alignment with the dominant ideology of heterosexuality as a means of affirming that they are accepted and acceptable among their peers. One can therefore imagine the therapeutic and liberating potential of gay and lesbian teen chat rooms for young persons. I have not analyzed these chat rooms here because among the teens in my study, experiences in these locations were not discussed except in instances in which the speaker was asserting his or her own heterosexuality. For instance, mention of gay and lesbian chat rooms surfaced in the discussion groups when the peer leaders asked them, "which is the worst chat room to meet boys or girls?" In each group someone answered, "The gay [or lesbian] lounge," followed by raucous laughter.

In addition to overt sexual advances and the sanctioning of homosexuality, there were also at least three potential hazards of Internet communication that further illustrated the borders of acceptability in teen chat room communication. These involved gender confusion, mistaking a person in "real life" for an anonymous converser on the Net, and, for females, avoiding the potential adult male stalker. The first story came about when Elizabeth was asked, "Do you ever make friends with girls on-line?" She replied,

> Yeah. A lot. Usually I'll post a BBS in some kind of folder, and it'll be like, "I'm new to the network. If you'd like to talk—." I'll like describe myself, what I like to do, and be like, "If you want to talk, then here's my address," and then I'll set up a time. And sometimes, most of the times, it was guys. 'Cause I think that's what a lot of people look for in relationships on the Internet. But sometimes I'd get a girl, and we'd talk about whatever. One time I was talking to this girl. . . . We both thought—I thought that she was a guy, and she thought that I was a guy. So we went in, and we started talking, and she goes, "Oh, I'm a model for *Teen* magazine." And I was like, "No way!" And she said, "Yeah, I'm gonna be in next month's." And I looked at it, and there was a girl on the front cover, and I was like, "Wait a minute!" So it got me weirded out, and I got back on the Internet, and I said, "Are you a girl?" And she said, "Yeah, is there a problem with that?" And I said, "Well, I'm a girl, too." She goes, "Oh, my gosh! I thought you were a guy!" So

sometimes you can get kind of confused if you don't specify who you
are.

After this initial confusion, Elizabeth attempted to e-mail the girl again
but noted that the "model" at first did not reply and then eventually
explained that she did not have time to keep in touch with Elizabeth. The
preferred method of communication on-line is apparently that of a heterosexual dyad, and while friendships between girls are permitted, the
potential for misunderstood motives makes them more risky owing to
the fears of homosexuality noted above. The mistaken identity problem
also extends to on-line communication between two people who believe
that they do not know one another, but actually do, as in these two stories
offered during the girls' discussion group:

— Vickie: My friend goes to school with this guy who she had had
  a crush on for like, years. Since 6th grade she's had a crush on
  this guy, and they've just been friends. One day she was on the
  Internet in a chat room, and she was sitting there talking and they
  were talking back, and all of a sudden—she has this thing about
  slinkies, and she gave her friend a slinky for good luck at his
  swim meet. And she's sitting there, they're talking, and he goes,
  "do you have a slinky?" She goes, "Matt?!" [uproarious laughter]
— Elizabeth: My cousin did that. He was talking on the Internet,
  it's like a small one, it's not all over the United States, it's just in
  Colorado or something, and she's talking to this guy. One thing
  led to another, and she asked if he likes "If They Were Giants."
  And he's like, "yeah," She goes, "Wow, my younger brother likes
  them, too." Turns out that she was talking to her younger brother
  on the Internet. She didn't even know! She's like, "Tristan?"
  [momentary silence]
— Lisa: How weird.
— Allyson: Weird.
— Betsi: That's odd.

The Internet offers risks, therefore, that not only hold the potential of
threatening one's cyberspace identity but of invading and confusing
"real-life" relationships, as well. But perhaps the most fearsome example
of how Internet relationships might disrupt real life were discussed in
terms of an Internet stalker. This shadowy figure emerged when the

leader asked, "What do your parents think about dating on the Internet? And if they don't know about it, what do you think they would think about it?"

— Allyson: No! Absolutely no! They won't let me date at all. They're mean, evil people.
— Betsi: My parents think it's gross.
— Lisa: They wouldn't care, they'd think it was weird. They'd be like, "Okay, if you think so." But . . .
— Elizabeth: My mom didn't have a problem with it, because she knew that I couldn't do anything with this guy. Specially since most of the guys I met were like . . .
— Allyson: But you don't know . . .
— Lisa: Yeah, I don't think my parents would . . .
— Betsi: Well, I mean—are you crazy??
— Allyson: Some of them can be really gross perverts, and they can find out where you live, and stuff, which is really quite dangerous.
— Elizabeth: Yeah. That's the only thing my mom's paranoid about. She's like, "don't give them your phone number. Don't give them your real name."
— Vickie: And don't give them your address.
— Elizabeth: And don't tell them even what state you live in. I always do it anyway. They're like, "where do you live?" I'm like, "Colorado." Big deal. [sarcastically] It's a big state, people, come on!
— Lisa: "Where do you live? I live in . . . "
— Allyson: I'm sure they're gonna go door-to-door and ask, "has anyone gone on the Internet with this name? You don't have a computer? Okay, next house!" [uproarious laughter]
— Betsi: [laughing] I'm sure!

In this situation, the potential stalker is not discussed within the context of what has happened to someone's friend (as was the case in the earlier example of border patrol) or to one of the girls themselves but in relation to what *could* happen. Whereas parents are clearly not involved in the teen chat rooms, their influence is felt in their ability to convincingly warn their children of the potential dangers of the practice of dating on the Net. Yet, also in this instance, the teen chat room is affirmed as a place for those of their own age, as they discuss deflection of potential intruders while simultaneously assuming greater expertise over their environment than that displayed by their parents.

The norm of interaction in teen chat rooms, therefore, to extend the earlier argument, is of heterosexual dyads between two persons of the opposite sex and approximately the same age who did not know one another in other contexts. This of course echoes the norms of romantic interaction occurring in the high school. Yet chat room and follow-up e-mail experiences have afforded teen participants an opportunity to experiment with heterosexual relationships in ways that are rather different from, and in certain ways less risky than, those occurring in their junior high and high schools. Even with their limits in terms of overturning gendered hierarchies, therefore, these relationships suggest changes that are occurring in the adolescent interactions and expectations between males and females.

Dating and the "Pure Relationship" in a "Risk" Society

Much like the dance halls 70 years earlier, today's cyberculture affords teenagers new opportunities to experiment with gender relations, with results potentially as far-reaching as those initiated during that time period. I would like to suggest that the relationships on-line are characteristically different along both physical and emotional lines. The *physical* hazards of relationships, at least in terms of consensual premarital sex, were limited more than 30 years ago with the introduction of "the pill" and the consequent rise in acceptability of other forms of birth control to avoid pregnancy and sexually transmitted diseases. It is almost too obvious to state that the Net introduces disembodied relations, thereby limiting physical contact between most teens. After all, even if they had wanted to meet their Net romance in person, the challenges of distance and a lack of transportation or resources limit this to a significant degree among teens. Net relationships, therefore, operate in tandem with or as verbal "practice" for the actual events in "real life" rather than eliminating or restructuring the sexual mores that preceded them. Yet in the contemporary situation, "Internet dating" emerges as an alluring option for intimate hetero- and homosexual experimentation that holds the possibility of decreasing the potential *emotional* hazards of intimate relations.

Someone from an older generation might wonder why teens would feel that dating is an emotional minefield to be navigated carefully. After all, those older than teens might look back on the youthful dating scene as carefree. Yet dating, like other cultural institutions, must be considered in context. Borrowing the term from Ulrich Beck, Giddens referred to the current situation as a "risk society." (Beck, 1986, cited in Giddens, 1991). Giddens noted that this implies more than the increased exposure to new forms of danger:

> To accept risk as risk, an orientation which is more or less forced on us by the abstract systems of modernity, is to acknowledge that no aspects of our activities follow a predestined course, and all are open to contingent happenings. . . . Living in the "risk society" means living with a calculative attitude to the open possibilities of action, positive and negative, with which, as individuals and globally, we are confronted in a continuous way in our contemporary social existence. (p. 28)

As a part of their developmental process, therefore, teens must garner the skills necessary to envision various possible outcomes to their actions. Even as this has occurred, the decline of the authority of adult institutions throughout culture in general has left young people with more autonomy and hence more authority over their own behavior. Moreover, with the rise of part-time employment hours, young people themselves now have greater control over resources (financial and educational) that allow them to choose the timing of the events in their own life course to a greater extent than in previous generations. This combination of factors results in a strikingly different approach to the future than the concept of one's "fate," which teens of earlier generations had been taught to accept, even if implicitly. Perhaps in the past teens felt that society held a specific place for them and their task was simply to find out what that was by undergoing an "identity crisis" of some kind, as Erickson (1968) postulated. Instead, with the rise of a plethora of potential courses of action, teens learn that they will, throughout their lives, continually be called on to choose between "possible worlds." They have witnessed their parents and other adults in their lives changing their minds about mates, careers, and home locations, after all. Teens therefore have come to expect that while intimate relationships may offer fulfillment, such satisfaction may be ephemeral. Relationships are pursued as a part of a self-reflexive process in this context and may be understood in terms of what Giddens (1991) characterized as a "pure relationship":

> [Pure relationships] offer the opportunity for the development of trust based on voluntary commitments and an intensified intimacy. Where achieved and relatively secure, such trust is psychologically stabilizing, because of the strong connections between basic trust and the reliability of the caretaking figures. (p. 186)

The "pure" relationship, therefore, is not necessarily constrained by the structures of social or economic life, although of course, one's life *choices* are greatly conditioned by one's life *chances* (the latter referring to the Weberian phrase in which work is acknowledged as an economic, and hence social, determinant of the lifestyle options one has). The "pure" relationship, Giddens argued, is justified not in reference to one's kinship or other social ties but in reference to romantic love. Indeed, it is considered "pure" because it is no longer constituted within the social context of kin and community. Persons are no longer constrained in their selection of romantic partners by the social mores of their families or communities. Instead, relationships are sought out and maintained solely for the gratifications they provide to the persons involved. Therefore, these relationships of modernity, Giddens argued, are always organized in relation to the reflexive self who asks, "how is this relationship fulfilling to *me*?" With the lowering of sexual inhibitions through the social transformations of the last four decades, sex has come to be more closely aligned with contemporary concepts of intimacy and even identity and thus is a key aspect of the "pure" relationship. This is illustrated in Modell's (1989) argument:

> In the 1950s love had been defined in terms of meeting role expectations. Now it was "characterized by 'meeting the needs' of the other through interaction, commitment, affection, and non-possessiveness." Mutuality was no longer a theme of "coming together" in mystic sexual union but rather of each partner enhancing the other's happiness. Each couple represented a fresh negotiation of promising but uncertain potential that would endure while each partner gratified the openly pleasure-seeking *self* of the other. (p. 303)

Thus to some extent, by Giddens's definition at least, we would expect to find that sex among teens has been transformed from the externalized "thrill" of the 1950s "date" to something much more consensual, intimate, and important in the construction of self-identity. Selfhood, Giddens argued, emerges in relation to the negotiation of self-gratification in relationship.

Because the "pure" relationship is not anchored in anything beyond itself, Giddens argued, voluntary commitment plays a central role, and therefore the ability to trust the other becomes central to its continuance. Intimate communication that validates and develops the self, therefore, seems to be an integral goal of the "pure relationship" of which Giddens wrote. Conversely, therefore, I would argue that teens—much like adults—seek to avoid emotional risk because they see it as a potential threat to the self. Some of the teens and their parents with whom I spoke noticed this tendency among teens to avoid emotional investment. One parent contrasted this with her own generation's proclivity to seek "deep" relationships:

— Mother: My kids, this generation, they're very surface. They don't get deep.
— Michael (15 years old): See, we're mellow.
— Mother: Back in the '60s, everybody got real deep. Even though they were into the free love and all that, they got into it real deeply. But this generation is more of, "don't make me go that far down into the situation."
— Interviewer (to the teens in the family):Do you think that's true?
— Paula (19 years old): I think that's true, and I think that's because of the way things are now. I feel that even with me, and a lot of my friends, there's so much violence, it's like, I don't know anybody that hasn't lost a good friend or brother or cousin or whatever to violence, so it's like, we don't try to get real deep in stuff. Everything's like, "whatever." If something happens it's like, "I don't care."
— Michael: And like, when a movie that comes out like that's all silliness, it kinda lets you escape from all the seriousness and stuff like that.
— Paula: But even most serious movies, that are supposed to be real violent, my mom gets mad at us, 'cause she gets all senti-

mental about it, "oh, it's so terrible," and we're all like laughing at her. She always says we're morbid. And I'm like, well, you can't really get that into it, 'cause with the everyday thing, you'll just go crazy. You gotta kinda go with the flow.

— Interviewer: So, is there something that gives you hope that things will be different sometime?

— Paula: I don't know. [chuckles] Well.

— Michael: Well, hope's just one day at a time.

In this exchange, the older teen explains the motivation for the avoidance of emotional risk, or "depth" in relationships, in terms of violence and the potential for loss. In fact, there is so much loss in "the everyday thing" for her that she explains her own desensitization to media portrayals of violence as a part of her position of self-defense. In doing so, she demonstrates the way in which self-construction and self-preservation play an important role in determining personal relationships and in "reading" the cultural and mediated texts of relationships, as well. Thus dating as a social practice must be seen within this wider cultural reality in which risk to oneself, and the seeking of intimacy that validates the self, have become important aspects of teen discourse on relationships.

This would imply that the character of the relationships formed on-line may be quite different from those of the past owing to fundamental shifts in how individuals relate to one another along the axis of intimacy. Of course, there is the obvious difference of a lack of physical sexual intimacy as an aspect of the on-line form of the "pure" relationship. As noted earlier, one could imagine that such relationships might be more egalitarian as the restraints of power issues in sexual relations between males and females are bypassed. Teen chat room relationships therefore would be expected to favor intimacy that is achieved through conversation and self-revelation, which were important aspects of Giddens's (1991) "pure" relationship, as noted here:

> The "pure" relationship depends on mutual trust between partners, which in turn is closely related to the achievement of intimacy. . . . To build up trust, an individual must be both trusting and trustworthy. . . . What matters in the building of trust in the pure relationship is that each person should know the other's personality, and be able to rely on regularly eliciting certain sorts of desired responses from the other. This is one

reason (not the only one) why authenticity has such an important place in self-actualization. (p. 186)

Giddens suggested that trust and "authenticity," or truthful and open self-revelation, are central to self-gratifying relations.

In contrast, trust and "authenticity" are *not* central to teen chat room relationships; "fun" is. In fact, one important aspect of the "fun" is in working within the "mysterious" element, as Jake terms it, of not knowing the other person in the on-line relationship at all. As Jake noted, "It's pretty fun. 'Cause it's like, you don't really care, 'cause they don't know who you are, you don't know who they are. It doesn't matter, you're just talking about all this stuff." Michael concurred, as did Elizabeth, who noted,

> You can be whoever you want to be, and the guys can be whatever they want to be. So it might not necessarily be an *honest* relationship, but it's fun. Because you don't get really serious, because, obviously you couldn't easily get involved with a guy on the Internet [when compared with one] you could actually talk to and see. So I think it's just for fun.

These relationships, therefore, are constantly renegotiated between honesty and dishonesty, even as they evolve over time. Dishonesty, as Michael noted earlier, is not sufficient reason to discontinue the relationship. Is this solely because teens are less invested in these relationships? In part, of course, that is true. But I would also suggest that the type of relationship pursued by teens on the Net is perhaps best understood as an extension of the "pure" relationship, regardless of whether or not its content is perceived as primarily one of romance or of friendship by its participants. In fact, these teens suggest that even these distinctions are less important on the Net than they may be in other contexts. This is due to the fact that the function of the relationship has shifted even further toward the affirmation of self, its gratifications resting in its ability to provide opportunities for self-reflexivity and even self-consciously imagined (or constructed) intimacy. The other person is important to this project but obviously to a much lesser extent than in the "pure" relationship described by Giddens. Whereas the on-line relations are connected to the lived experiences of the participants through the social contexts and mores in which the individuals are situated on a local level, there are even fewer possibilities for social constraints in these on-line relations. The peers of those who participate in Internet dating only know what their friends choose to reveal about these relations. The participants in the relations experience a satisfaction in relationships that have no reference to their peer group or social status and may be considered more individualistic as a result. Moreover, it is not a complete lack of commitment but a tenuous and ephemeral commitment that links the participants in the Internet date and provides satisfaction for its participants. In this context, it is perhaps not surprising that it does not matter whether or not the participant in the relationship is accessible in "real life," and why in some cases such connection is studiously avoided, as was illustrated in Elizabeth's avoidance of the male Net friend who wanted to speak with her on the telephone. The lack of accessibility fulfills a function in keeping such individualized expressions of intimacy and self-gratification from impinging on one's local, lived experience. In essence, the relationship has many of the benefits of the "pure" relationship but without the restraints of a commitment of time or emotional resources. In this sense it might be said to be a postmodern "pure" relationship: one comprised of self-reflexivity in which experimentation and self-construction are central. Unlike adult participants in chat rooms, teens are limited in their ability to parlay an emotional tie forged on the Net into something that would have material consequences in the local context. Thus, the relationships that emerge transcend time and space to deliver satisfaction through the medium of a disembodied, "surface" communication, allowing the teen to feel connected to others while allowing them to experience affirmation in an environment that does not risk their current social position.

Conclusion

What, then, might be the implications for a teen community on the Internet in this environment? I have argued that whereas teen dating relationships in chat rooms mirror the relationships of "real life" in their adherence to norms of heterosexism and sexism, we also see a difference in the role of trust and intimacy in these relations when compared with those of the past and in "real life." Internet dating, despite its possibilities for verbal intimacy and egalitarian relationships, is in actuality more frequently employed for fleeting, "fun" relationships that hold little consequence in the "real" lives of the teens who engage in them beyond self-gratification. Further, the emphasis on "fun" and inconsequentiality suggests that the norms of conduct for teens on-line may be localized to such an extent that teens feel no need to consider how their own participation might influence others. Because the focus in the Internet date is on individual gratification, teens experience no sense of obligations to the person with whom they are ephemerally committed; as Elizabeth noted, if a person fails to show up at the preappointed time, there are no consequences. Of course, this assumes that both parties agree to the lack of seriousness with which such relations are entered into. Denial of a more intimate connection is not out of maliciousness; those who believe that they are experiencing more than simply a "fun," ephemeral connection are assumed to be not "playing by the rules," as it were.

Teens participating in Internet dating also seem to feel no need to justify their actions among their "real-life" peers, as they might for other, more widely observable actions. In the Net environment, teens are unmoored from local peer groups in which so much of identity is constituted among this age group. Peers are only involved when the participant chooses to involve them, either by conversing about one's individual experiences on-line or, on frequent occasions, watching over one's shoulder as a friend converses with others on-line. Most frequently, however, teens on-line experience themselves as individuals removed, to some extent, from their local social context. As autonomous persons in interaction, teens are like the adult counterparts to Giddens's (1991) "pure" relationship in their search for connection yet are very different in that trust is not a factor in the relationships achieved, nor must they risk "authentic" self-revelation to achieve gratification.

It is also worth noting that much like the teen dating experiences of the midcentury, there is a noticeable absence of other classes and races beyond the Caucasian, middle-class norm of the Net. Participation in teen chat rooms is increasingly forbidden in school and community center contexts, and thus young people with limited means are less likely than their middle-class counterparts to have access to the technology.

This research, therefore, leaves us with several more questions regarding the future of the Internet as a possible site for community building, particularly among teens. If these postmodern "pure" relationships might be considered a youthful precursor to the more serious, "pure" relationships its participants will presumably enter on adulthood, one wonders: will authenticity in the lived environment appear less—or perhaps more—important as a characteristic of these meaningful relationships as a result? I think the fact that the "other" in the relationship is hardly considered, or is assumed to share one's level of commitment and self-gratification, is telling. Teens in chat rooms, after all, experience themselves as a gathering of unconnected individuals, seeking others (or usually one other) with whom to converse and thereby achieve gratification. Perhaps these individualistic relationships under-score the increased localization of caring, thus implying the increased lack of any communal sense of identity. Teen chat rooms become a space outside the stream of everyday life, a space for the development of the ideal "pure" relationship of the contemporary age: one with imagined intimacy but no need for trust or commitment; thus one that is fulfilling and liberating, ultimately and primarily, to the self. In this sense, then, the self-gratification of dating on the Net can be seen as a natural outgrowth of current cultural conditions. The technology does not enable a wide-scale social change toward greater self-reflexivity but allows this already occurring practice to find a new avenue for its expression and development.

Notes

1. I serve as Associate Researcher on the Lilly Endowment funded project, "Media, Meaning, and the Lifecourse," which is under the direction of Stewart M. Hoover at the Center for Mass Media Research, University of Colorado. I gratefully acknowledge the funding for the research in this chapter, which has been provided by the Lilly Endowment and by a dissertation fellowship from the Louisville Institute.

2. I paid each of the leaders $25 for their efforts and paid each of the participants they recruited $8. I also provided money for pizza, which the leader purchased at the conclusion of the discussion.

3. For an illustration of warnings in the popular press, see, for example, Rozen, L. (1997, November). Undercover on the Internet. *Good Housekeeping*, pp. 76-78, 82.

4. It should be noted, however, that while the teens in my study by and large noted preferences for the teen chat rooms, many of them had experimented with the more racy adult chat rooms, as well.

References

Austen, J. (1989). *Sense and sensibility*. New York: Signet. (Original work published 1795)

Bailey, B. (1988). *From front porch to back seat*. Baltimore, MD: Johns Hopkins University Press.

Baym, N. (1995). The emergence of community in computer-mediated communication. In S. G. Jones (Ed.), *CyberSociety: Computer-mediated communication and community* (pp. 138-163). Thousand Oaks, CA: Sage.

Blumer, H. (1933). *The movies and conduct.* New York: Macmillan.

Brown, L., & Gilligan, C. (1992). *Meeting at the crossroads: Women's psychology and girls' development.* Cambridge, MA: Harvard University Press.

Erickson, E. (1968). *Identity: Youth and crisis.* New York: W.W. Norton.

Fass, P. (1977). *The damned and the beautiful: American youth in the 1920s.* New York: Oxford University Press.

Friend, R. (1993). Choices, not closets: Heterosexism and homophobia in schools. In L. Weis & M. Fine (Eds.), *Beyond silenced voices: Class, race, and gender in United States schools* (pp. 209-235). Albany: State University of New York Press.

Giddens, A. (1991). *Modernity and self-identity: Self and society in the late modern age.* Palo Alto, CA: Stanford University Press.

Illouz, E. (1997). *Consuming the romantic Utopia: Love and cultural contradictions of capitalism.* Berkeley: University of California Press.

Jones, S. (1995). Understanding community in the information age. In S. G. Jones (Ed.), *CyberSociety: Computer-mediated communication and community* (pp. 10-35). Thousand Oaks, CA: Sage.

Kiesler, S., Siegel, J., & McGuire, T. (1984). Social psychological aspect of computer-mediated communication. *American Psychologist, 39*(10), 1123-1134.

Kramarae, C. (1995). A backstage critique of virtual reality. In S. G. Jones (Ed.), *CyberSociety: Computer-mediated communication and community* (pp. 36-56). Thousand Oaks, CA: Sage.

Modell, J. (1989). *Into one's own: From youth to adulthood in the United States 1920-1975.* Berkeley: University of California Press.

Rakow, L. (1988). Gendered technology, gendered practice. *Critical Studies in Mass Communication, 5*(1), 57-70.

Rakow, L., & Navarro, V. (1993, June). Remote mothering and the parallel shift: Women meet the cellular telephone. *Critical Studies in Mass Communication, 10*(2), 144-157.

Rheingold, H. (1991). *The virtual community: Homesteading on the electronic frontier.* Reading, MA: Addison-Wesley.

Rozen, L. (1997, Nov.). Undercover on the Internet. *Good Housekeeping, 225*(10), 76-78, 82.

Seabrook, J. (1997). *Deeper: My two-year odyssey in cyberspace.* New York: Simon & Schuster.

Yin, R. (1994). *Case study research: Design and methods* (2nd ed.). Thousand Oaks, CA: Sage.

7

Virtual Ethnicity: Tribal Identity in an Age of Global Communications

Mark Poster

Ethnicity and race are today much contested terms. Once, when Enlightenment discourse retained its hegemony, these terms were easily dismissed as idols of outmoded eras and primitive societies, as irrational myths, at best as regrettable ideals of minds incapable of ascending to their own humanity. Today, spontaneous identification with one's local group, a sort of natural parochialism, is precluded by the saturation of daily life with globalized media: One is continually confronted with people who are not of one's tribe, kin, ethnicity, race, or community in any sense. Yet the desire for ethnic identification, at least in some quarters, is strong. Perhaps this is a postmodern ethnicity, mediated by an increasingly technologized social world.

The celebration of what some call neoethnicity extends to critical discourse. With a purpose of supporting oppressed groups in their struggles against domination, many critical thinkers wary of essentializing ethnicity as a stable, presocial center of identity nonetheless discover there a resort for resistance to domination. For example, Lisa Lowe (1996), in *Immigrant Acts*, recognized that "oppositional solidarity movements have been organized around racial identities because of social and economic oppressions that have targeted those identities" (p. 15). Yet this defensive identification did not prevent her from attributing to such communities "resistance cultures" on the basis of those identifications (p. 23). She argued that inequalities of class, race, and gender contravene absorption into the abstract position of national citizenship. "Asian American particularity," she contended, "returns a differently located dialectical critique of the universality proposed by both the economic and the political spheres" (p. 28). And at the cultural level, she continued, "the contradictory history of Asian Americans produces cultural forms that are materially and aesthetically at odds with the resolution of the citizen to the nation" (p. 30). For Lowe, race and nation are in antagonism.

But race and nation are not in singular opposition. A global economy and communication complicates and disrupts this site of struggle. When Lowe (1996) added the global into the stew of cultures of resistance the dish changed flavor: ethnic and racial identification became questionable supports of emancipation. She wrote,

> The current global restructuring—that moves well beyond the nation-state and entails the differentiation of labor forces internationally—constitutes a shift in the mode of production that now necessitates alternative forms of cultural practice that integrate yet move beyond those of cultural nationalism. (p. 171)

When the reference point is global, ethnicity becomes an impediment to alliances of solidarity, not an inspiration to resistance.

Local identifications are increasingly linked with planetary configurations of economy and media. Ethnic differentiation now mixes with transnational formations. Ethnocentrism becomes ethno*ex*centrism. A culture of resistance must engage with the other in global configurations. Instead of a localism oriented to an original, pure ethnicity, globalism impels us to conceive a new localism profoundly affected by the grace of the link with others. In *Primitive Passions*, Rey Chow (1996) offered a concept of translation as a model for such cultural restructuring. Chow took the linking of nations, races, and ethnicities in global configurations as an opportunity, not a threat. The occasion was now offered to us to understand how our language, heritage, traditions partake, in their specificity, of the general capacity for such phenomena. When we translate we learn new things about ourselves, not simply about the other we encounter. To translate is not to copy an original, represent it, appropriate it as our own, or to fail to do so. It is the chance, Chow reminded us, borrowing from Benjamin (1935/1969), to enhance our experience of our own culture. Understood in this manner, ethnicity becomes neither an originary resort of identification nor a primitive incapacity to attain universality. It becomes a moment of self-construction through the other, just the sort of practice fitting with a thickening global landscape.

The term "virtual ethnicity," like Chow's translated ethnicity, suggests one of the great questions confronting us at the close of the 20th century: Is there a new form of planetary culture alongside existing ones that appears in the "space" of electronic communications? Does "globalization" imply a "noosphere" in Teilhard de Chardin's (1955/1959) sense, a new layer of hominization, as he calls it, that inhabits the Earth in underground wires, floats in the air over the planet as high frequency radio waves and under the water in cables; all variations of communications technologies? Can there be a form of culture that is not bound to the surface of the globe, attaching human beings to its particular configurations with the weight of gravity, inscribing their bodies with its rituals and customs, interpolating their selves with the force of traditions and political hierarchies? Is virtual ethnicity an alternative to the binaries of particularism and universalism, parochialism, and cosmopolitanism, inserting itself between nations and communities, earthly ethnicities and races? Is virtual ethnicity a transgression of essentialism in all its forms, including that of Western rationalism? Does virtual ethnicity betoken a new age, a "postmodernity" that spawns multiple, dispersed, heterogeneous subjects as well as global communities? These are some of the fascinating questions inspired in me by the emergence of forms of ethnicity in the global communications network known as the Internet.

An approach to these questions requires a double interrogation: first, of the term *virtual* and its formulation in relation to its apparent opposite, the real; and second, the term *culture* and its related terms *ethnicity, nationality, race.*

In Wellington, New Zealand in April, 1994 a Maori reporter for a Maori radio station asked me, in an interview about new technologies, what the implications were if a Western company produced a CD-ROM on Maori culture and sold it throughout the world? Could Maori culture survive if its sounds, images, and texts were controlled by a non-Maori entrepreneur? Could her social world survive if people from other cultures obtained the CD-ROM and learned the stories, customs, and secrets of her culture without participating in them in Real Life? It appeared to her that her world was being threatened by CD-ROM technology; that the integrity of her way of life was at stake in an era of high technology; that the autonomy and coherence of Maori identity easily could be shattered and dispersed by information systems that disseminated cheaply the sacred rites of her group, the secrets and precious beliefs and practices that defined and held together her ethnicity. She implied that ethnic identity and global information were incompatible. If Marshall McLuhan celebrated the spread of electronic media as the dawn of a "global village," a retribalization of humankind, this Maori feared that same future as the devastation of her tribe.

An altogether different attitude toward information technology was expressed at a different time, in a different place by a person of a different background. In this instance, the question of ethnicity evaporates before a universalist vision of rationality. Here are the words of one white American male of the mid-19th century (Briggs & Maverick, 1858):

> It has been the result of the great discoveries of the past century, to effect a revolution in political and social life, by establishing a more intimate connexion between nations, with race and race. It has been found that the old system of exclusion and insulation are stagnation and death. National health can only be maintained by the free and unobstructed interchange of each with all. How potent a power, then, is the telegraph destined to become in the civilization of the world! This binds together by a vital cord all the nations of the earth. It is impossible that old prejudices and hostilities should longer exist, while such an instrument has been created for an exchange of thought between all the nations of the earth. (pp. 21-22)

This sanguine vision of a pacified and unified Earth, shorn of ethnic particularism, as a consequence of the proliferation of communication technologies, exemplifies the dominant metanarrative of liberal thought, the hallmark of the telos of progress.

In the one case, the globalization of Maori culture through CD-ROM technology incites a threat of dissolution; in the other, the telegraph promises to unite into harmony the peoples of the Earth. Is this an opposition between tribal parochialism and Western Enlightenment,

between particularism and universalism, between difference and sameness, between localism and globalism? Are these the only alternatives
before us as electronic communications technologies multiply and
spread across the globe? What then is the fate of ethnicity in an age of
virtual presence?

Culture is now technologically processed. Machines that process
symbols, sounds, and images install mediations between human beings
that permit remote intimacy, exchanges at a distance, spatial simultaneity. The computer, communications satellites, telephones, and now television, are being linked into a new cultural processing assemblage. This
assemblage in turn is connected by a network architecture that extends,
however unevenly at present, over the globe. And this network is decentralized, so positions of speech and reception cannot easily be restricted
or even hierarchized. The assemblage is digital, so that messages travel,
when bandwidth is adequate, at the speed of light. And it is packet-
switched so that each message has no prescribed path but follows any
available route to its destination. What is known as cyberspace is sustained by this entire apparatus. Though it is not a finished product with
definite specifications and fixed features, one may characterize cyberspace, because of the characteristics that have emerged thus far in its
configuration, as the virtual territory. If an argument can be sustained
that a virtual realm has been set into place, can there be a "virtual
ethnicity"? Does such a virtual ethnicity imply a new articulation of the
relation of individual to community or is it a "false" ethnicity, as some
would have us believe? Are the Maori reporter and the Western progres-
sivist really in opposition or do they both present ethnic identity as
essentialist? Do virtual technocultures challenge this essentialism, and if
so, how?

Language and the Virtual

The first question confronting the analysis of virtual ethnicity is that of
language. To what extent and in what ways do virtual technologies alter
the gap or *différance* already inserted between identity and ethnicity by
language. Friedrich Nietzsche (1878/1986) theorized language as itself
a second or virtual world standing against and outside "the real."
Nietzsche wrote,

> The significance of language for the evolution of culture lies in this, that
> mankind set up in language a separate world beside the other world,

a place it took to be so firmly set that, standing upon it, it could lift the
rest of the world off its hinges and make itself master of it. (p. 16)[1]

Here language is not only separate from "the world" but also "master of
it." At every moment symbolic coding intercedes between individual
consciousness and experience, rendering human culture a double world
of mediated immediacy.

There are three separable assertions in Nietzsche's statement: (a) that
language mediates humanity's relation to the world, (b) that in doing so
it alters that world, and (c) that this alteration takes priority over any
immediacy of the world. Today, decades after the linguistic turn, the first
position may be accepted without argument. The third is essentially an
empirical question, one that is not at the heart of the issue in this essay.
The second, however, leads into my central concern. In what way does
language alter experience? More particularly, how does the form in
which language is exchanged between individuals and groups affect the
cultural construction of the world and subject positions within it? In
addition, this question must be expanded beyond language proper to
include all mediated symbolic structures, comprising, in addition to
language, images (both still and moving), animations, and sounds.

Walter Benjamin (1935/1969) argued that the technical[2] reproduction of art alters the nature of art by changing the relation of the audience
to the author, the conditions of reception, and the authority of the author.
A similar claim may be sustained for culture taken in the anthropological
sense of symbolization in general and in the Foucaultian sense of the
construction of the subject. The technical reproduction of culture then
transforms the constitution of identities,[3] even ethnic or national identities. If these claims are accepted, the next step in the argument is to divide
the term technical into its various aspects: mechanical or electrical and
broadcast or networked.

The mechanical or electrical distinction (for example, print versus
television) affects considerably the ease of diffusion of fixed materials.
In both cases production is greatly centralized and cut off from reception.
The mass distribution of objects requires, for technical reasons independent of their social location, a preformed content whose reception
may be contested and resymbolized as Michel de Certeau (1980/1984)
demonstrated but whose material form is not altered in the reception.
Even if I critique an advertisement on television or in the newspaper,
everyone still receives the same content, regardless of the brilliance of

my response to it. The ability to disseminate widely cultural objects appears to curtail the ease of their transformation. Both print and electronic mass media install a monologic discursive regimen in the heart of everyday life. Cultural and social critics, however, have tended to register complaints against such centralization, not with the advent of newsprint but rather with the spread of electronic media (Horkheimer & Adorno, 1944/1972).

The second distinction concerns broadcast versus networked wrappings of language. In this case cultural objects may be distributed centrally or not. In the case of the telephone and the Internet a highly decentralized practice of distribution replaces the hierarchy and monology of the broadcast model. Whereas the telephone generally confines decentralization to a one-to-one pattern of sending and receiving, the Internet allows broadcasting or multiple distribution in addition to decentralization. Various techniques available on the Internet, from asynchronous listserves and newsgroups to synchronous electronic cafes, with or without graphics and sound, permit a many-to-many dialogic practice to be instituted in a global environment of exchange. How might such an alteration of the way language is packaged and exchanged affect the constitution of ethnic identities?

One caveat is necessary before pursuing this question. These differences in the material inscription of language are not to be taken as technological determinisms. Technical forms are never "independent variables" but always already inscribed in social and cultural processes (Warner, 1992). Nonetheless, technical forms do open possibilities and do contain constraints. One cannot fly from London to Vienna on a cigar, however symbolically charged in the unconscious might be the relation between airplanes and cigars. Yet one might do just that in a virtual reality technology, except that "Vienna" would be computer generated and one's feet would remain firmly planted in London. It might be useful to distinguish and to bear in mind four levels of technological inscription:

1. The constraints of the medium, its material limits

2. The pretechnological conditions for the introduction of the medium; perceived needs that inspire innovation

3. The general *cultural* determinations of the medium, for example, the difference between the introduction of print in Europe and in China

4. The determinations of the medium through practices, that is, how people symbolize their experience with the medium

If these are kept in mind, the problem of technological determinism may be held at bay.

I will assume, as a working hypothesis, that technologies of symbolization are positioned in complex relations to other social practices, are mutually transforming through historically specific articulations but also have limits to their material forms that seriously affect the way they are so inscribed. Before developing this hypothesis in relation to the issue of virtual ethnicity, it is necessary to consider an opposing position: that the virtual is not real.

No Virtuality

There are many ways to deny the virtual, to elide it or repress it, to claim that it represents nothing new, that it does not challenge the existing order of things in any way. Here is Slavoj Zizek's version of such a stance (Lovink, 1996), one that may stand in not so much for psychoanalysis in general but for the propensity, widespread in many registers of discourse and daily life, to normalize and to disavow the strange and the novel:

> GEERT LOVINK: In your speech during the Ars Electronica conference, you emphasized the fact that after a phase of introduction, the seduction of the new media will be over and so will "virtual sex." So the desire to be wired will be over soon?
>
> SLAVOJ ZIZEK: The so-called "virtual communities" are not such a great revolution as it might appear. What impresses me is the extent to which these virtual phenomena retroactively enable us to discover to what extent our self has always been virtual. Even the most physical self-experience has a symbolic, virtual element in it. For example playing sex games. What fascinates me is that the possibility of satisfaction already counts as an actual satisfaction. A lot of my friends used to play sex games on Minitel in France. They told me that the point is not really to meet a person, not even to masturbate, but that just typing your phantasies is the fascination itself. In the symbolic order the potentiality already gives actual satisfaction. In psychoanalytic theory the notion of symbolic castration is often misunderstood. The threat of castration as to its effects, acts as a castration. Or in power relations, where the potential authority forms the actual threat. Take Margaret Thatcher. Her point was that if you don't rely on state support but on your individual resources, luck is around the corner. The majority didn't believe this,

they knew very well that most of them would remain poor. But it was enough to be in a position where they might succeed.

The idea that you were able to do something, but didn't, gives you more satisfaction than actually doing it. In Italy, it is said to be very popular during the sexual act that a woman tells a man some dirty phantasies. It is not enough that you are actually doing it, you need some phantasmatic, virtual support. "You are good, but yesterday I fucked another one and he was better." What interests me are the so-called sado-masochistic, ritualised, sexual practices. You never go to the end, you just repeat a certain foreplay. Virtual in the sense that you announce it, but never do it. Some write a contract. Even when you are doing it, you never lose control, all the time you behave as the director of your own game. What fascinates me is this *Spaltung*, this gap in order to remain a certain distance. This distance, far from spoiling enjoyment makes it even more intense. Here I see great possibilities for the VR stuff.

In the computer I see virtuality, in the sense of symbolic fiction, collapsing. This notion has a long tradition. In Bentham's panopticon we find virtuality at its purest. You never know if somebody is there in the centre. If you knew someone was there, it would have been less horrifying. Now it's just an "utterly dark spot," as Bentham calls it. If someone is following you and you're not sure, it is more horrible than if you know that there is somebody. A radical uncertainty.

In the first sentence of his reply to Geert Lovink's question, Zizek dismissed Internet communications: it is no "revolution." In the second sentence, he universalized it: everything is always already virtual so although it is everywhere, it is also nowhere. He did this by equating the virtual with the symbolic, an interesting proposition but one that dangerously occludes the material forms in which the symbolic is wrapped. Beginning in the third sentence, Zizek incorporated "virtual communities" within the principle of psychoanalysis: That virtual sex is real sex was already known to psychoanalysis in its understanding of the imaginary component in all psychic phenomena—that the threat of castration is, in a very important sense, castration. In this way the virtual becomes one more example of the truth of psychoanalysis, not at all a new register that might be the occasion for a rethinking or even restructuring of the Freudian position. Zizek's discursive move in this passage illustrates the classic gesture of ideology: When faced with an apparent novelty, a seeming "revolution," to use his term, place it under the cover of one's already existing position. Two feats are thereby accomplished: the threat of the new is dissolved and one's position is expanded and strengthened.

His last position, that the computer, far from sustaining a "revolution" in virtual communities, actually dissolves the virtual, goes one better. Now we find that actually existing psychoanalysis has not simply discovered the virtual in advance of modern technology but that modern technology destroys the virtual, in contrasts to psychoanalysis, which defends and sustains it. To achieve this theoretical reversal, Zizek switched the scene to Bentham's panopticon, hardly the latest development in Western technology but one that nonetheless represents to Zizek "virtuality at its purest." The "utterly dark spot," the "black hole in cyberspace,"[4] of the prison tower with its position of surveillant authority whose guard may be present or absent but in either case effectively real for the prisoner caged in his cell, this "virtuality" is somehow the "real" virtual, if this oxymoron will pass the reader's scrutiny, compared to the alleged false virtual community on the Internet. Zizek here moved outside of the psychoanalytic paradigm into that of deconstruction: a conflation of presence and absence replaced the effective power of the imaginary as absence. Such a conflation did not seem to give Zizek pause for reflection as the interview moved on to other matters. Yet it does illustrate an incoherence or, if one prefers, a *consistent* shifting of registers within the same argument, a shifting that reminds one of the movement of unconscious in Lacan's version of it rather than of the ego function of discursive method.

Perhaps the most interesting position expressed by Zizek in response to Lovink's query appeared just before the turn to Bentham when he announced that he sees great possibilities for "this VR stuff" because it "intensifies" the "gap" or "distance" between announcing an act and doing it. At last Zizek found an aspect of the virtual communities of the Internet that he defined as new (at least in its intensity even though Italian women have already mastered the art for the pleasure of their men) and as positive, as something that contains "possibilities." But at precisely this point in his answer to the question Zizek slipped from speaking of the virtual in any meaningful sense. He was simply presenting the imaginary, the "symbolic fictional," as he previously said. "This VR stuff" must be taken as the real in order for it properly to be virtual. When one is on-line in an erotic exchange with a partner, one must play the game of the conversation as a form of "virtual" conversation. Instead Zizek reduced Internet sex games to being a "director" of one's own play, of simply exaggerating the real with special effects for the purpose of manipulating the audience that is oneself into greater orgiastic pleasure. The problem is that one does not control or "direct" conversations on bulletin boards any more than one does in RL, face-to-face dialogue or on the phone. What is virtual about Internet community is not the intensification of the role of director but the simultaneity without physical presence, even the physical presence of the voice.

I have taken this digression from the discussion of virtual ethnicity to the path of Zizek's answer to the question of the virtual not to expose the limitations of his thought—his text comes from an off-the-cuff interview, after all, not a carefully prepared statement—but to illustrate the practice of the denial of the virtual. We must acknowledge the possibility that the globalization of a new communications network may not amount to much except the instrumental purpose of speed of interchange. Because the installation of virtual technologies is at an early stage, no firm judgment about its effectivity is possible. Nonetheless, I will assume the opposite of Zizek, that is, that virtuality represents an occasion for the articulation of new figures of ethnicity, nationhood, community and global interaction. Only on the basis of this assumption is it possible to perceive the novelty of virtual ethnicity and evaluate its import. And I will attempt to avoid the naturalization or normalization of the virtual, the discursive practice through which it emerges in writing as always already given. For the "natural" is only what we are used to, but it is so in the form of denying that we are used by it, transformed and constituted into something historically articulated, something emerging in time, something new; in short, an event.

"Real" Ethnicity

Is there a real or true ethnicity against which a virtual ethnicity may be measured as a fall or an advance? My aim is not to pose this question but instead to construct a theoretical object of ethnicity as a multiple historical articulation without privileging any of its specific configurations except to highlight the emergence of a new form of ethnicity in the age of electronically mediated communications and to examine its political import in relation to contemporary claims of ethnic authenticity. Virtual ethnicity then is an historically emergent form that, as all cultural figures, bears a relation of force to what has preceded it. The problem then is to define the specific categories of communication that render intelligible the pertinent forms of ethnicity in their differential aspects. The understanding of ethnicity found in electronic communities on the Internet must be able to delineate its difference from low technology, tribal ethnicity.

The historian, Pierre Nora, in *Les Lieux de Mémoire*, provided a useful starting point for this analysis. Nora wished to theorize a new kind of history, one that is self-reflective and has come to terms with the deeply transformed conditions of writing history at the waning of the 20th century, conditions that profoundly discourage the sort of history written when it could be assumed that individuals formed their identities in good part through an attachment to a national past. He distinguished what could be called a "modern" practice of writing history, in which the historian innocently constructs in discourse the past of the nation, from a "postmodern" practice of history in which the narrative link of the individual to the nation is problematic at best (Nora, 1989). In doing so, however, he first distinguished the prehistorical from the historical as a distinction between a context in which individual identity is formed into ethnicity through "real environments of memory" (the prehistorical) and one in which it occurs through "sites of memory" (the historical) (p. 7). French peasant culture was his chief example of the former and it was presented as "true" and "immediate." Here the identification of the individual with the group or ethnicity, is formed "in gestures and habits, in skills passed down by unspoken traditions, in the body's inherent self-knowledge, in unstudied reflexes and ingrained memories" (p. 13). By contrast, historical, national, modern identity is "indirect" and mediated. The salient mediation of national identity, for Nora, was the material trace, particularly the written trace found in the archive. For the modern individual, national identity is principally constituted in historical discourse, Nora contended, perhaps betraying to some extent the myopia of the historian. Today a third stage in the story has emerged "with the help of the media." Electronic communication "has substituted for a memory entwined in the intimacy of a collective heritage [the modern] the ephemeral film of current events" (pp. 7-8). Today "a completely new economy of the identity of the self" (p. 15) disrupts and reconfigures ethnicity through electronic encoding and storage of memory in "the omnipotence of imagery and cinema," in "televisual memory" (p. 17). As a result, ethnicity is no longer a collective phenomenon but is individualized: it is "as if an inner voice were to tell each Corsican 'You must be Corsican' . . . [or] to be Jewish is to remember that one is such" (p. 16).

From the standpoint of the practicing historian, Nora (1989) searched for a way to theorize changing forms of ethnicity in relation to the configurations of memory as they in turn changed from face-to-face, to print and finally to electronic communications.[5] He wanted to open a project of rewriting history for a postmodern age. No doubt there is much of value in his proposal as testify the full volumes of Nora's *Les Lieux de Mémoire,* with their rich analyses of reconfigured historical objects. For an understanding of virtual ethnicity, however, Nora in one sense did not go far enough and in another went too far. He did not go far enough because his consideration of postmodern ethnicity included only mass media (film and television) not newer technologies of the computer— their network of communications and virtual reality systems. He went too far in the sense that his opposition "true" and "indirect" sites of ethnic identification first privileged the premodern, peasant structure and then, when the comparison was drawn between the modern and the postmodern, privileged the modern, nationalist phase.

We cannot begin with an opposition of immediate or mediated because this discursive move misconstrues the premodern as the authentic, which is exactly what Nora (1989) did. Such a binary opposition fails to account for the *mediations* within face-to-face communities, the way they are technologies of power that constitute subjects and their ethnic identities through material, symbolic practices. In the passage cited above Nora erred in attributing to peasant culture "unspoken traditions" whereas these cultures have specific narratives of origin that are spoken, performed, and repeated time and again in barns and churches. We must understand these premodern ethnicities not through a binary opposition of immediate or mediated but through different configurations of mediation, with particular attention to the material element in the mediation. Whereas it certainly appears to be the case that premodern ethnicities, in their predominately verbal pattern of symbolic formation, were relatively stable, providing the individual with a fixed ethnic identification, this ethnicity still had to be produced and reproduced in discourses and practices, and it remained subject to change, to doubt, and to alteration. It had to be inscribed.

By the same token, Nora's premature ending in film and television preempted the innovation of computer mediated communication, leading him to sketch the present conjuncture in seriously limited ways. He understood contemporary forms of ethnic identity through the model of consumption: One chooses one's ethnic heritage the way one chooses a pair of shoes or an automobile. He conceded far too easily the voluntary character of the process, thereby losing sight of the socially constituted material patterns at play in such practices. In addition, he comprehended the late 20th century to some extent as no more than an extension of the modern period, with its practice of archiving written materials. "What began as writing ends as high fidelity and tape recording," he wrote, continuing to avoid the computer as a model of storage (Nora, 1989, p. 13). We need to ask, then, how do tape recording, e-mail, and electronic communities constitute a structure through which, to take his example, the Jew remembers to be a Jew? Nora noted the recent phenomenon of nonpracticing Jews reviving their ethnic heritage, but he in no way accounted for the material communicational and political structures through which this became a possibility or even an urgency. In the end the outer chapters of Nora's story, the premodern and the postmodern, were dependent on and determined by the historian's predilection for the modern, for the period of national identity, for the time when it fell to the historian to narrate the past of the nation—at least this is the view of the historian—as a discursive interpellation for national identity. The task for us, then, is to extract from Nora's account the problematic of ethnic identity in relation to material, symbolic configurations and to reshape this category, articulating its attributes, to allow the comprehension of virtual ethnicity in relation to earlier ethnicities, and, finally, to open this project with a sense of the political dimension of new formations, the relations of force necessarily at play, and the pathos of individuals searching for a better life.

The Global Village Reaffirmed

To comprehend the phenomenon of virtual ethnicity, it is necessary to approach contemporary forms of social life at least to some extent on their own terms, to view them without the modernist lenses through which they are perceived as massified, inert, passive. This is the important achievement of the current of cultural studies of recent decades (Grossberg & Nelson, 1992), of urban anthropology and of some individual figures, such as Michel de Certeau (1980/1984). Although risking a new romanticism of the popular and the everyday, these intellectual strains bring us closer to the strange new world of the postmodern quotidian, enable us to glimpse the contours of mass society without the defensive reaction of Olympian disdain that marks so much of critical theory. By the same token, other thinkers, such as Marshall McLuhan (1994), Jean Baudrillard (1995), and Paul Virilio (1995), also pioneered the "descent" in mass culture. McLuhan in particular opened a promising path to virtual ethnicity with his celebration (at times ambivalent to be sure) of a new tribalism, a global village of electronic communication in which the sense ratio of individuals alters from a dominance of the visual in modernity to a dominance of the tactile in what we may now call postmodernity. McLuhan's position, developed mainly in the early 1960s, was limited by, among other things, its focus on the broadcast media, appearing before the dissemination of computers and their communication networks.

Writing in the late 1980s, Michel Maffesoli (1988) suffered no similar handicap. In *Les Temps Des Tribus* he renewed McLuhan's (1994) initiative in a more developed postmodern environment, opening critical discourse to an understanding of virtual ethnicity. Maffesoli began by reaffirming McLuhan's claim of a change from "an optical period" to "a tactile era of proximity, from the global to the local" (p. 51). Very much like McLuhan, he also discerned a new "orality" in daily life amidst a chaos of "microgroups" he calls tribes. More clearly than McLuhan, Maffesoli perceived the social as a realm of increasing massification but also, and at the same time increasing heterogeneity, increasing "sameness" *and* increasing differentiation at the micro level. Maffesoli located the new tribalism "in diverse sports gatherings . . . in consumerist fury in department stores, supermarkets, commercial centers . . . on the avenues of large cities" (p. 125). Although he provided no detailed analyses of these "pivots" of postmodern daily life, he discerned within them "a constant going and coming between tribes and masses" (p.126).

According to Maffesoli (1988) the new tribalism is characterized by proximity, "the unsaid," "the residue," very much along the lines of Nora's community of "true memory." Maffesoli insisted that the tribes are beyond modern "individualism," are determined by forms of feeling, "auras" of togetherness that refute the logics of identity and subject or object dualism. The tribes are "nonrational" not "irrational" but also contain "a new form of rationality" that is a combination of proximity, intensity, "both linking people and letting them be" (p. 178). The tribes represented a new Fourierism of postmodern passionate attraction. They were characterized above all by mobility of connection, Charles Fourier's "butterfly passion," the desire constantly to change partners and associations. In this respect they were, for Maffesoli, different from the counterculture of the 1960s with its dream of stable communities. Although Maffesoli based his understanding of the tribes on premodern, even archaic principles of closeness, contact, exchange of feeling, he avoided

Nora's ideology of presence: "The fusion of the community . . . does not imply a full presence to the other . . . but establishes rather . . . a *tactile relation*," (p. 94). Even with this caution he slipped at times from his own analytic perch. He did, in places, ontologize the tribes, finding in them a new realization of fullness of being: "Participating in a multiplicity of tribes . . . each person will be able to live his [sic] *intrinsic* [italics added] plurality" (p. 182). Here the postmodern vision of the multiple, decentered self amplified into the redemption of man, the recuperation of lost unity, the completion of the metanarrative of progress as "plurality" becames "intrinsic." The tribes were, for Maffesoli, clearly an improvement on the autonomous, rational subject of modernity. The edge of a differential analysis was given over to a comic trope of a happy ending.

The use of the term *tribe* is perhaps one source of the problem. In the postmodern context *tribe* cannot designate the anthropologist's society of kinship. Maffesoli's tribes were urban, not rural; dispersed within wider relations, not isolated; subject to the modernizing processes of the division of labor and institutional differentiation, not combined in the unity spatial and functional solidarity; penetrated by processes of commodification and telecommunications, not restricted to production for use and face-to-face symbolic exchange; disciplined by the nation-state, not governed by hereditary hierarchies. Nothing could be farther apart than the human ecologies of the late-20th century Western world and the hunter or gatherer societies normally known as tribes. Even Maffesoli's insistence on the emotional ties of the new tribes suggested a break, not a continuity from the old tribes. The former after all gather into groups on a purely voluntary basis not through the prescriptions of local myths.

These cautions aside, Maffesoli (1988) was able to incorporate a sense of computerized communications into his vision of the proximate, local new tribe. He surmised,

> The feeling of tribal belonging can be comforted by technological development . . . potentially, "cable," electronic bulletin boards (playful, erotic, instrumental, etc.) create a communication matrix where groups with diverse configurations and objectives emerge, are fortified and disappear; groups which recall the archaic structures of tribes or village clans. (pp. 171-172)

Global relations on the Internet became local neighborhoods for Maffesoli, very much in the spirit of McLuhan (1994). Maffesoli found the

sociability and amorousness of the Minitel's *messageries* compatible with
shopping at malls, attending football games and rock concerts, joining
raves, and hanging out on street corners. His new ethnicity was one
without virtuality, a tribalism that conquered the alienations and isola-
tions of life in postmodern capitalism, overcame the loneliness and pas-
sivity of mass culture in a novel flexible and multiple individualism, a
sociability that, shorn of bourgeois individualism, celebrated what is after
all predominantly youth culture with no sense of its difficulties, suicides,
drug abuse, identity confusion, racism, gang warfare and so forth. His
generous appreciation of "new tribalism" failed to provide a materialism
of the mediation, an articulation of the complex structuring of each aspect
of everyday life, a sense of how, for example, watching a television show
like *The X Files* and, during the commercial break, connecting by computer
modem to a Usenet group on that subject to enter one's comments or see
what others are saying and finally going to the mall to buy an "X Files"
T-shirt, are each differential engagements that constitute subjects in highly
heterogeneous ways. I want to ask not how a new, unified image (new
tribalism) is emerging but how specific figures of ethnicity are altered by
their electronic constitution in virtual spaces.

Undetermination

At what point in the history of technologies of symbolization is it
appropriate to speak of "the virtual"? Everything depends on how the
virtual is understood. There are currently many concepts of the virtual
to clarify this issue (Baudrillard, 1995; Derrida, 1995; Heim, 1993, in
press; Virilio, 1995), but I will turn to the work of Pierre Lévy (1995),
Qu'est-ce que le Virtuel?, because of the way it deals with the basic
distinction, real or virtual. Two tendencies above all must be avoided: to
celebrate the virtual as an evolutionary or dialectical "next stage"
beyond the real or to dismiss the virtual as a false instantiation of the
real. Instead, the virtual must be understood as an historical articulation
of the real, fully as actual as any other such articulation but one connected
specifically with computer-mediated communication technologies.
Lévy productively theorized this relation by distinguishing between the
opposition real or potential versus actual or virtual, which he found in
the Western philosophical tradition. The difference between the two sets
of terms is that the former is more algorithmic; that is, the potential easily
becomes the real, or better, its possibility to become real is "predefined."
In the latter case the relation is more "problematic," requiring more

"invention" for the virtual to become actual. This distinction was useful merely to indicate relative degrees of uncertainty and complexity. Lévy's innovation was to argue that today a reversal is taking place: Instead of the virtual becoming actual, the actual is becoming virtual. We have moved to a condition in which what is actual is now virtual, articulating an undefined set of possibilities rather than a fixed state of things. "Virtualization," he contended,

> is not a derealization (the transformation of a reality into an ensemble of possibilities) but a mutation of identity, a displacement of the center of ontological gravity of the object in question: instead of being defined principally by its actuality (a "solution"), the entity henceforth finds its essential consistency in a problematic field. (p. 2)

He gave the example of a hypertext (Landow, 1992) in which the determination of the text, its sequential structure and meaning, its logic of associations, are, in comparison with the book, to a great extent at the discretion of the reader. We thus find objects before us whose determination is to a very considerable extent underdetermined.

Louis Althusser (1965/1970), with some reluctance, adapted the psychoanalytic term "overdetermination" to the context of social theory. In Freud, overdetermination designated the multiple causes of the onset of neurotic symptoms. A patient suffered because immediate traumas combined with older ones to produce symptoms. The "cause" of illness was not singular but wrapped up in the patient's long psychic history. For Althusser, the term served to help differentiate Marx from Hegel. The question concerned the unity of phenomena in their contradictions. Althusser argued that the Hegelian dialectic was too unified to allow for contradiction. The process of negation was sublated into the center of consciousness, whereas in Marx determinations of an object could not be so homogenized. Superstructural or ideological determinations, for example, were distinct from those of the base yet combined with them and related to them to form a conjuncture. Ideologies "reactivated" older elements that merge with new class conflicts as the republicanism of ancient Rome was overlaid on the French revolution of 1789 or Pauline theology was invoked to Luther's break from Rome. A historical object then was a complex of distinct aspects, all combining, through the engine of contradiction, to "overdetermine" an outcome. Although this outcome may, for Althusser, either be a blockage of political change or an eruption of revolution, the term overdetermination has come to suggest the contingency of events. Because social objects consisted of many discrete determinations, causality is not unilinear and history is governed by a law of complexity.

With the term "underdetermination" I contend that certain social objects that I call virtual (hypertexts, for example) are overdetermined in such a way that their level of complexity or indeterminateness goes one step further. Not only are these objects formed by distinct practices, discourses, and institutional frames, each of which participates in and exemplifies the contradictions of capitalism and the nation-state, but they are open to practice; they tend not to direct agents in clear paths; they solicit social construction and cultural creation. In a museum one contemplates a painting or even enters into an installation. In the former case one is moved by the sublime, the unpresentable in the work of art. In the latter case one forms the work of art while observing it, because by moving within it one may instigate changes in lighting or sound that are part of the installation. Downloading an image of a painting on the Internet, one may find the image within a program (such as Lview) that allows the viewer to alter any aspect of the image, not just to signal a light or sound as in the programmed structure of the installation, but to reconstruct the image from inside out, displacing it into a text, adding sound to it or combining it with other images. The image on the Internet is virtual in the sense that it only becomes actual through the countless transformations it undergoes as people copy it and change it. A type of object thus emerges into social space that is overdetermined in the sense of being structured through multiple contradictory practices but is also underdetermined in the sense that it remains an invitation to the imaginary.

One may argue that this is always the case, that "virtualization" is the normal, not the new state of things, that books are as indeterminate as hypertexts, for instance. Lévy (1995) considered this question and argued, as a philosopher, for the transcendental possibility of the always already, that what may be conceived now, may be conceived at any time. Whereas in principle one cannot disagree with the philosopher, as a historian, I would rather assert that the transcendental is a condition of thought, not a condition of history. I prefer to acknowledge the logic of the transcendental but defend against projecting it as a conceptual tool for historical analysis, in short, ontologizing it. Thus, in the realm of the actual and the real, the structure of objects and subjects, although never absolutely fixed but always open to resymbolization, maintains a consistency of presence in space and time. In modern society, for example, objects and subjects appear as never a full presence but as a presence whose absence is rendered difficult by its material root in space and time. The phenomenon of virtualization, what I call "a mode of information," enables subjects and objects increasingly to appear in configurations of space and time, mind and body, human and machine that disaggregate the real or actual into constellations of indeterminate—not amorphous—complexity. What is, above all, necessary is to specify the parameters of these "virtual" configurations. What are objects like in electronic communities? What are they like in helmet-and-glove virtual reality technologies? What are they like on e-mail, computerized databases, World Wide Web pages, Internet Relay Chat channels? How are identities associated with the body, such as gender and ethnicity, configured in these virtual "places"? How are these genders and ethnicities different from and similar to those on television shows, telephone conversations, synchronous meetings, serendipitous urban encounters, massed refugee camps, and rural dwellings?

Jews in Space

The Internet is not a homogeneous social object. It contains records of information, databases, which construct identities of individuals outside their consciousness, with their (unwitting) participation, yet inscribed in institutional and practical contexts. I have called this phenomenon the "superpanopticon," modifying Foucault's analysis of disciplinary surveillance (Poster, 1995). In these electronic interpellations, ethnic identities are sutured or attached to individuals, in some cases multiplying but always dispersing their selves. Yet these inscriptions are not fully virtual because they are relatively fixed, formed by the objectified processes of computer-generated files. The Internet also includes electronic mail exchanges where individuals and groups exchange messages generally with fixed addresses attached, addresses that refer to the identity the individual has already determined in nonelectronic, social space. Here, ethnicity, to the extent that it emerges at all, is associated with the legal name of the individual. The situation becomes more ambiguous in the hypermedia zone of the Internet known as the World Wide Web. In the Web, individuals compose "home pages" that present them to anyone who is on-line. A person may include pictures, sounds, and texts that offer a version of who they are, including their ethnicity either inherited or self-defined. Still other sectors of the Internet are more prone to virtualizing ethnicity. These are bulletin boards and MUDs and MOOs (Multi-User domains, Object Oriented) where real-time exchanges of textual messages occur. In the MOOs, identities are constructed by participants requiring a name and a gender, but self-descriptions may include ethnic characteristics. Such identities are further formed and reformed in the actual exchanges of messages, in dialogues with others and are not therefore simple expressions of interior consciousness. Because the bodily markers of ethnicity (physical attributes and vocal accent) are invisible on MOOs, such ethnicity as exists in these electronic communities is fully virtual,[6] although the predominance of white American users often leads to the presumption that one is interacting with a white American person.

It would seem, then, that interactions on the Internet would tend to dissolve ethnicities to the extent that they are based, as Nora (1989) argued, on presence in space and on ancient, common rituals. The fixity of ethnicity as an attribute of the self would appear to be the opposite of the identities constructed in the virtual spaces of the Internet. I explored this question by subscribing to a listserve,[7] a messaging system in which all subscribers receive messages sent by any other subscriber, called "CyberJew." Initiated by someone in Israel but including individuals from the United States and other countries, CyberJew explicitly raises the question of ethnicity on the Internet. One participant asked if a "cyber Seder"[8] is a real Seder? "How and what aspect of the high touch aspects of the Mitzvot (blessing) are at all possible in a cyber mode?," he asks. To what extent is the intimacy of face-to-face presence a requisite for the spiritual effects of the meal?

I was raised in a family of Eastern European Jewish working-class immigrants. My grandfather's generation was secular so we did not perform Jewish rituals like Seders, but when his siblings and other relations visited Jewish ethnicity permeated the air. They spoke Yiddish, ate Jewish meals and also reflected ways of being that were clearly different from that of "America." My father, however, was a thorough-going Americanizer. He wanted to have no accent, to dress in the latest fashion, and raise his socioeconomic standing. He remarried (my mother had died) a woman from a more religious Jewish background. In her family I began to attend Seders. Yet I saw them almost as an outsider because I came to them late (around age 10) and I experienced them through what I imagined was my father's dislike and my grandfather's politically motivated disdain. Even with these contradictory mediations, the Seder was somehow a natural, necessary event for me . I had become a Jew in America.

Years later, after not practicing any Jewish rituals nor attending any religious service for decades, I still passively regard myself as Jewish. I believe this ethnic identity "stuck" with me because of my early presence before people of my grandfather's generation who, without believing in any religious doctrine, were steeped in Jewish culture from Europe. The smells of food, intonations of voice, bodily gestures and ways of touching (pinching my cheek and calling me "boychick"—a practice I did not very much appreciate)—these "micropractices" of everyday life made me Jewish and these are, I believe, the factories of ethnicity. To answer my question posed above, then, the intimacy of face-to-face presence during childhood appears to be a sufficient condition for ethnic identification. If that is the case, is a "CyberJew" possible?

The "CyberJew" quoted above hypothesized that the Internet is not a dissolvant of ethnicity but represents a new stage in the history of the Jews. He wrote,

> My sense is that we are in an analogous period when the Temple was destroyed and the Rabbis had to reinvent Jewish worship and came up with tefillah[9] and what later became the Synagogue. Are we in a new Yavneh[10] time period?

The question is more pertinent than might at first appear because one of the stages of Jewish history is the diaspora, a time precisely when Jewish ethnicity was not associated with spatial proximity. In fact anti-Semitic writings in Europe often rebuked Jews as the deracinated people, those without a homeland, without roots in the soil, without the conditions that Nora (1989) thought are essential to ethnic identity. Jews are thus the displaced people par excellence. Unlike nomads, whose relation to space is one of movement and change, Jews, until the establishment of Israel, precisely had no space. When Nora wrote that Jews must remember to be Jews, as we saw above, he dissociated ethnicity from place in a manner that opened the possibility that remembering might occur through non-spatial mediations, such as the Internet.

This is precisely the argument of many CyberJew participants: the Internet, far from dissolving ethnicity, enables all Jews, wherever they are on the planet, to connect with one another. The Internet here is a

neutral instrument of community, connecting preestablished ethnic
identities. Numerous home pages established by Jews, such as The
Federation of Greater Toronto (http://www.feduja.org) and Chabad
(http://www.utexas.edu/students/cjso/Chabad/houses.html) and by
other ethnic and religious groups, as well as the Roman Catholic Pope,
testify to the powerful expectation that cyberspace provides a neutral
arena of community solidarity, a place of stabilizing individual commitments to groups, of congealing ethnic identity in a gossamer, electronic
medium. As one participant in CyberJew put it, "Modern communications, including airplanes and computer networks, are doing something
else: creating the potential for Jews the world around to be part of an
integrated Israel (the people, not the state)." A further example of the
facilitating character of the Internet is the exploration of distance learning in MOOs. One participant reported,

> So, let me tell you briefly about the Judaic Studies Center that I am
> building on Diversity University. So far, I have built a classroom, a room
> focusing on the Hebrew calendar, and a room focusing on Jewish stories
> where the person reading the story becomes a character in the story and
> occasionally has to talk to the other characters in the story. A few
> members of DU from Connecticut to Hawaii gathered last Chanukkah
> to light candles together, eat latkes, and so forth.

In MOOs, one may learn about Jewish history but also enter into the bible
as a character. In cyberspace, past and present ethnicities merge into the
bitstream of pixels on the screen. In the words of Barbara Kirshenblatt-
Gimblett (1996), an anthropologist examining Jewish virtual ethnicity,
"New communication technologies have made possible the gathering of
vast and far-flung following in new forms of assembly" (p. 32).

Countless difficulties confront the would-be CyberJew. How is one
to know that participants in electronic communities are Jews? Or does
participation constitute ethnic membership? How can traditional practices of Judaism subsist in cyberspace? Otherwise trivial practices
become impossible predicaments when transferred to cyberspace where
not only space but also time is problematic. One participant in the listserv
asked,

> The time for prayer is tied to earth time and it is tied to the cycle of a
> day experienced by someone standing on the earth—in other words the
> 12 or whatever hours between sunup and sundown. Being in space

would change one's relation to the sun, but it wouldn't need to change the concept of a "day."

Conundrums over the basic features of Jewish practices assail ethnicity in cyberspace. It would seem that the transplantation of social forms that arose in preindustrial contexts into high-tech contexts would have great difficulty. As one skeptical CyberJew participant wrote, "precisely because in cyberspace we do not meet face-to-face, the standards of decent communication break down far more easily." Many had suspicions that cyberspace was not conducive to any form of ethnicity.

Others were more sanguine but placed their hopes for the Internet in a global spiritual renewal, rather than in a simple transformation of Judaism. Here is one participant's formulation of the new possibilities:

> We have been treating "cyberspace" as possibly an important new technology thru which the Jewish community around the world may have to reexamine and reshape its communal form.
> I want to ask whether it may be EVEN MORE than that: a token, along with many others, of a great surge of God-consciousness into the world, which requires us to shape not only new forms of Jewish community but new Jewish images (i.e., Names) of God, new forms of prayer, new ethical understandings, new shapes of Torah as different from the Oral Torah of the Rabbis as that was from the Written Torah of Tanakh . . . inventing the Internet and Cyberspace. This is not just a change in human history, but in its fabric—a shift in the life-cycle of God . . . a "new paradigm" of Judaism.

A "shift in the life-cycle of God" poses the question of virtual ethnicity in its most extreme form: If the Internet represents the possibility of a spiritual "change in human history" are we still speaking of ethnicity in any recognizable form or are we speaking of some new global consciousness, such as Teilhard de Chardin's (1955/1959) "noosphere" or Pierre Lévy's (1996) "collective intelligence"? If cyberspace is the occasion of a great spiritual renewal of the planet, have we not surpassed in some sense the historic forms of ethnic identity toward some as yet unknown relation of individual to group. In the following passage Lévy envisioned a new collective intelligence in cyberspace far different from any historical or even conceivable ethnicity:

> If we were to take the route of the collective intelligence, we would gradually invent techniques, systems of signs, social forms of organi-

zation and of regulation permitting us to think together, to concentrate our intellectual and mental power, to multiply our imaginations and our experiences, to work out practical solutions for the complex problems affronting us in real time and on all levels. We would progressively learn to orientate ourselves in a new cosmos, constantly transforming itself and drifting, to become its authors as much as we can, to invent collectively ourselves as a species. Collective intelligence does not aim at the mastery of selves through human collectives but at an essential loosening of the grip [and] changing the very conception of identity, the mechanisms of domination and of the breaking out of conflicts, the unblocking of confiscated communication, the mutual launching of isolated thoughts.

Lévy's perhaps breathtaking concept of the Internet as "collective intelligence" situates the individual in a virtual object, an unfinished, contingent state in which identity is a temporary, fluid link to a process of creation, an *underdetermined* entity whose recognition is never a mis(s) because it never congeals into permanence, a subject position that is "never before" rather than "always already." Linked to continuously shifting global processes of textual, graphic, and aural formations, individuals in cyberspace cannot attach to objects in the fixed shapes of historic ethnicity.

Notes

1. I am indebted to Michael Lang for drawing my attention to this passage.

2. Samuel Weber in *Mass Mediauras* argued persuasively that the translation of Benjamin's essay as "The Work of Art in the Age of Mechanical Reproduction" does not render the German *technischen* as well as the English "technical." For the Benjamin (1969) essay, see *Illuminations* (H. Zohn, Trans.). New York: Schocken, pp. 217-252.

3. The term "identity" is widely used in critical theory and cultural studies today, yet it remains a problem. In its psychological version "identity" entered the discursive scene with Erik Erikson's *Identity: Youth and Crisis* in 1968. In the philosophical tradition, identity is a fundamental category of logic and ontology. In social theory, it emerged in Theodor Adorno's work, especially in *Negative Dialectics* (1973) as part of the critique of the cultural figure of the individual as subject. This line of criticism continues, with important changes, in poststructuralist positions as well as in postcolonial writings.

The problem is twofold: first, the category is Western yet appears in discourse as universal and, second, it presumes what it needs to demonstrate, that the subject as a coherence, unity, foundation. On the first issue see the important essay by Roger Rouse (1992), "Questions of Identity: Reflections on the Cultural Politics of Personhood and Collectivity in Transnational Migration to the United States" with essays by Homi Bhabha, Ernesto Laclau, Jacques Ranciére, Joan Scott, and others. Here I wish only to add a serious caution to the use of the term.

4. This phrase is used by J. Hillis Miller in an as yet unpublished essay on Anthony Trollope's *Ayala's Angel*.

5. Many Jews agree with Nora's assessment of their situation regarding memory. One, Joel Rosenberg, says, "I marvel at the resilience of the Jewish people. Their best characteristic is their desire to remember. No other people has such an obsession with memory!" (Eshman, 1996, p. 8). I am indebted to Jonathan Judaken for showing me this essay.

6. For an analysis of ethnicity and race on the Internet see Nakamura (1995), who argued that race persists on MOOs but is constructed differently from "real life."

7. The coodinator of the listserv is Moshe Dror and CyberJew is found at CYBERJEW@bguvm.bgu.ac.il. He is a member of World Futures Society-Israel Chapter and World Network of Religious Futurists. There is a sci-fi tone to some of the messages, such as one member who pondered the first synagogue in space. I began my subscription in April 1996. On the Web CyberJew is found at http://www.jewishnet.net/

8. A Seder is a ritual meal eaten during the Passover holiday that commemorates the exodus of the Israelites from Egyptian captivity.

9. Tefillah are leather straps donned by Jewish males each morning when certain prayers are recited.

10. Yavneh time suggests a period of fundamental political and social reorganization, as in the shift from the Synagogue system to the Rabbi system.

References

Adorno, T. (1973). *Negative dialectics* (E. B. Ashton, Trans.). New York: Seabury. (Original work published 1966)

Althusser, L. (1970). Contradiction and overdermination. In *For Marx* (B. Brewster, Trans.) (pp. 87-128). New York: Vintage. (Original work published 1965)

Benjamin, W. (1969). *Illuminations* (H. Zohn, Trans.). New York: Schocken. (Original work published 1935)

Baudrillard, J. (1995). *Le crime parfait*. Paris: Galilée.

Briggs, C. F., & Maverick, A. (1858). *The story of the telegraph, and a history of the great Atlantic cable*. New York: Rudd & Carleton.

Chow, R. (1996). *Primitive passions: Visuality, sexuality, ethnography, and contemporary Chinese cinema.* New York: Columbia University Press.

de Certeau, M. (1984). *The practice of everyday life* (S. Rendall, Trans.) Berkeley: University of California Press. (Original work published 1980)

de Chardin, T. (1959). *The phenomenon of man* (B. Wall, Trans.). New York: Harper and Row. (Original work published 1955)

Derrida, J. (1995). Archive fever: A Freudian impression. *Diacritics, 25*(2), 9-63.

Erikson, E. (1968). *Identity: Youth and crisis.* New York: Norton.

Eshman, R. (1996). Caught in a net of controversy. *The Jewish Journal,* p. 8.

Grossberg, L., & Nelson, C. (1992). *Cultural studies.* New York: Routledge.

Heim, M. (1993). *The metaphysics of virtual reality.* New York: Oxford University Press.

Heim, M. (in press). *Virtual realism.* New York: Oxford University Press.

Horkheimer, M., & Adorno, T. (1972). *Dialectic of enlightenment* (J. Cumming, Trans.). New York: Continuum. (Original work published 1944)

Kirshenblatt-Gimblett, B. (1996). The electronic vernacular. In G. Marcus, (Ed.), *Connected: Engagements with media* (pp. 21-66). Chicago: University of Chicago Press.

Landow, G. (1992). *Hypertext: The convergence of contemporary critical theory and technology.* Baltimore, MD: Johns Hopkins University Press.

Lévy, P. (1995). *Qu'est-ce que le virtuel?* Paris: La Découverte.

Lévy, P. (1996). *Toward superlanguage* (R. Stewen, Trans.). Available at: http://www.uiah.fi/bookshop/isea_proc/nextgen/01.html

Lovink, G. (1996, Feb. 21). Civil society, fanaticism and digital reality: A conversation with Slavoj Zizek. *Ctheory: Theory, Technology and Culture, an Electronic Journal, 19*(1-2).

Lowe, L. (1996). *Immigrant acts.* Raleigh, NC: Duke University Press.

Maffesoli, M. (1988). *Le temps des tribus: Le déclin de l'individualisme dans les société de masse.* Paris: Meridiens Klincksieck.

McLuhan, M. (1994). *Understanding media.* Cambridge: MIT Press.

Nakamura, L. (1995). Race in/for cyberspace: Identity tourism and racial passing on the Internet. *Works and Days, 13*(1-2), 181-193.

Nietzsche, F. (1986). *Human, all too human* (R. J. Hollingdale, Trans.). (Original work published 1878)

Nora, P. (1989, Spring). Between memory and history: Les lieux de mémoire. *Representations, 26,* 7-25.

Poster, M. (1995). *The second media age.* Cambridge, MA: Blackwell.

Rouse, R. (1992). *Questions of identity: Reflections on the cultural politics of personhood and collectivity in transnational migration to the United States.* Unpublished manuscript.

Virilio, P. (1995). *La vitesse de libération.* Paris: Galilée.

Warner, M. (1992). *The letters of the republic: Publication and the public sphere in eighteenth-century America.* Cambridge, MA: Harvard University Press.

Weber, S. (1996). *Mass mediauras.* Palo Alto, CA: Stanford University Press

8

Dissolution and Fragmentation: Problems in On-Line Communities

Beth Kolko and Elizabeth Reid

The proliferation of virtual communities in recent years has resulted in the creation of new social spaces, and new forms of interaction and identity formation. While virtual communities have been the focus of much research, the majority of these assessments have left many assumptions unarticulated and have avoided the question of what it means to fail in cyberspace as a virtual self and as a virtual community.

Those failures are the chief subject of this chapter. The histories written of a number of on-line communities catalogue a variety of communicative failures: incidents when breakdown in the ability of the community to collaborate disrupted the social fabric. In examining instances of virtual community failure, we work toward a more complete understanding of the tension between written and spoken language within virtual environments. In so doing, we examine both the language of interaction and also the language of spatial construction. Language, as the building block of what occurs in cyberspace, is more ephemeral than the written word and more fixed than the casual spoken word. This tension can pose problems for on-line communities where words have both the spontaneity and immediacy of social speech and the permanence of writing.

As Mark Poster (1995), Allucquere Rosanne Stone (1991), Sherry Turkle (1995), and others argue, the self in cyberspace is fragmented and multiple. Cyberspatial freedom to obscure or recreate aspects of the self has been written of as allowing greater exploration and expression of the self. For all the positive potential of such self-recreation and reinscription, the tales of relationships formed under these circumstances also can contain less celebratory themes. In *Life on the Screen*, Turkle asserts the positive potential of this multiplicity of personality as she chronicles a number of user's experience with virtual communities and personae. Her profiles of Gordon (p. 189) and Matthew (p. 190), for example, are two narratives that illustrate the different ways people use the flexibility of on-line identity to negotiate the challenges of the face-to-face world. Both participate in virtual communities to simultaneously broaden and hone their conception of their selves, and to achieve a real-life emotional equilibrium. Whereas these and other characterizations in the book relate a largely positive relationship with virtual existence, Turkle also acknowledges cases such as those of Stewart, a young man who ultimately experiences no positive effects from his on-line personae and who feels that these experiences "have stripped away some of his defenses but have given him nothing in return" (p. 198).

Despite these caveats in her work, as other researchers have used Turkle's (1995) arguments in their own meditations on cyberspace they have most often focused on her liberatory pronouncements regarding the adoption of virtual selves. In contrast, in this chapter we seek to explore themes of more qualified approbation regarding cyberspatial interaction and discuss the ways in which the counternarratives we propose—stories of dissolution—suggest that fragmented projections of the self can become fixed and invariable, and can preclude flexible social interaction. In contrast to Turkle's psychoanalytic focus on individual effect and affect, we wish to focus on the sometimes negative relationship between the construction of the cyberspatial self and the formation of on-line community.

The visions of fragmentation and inflexibility in cyberspace that this chapter examines relate to a series of collaborations in cyberspace that we have participated in or observed. We explore community failure by first examining an on-line governance experiment, one which at its conclusion framed larger issues mirrored by other attempts in cyberspace to establish governing structures and justice systems. The debates that have emerged from these experiments form an interesting and powerful critique of current notions of virtual communities. As these discussions illustrate the inadequacy of traditional notions of individual and cultural boundaries to address the needs of virtual communities, we work toward a perspective on language use that emphasizes the rhetorical nature of virtual space.

Case Studies of
Collaboration and Community

In 1993 a graduate student started a virtual community for media researchers, a membership-only MOO. As of January 1997, almost 4 years into its existence, this MOO had 919 members, 37 countries represented among the membership, and an average daily login maximum of 13 users. Membership was by a formal and yet not very strict application process. Many participants were academics; the group also included programmers, students, artists, and a variety of that self-identified "other" category. About a year into its existence, this community embarked on an experiment in virtual governance; until that point it had been operating—as many such virtual environments do—under the benign dictatorship of its chief administrator, or arch-wizard. The roots of the decision to change the structure of the community were tangled and complicated by the vastly different ideas and expectations of the parties involved: the wizards, the handful of members who first raised the issue of alternative modes of governing the community, the group that participated in an initial town meeting to discuss the idea, and the greater number of those who remained uninterested and uninvolved with the discussions.

It is possible to claim that this experiment was doomed from the outset because of the particulars of how the decision was made to create what came to be known as "the council." We suspect that particular analysis would be an important one to conduct at some point. It is not, however, the story we are going to tell here. Rather, we want to focus on the dissolution of the council, and the series of events that led its members to their final stages of frustration. In ethnographic terms, this story comes down perhaps too heavily on the participant side of the participant-observer relationship; one of the authors was on that council and the other was a member of the MOO. This chapter grew out of nearly 3 years of trying to make sense of what happened during those months. One might also claim that, given what we know of ethnographic methodology, what follows is a story; one version only of the many possible narratives that could be told of these events.

The particulars of the case that led to the end are less germane. It was a case of harassment, complicated by evidence and testimony that spanned several different virtual communities, by the differing nationalities of the plaintiffs, accused, and council members, and by two council members' personal involvement with the case. Members of the council cast about for some legal guidelines but could rely on neither institutional nor national boundaries to provide a framework. In addition, because two of the six council members were involved in the case, they recused themselves, leaving four to adjudicate. The council members had no precedents, no legal backdrop, and not even much of an indigenous social code to guide the decisions. Councilors talked to people, read logs that were submitted, reinterviewed participants and also established a mailing list that allowed the four to facilitate conversations, weigh evidence, and tentatively spin out some decisions and rationalizations for those decisions.

The process was frustrating to those at the center and on the margins. But what grew most disconcerting was not the actual process of coming to some sort of judgment, which some council members largely believed was a valuable use of time. The case was fascinating, challenging, and demanded a great deal of creative thinking and charting of new ground; by and large the councilors perceived themselves as being engaged in something important, something worthwhile. It was the aftereffects of the decision, however, that were so excruciating, because the council reached a decision that met with objection from some community members. The particular fault lines of disagreement are not the concern of this chapter—our concern is the fact that such fault lines persisted despite best efforts at discursive negotiation.

The basis of our chapter is a view of MOOs (and MUDs in general) as writing environments, places where discourse is all-powerful and linguistic negotiation is the only real weapon. It is in this light that we read the aftermath of the council's decision, a time when different versions of how the council proceeded circulated. One example of how contradictory narratives persisted concerns the fact that two council members were part of the plaintiff collective. One of the first decisions the council made was to have those two members recuse themselves. Their testimony was subsequently disregarded out of awareness of the potential conflict of interest and the ways in which personal relationships could affect the outcome. Whether or not the council protected itself sufficiently from claims of bias is not the case here. What is crucial is that the council's attempts at self-representation in terms of the decision-making process were nullified by relegation to M. Christine Boyer's "zones of silence" (1996, p. 80). Stupefying amounts of text were posted to internal mailing lists; accusations were relentless. Despite the numerous posts put forward by council members regarding the process followed, no middle ground was ever identified. Resentment on all sides grew, and the resulting acrimony made it difficult to reclaim any sense of community spirit or any sense of shared objectives.

In the wake of the furor over the council's decision, we were forced to ask what led to this particular failure. We could provide a variety of possible explanations. It might be that the council just did a bad job. It might be the result of the MOO's members being drawn from a variety of countries and having a diversity of experience with and expectations of governance systems. It could have been tied to the MOO being populated by people with wildly diverging ideas on what the goal of the MOO should be. The failure also could be related to an ultimately flawed sense of public versus private within the community, a blurring of virtual space that made it impossible for clear function to follow unclear form.[1]

From the perspective of a rhetorician, this ultimate breakdown seemed to be a quite clear lesson that virtual communities are *not* the agora, that they are not a place of open and free public discourse. It is a mistake to think that the Internet is an inherently democratic institution or that it will necessarily lead to increased personal freedoms and increased understanding between people. After all, no sooner did Internet users realize that when on-line they were unable to see someone's age or office door plaque, but they began to divide people into new categories with new status symbols and new languages of social domination and subordination. The IRC operators, MUD wizards, FAQ (Frequently Asked Questions) list maintainers—and virtual councilors—all entered the stage, creating social hierarchies that can be every bit as restrictive and oppressive as some real life ones.

While we are loathe to accept any one failed experiment as evidence that on-line communities *cannot* be a space of constructive public discourse, the narratives of LambdaMOO substantiate similar claims. Julian Dibbell's (1993) article "A Rape in Cyberspace" is perhaps the best known story about LambdaMOO, and while his narrative is ostensibly about the *creation* of a community, closer reading reveals that the creation was predicated on dissolution. In other words, it was transgression and the resultant attempts at justice and governance that Dibbell reads as the force that brought members of LambdaMOO together. In the course of his narrative, Dibbell chronicles a remarkably rapid fragmentation of a community. Jennifer Mnookin (1996b) and Charles Stivale (1995) have written similar stories about LambdaMOO; their pieces chronicle in detail the ways attempts at on-line governance ultimately have failed to adjudicate disagreements without provoking resentment within the community. Mnookin pays particular attention to the development of "Lambda Law," whereas Stivale addresses harassment narratives. Their arguments illustrate the seeming ineffability of community collaboration in cyberspace, a failure to achieve the vision of cyberspace as public sphere that writers, such as William Mitchell (1995) and Howard Rheingold (1993), evoke.

The circumstances which Dibbell chronicles incited, energized, and ultimately polarized members of LambdaMOO. Participants in the community devoted substantial energy to analyzing the event, understanding the philosophical and legal import of the incident and people's reactions to it, and developing appropriate guidelines for dealing with future disruptions. In the wake of this, the shape of the on-line society shifted dramatically. It is not our task to evaluate the success of LambdaMOO's introduction of governance tools, but we suggest that the perceived necessity of reforming the community as a legislated virtual body can be read as a version of community breakdown—as a point against the vision of virtual communities as liberatory, radically democratic, and positively transformative.

Multiple and Fragmented Selves

The freedom to obscure or recreate aspects of the self on-line allows the exploration and expression of multiple aspects of human existence. The research on virtual communities is filled with tales of masks for age and race, gender and class; masks for almost every aspect of identity (e.g., McCrae, 1996; Ullman, 1996). These are tales that do not always have happy endings. The stories of on-line cross-dressing that abound, for example, often culminate in narratives of betrayal. In this accumulated body of scholarship, participants talk of how their notions of the world and of their selves have been destabilized, rocked beyond recognition, leaving them emotionally and socially adrift. In this unanchored state, the basis of all social contracts is uprooted: participants feel that they cannot trust anyone, that everything on-line can be a lie, and that no one tells anyone who they really are.

Warnings of such scenarios are now part of the folklore of cyberspace; even usage agreements from many providers now alert new members that they cannot always trust virtual appearances. This separation from the seeming fixity of the "real-world" self rests at the core of conceiving the on-line self as fluid, and it is also responsible for both the liberatory and alarmist narratives that alternatively dominate the popular press. The fluid self in a text-based virtual community depends on interruptive practices and discursive resistance as a way to negotiate and reform a world. Linda Brodkey (1996), situating language within a social matrix, characterizes discursive resistance as the dynamic by which people "interrupt the very notion of the unified self—the traditional Cartesian notion that the self is a transcendent and absolute entity rather than a creation of language and ideology—in their spoken and written texts" (p. 90).

Whereas the fluidity of the self has garnered attention from scholars, less work has examined ways in which the fluidity of space in on-line environments might relate to the disruption of the self. We suggest that the interruptive practices associated with fluid identity relate to the construction of virtual space, where the fragmented self becomes dispersed, and that both make difficult the evolution of resilient on-line personae and communities. It is crucial to realize that on-line experiments with identity are often highly focused and ephemeral. It is extremely common for users of MUDs, for instance, to have numerous characters. There might be an intellectual character on LambdaMOO, a fluffy sexpot on FurryMUCK, a sardonic Vulcan on TrekMUSE—a different persona for every mood and every day of the week. In total, these multiple instances of the self may allow the individual projecting them to experience a greater diversity of himself or herself than would otherwise be the case, but each single instance operates on a very limited psychological and social plane.

The fragmentation of the individual hinders the formation of flexible and resilient on-line personae. Interpersonal problems require flexibility for resolution. Compromise, change, empathy and negotiability are qualities vital to the continuance of relationships. Without these qualities all relationships are at risk. At the same time, the negotiation of change must allow continuity. Virtual presence often can preclude change or only allow it at the expense of continuity. To some extent we operate in such a fragmentary fashion in the corporeal "real world": Many of us exhibit different personae in professional or personal circumstances. Nonetheless, for most of us these fragmentary social faces are integrated into a visceral sense of a single self. In this integration we are aided by the practical difficulty of physically isolating our social faces: All inhabit the same space and are identified as one person by those around us. By contrast, on-line personae are not spatially integrated, and from the individual's point of view there can be a definite psychological disjuncture between the experience of being one persona and of being another. This psychological disjuncture is permitted by the discrete nature of on-line spaces. Various on-line social spaces may overlap in the real-life identity of participants, but on-line personae cannot be readily unified by others as being operated by one physical individual.

This lack of integration does not allow much flexibility for negotiation in interaction with other on-line personae. The range of expression that any one persona can draw on is commonly far less than the range of the individual in the real world, just as the aggregate psychosocial range of an individual's collection of personae may exceed his or her real-life range. In the real world it is our plurality—our multiple moods and changing opinions—that allows individual psychic resilience and the creation of a vibrant and vital culture. Virtual communities often encourage multiplicity but not flexibility, with each individual persona having a limited, undiversified social range; this cultural schizophrenia makes the on-line community brittle and ill-equipped to evolve with the demands of circumstance. Virtual communities often fail to heed the lessons learned by the original designers of the Internet's underlying technical protocol. Whereas Paul Baran realized that a robust network must have multiple connections, many custodians of on-line communities fail to realize that there must be multiple aspects to personae and multiple social connections between personae if the group is to survive.

In consequence, the individual virtual persona is at once too committed to the particularity of the self it projects and too uncommitted to the continuity of that self. One of the authors (Reid, 1992) of this chapter once quoted a user of IRC (Internet Relay Chat) as commenting that if an on-line interaction became too awkward or unpleasant it was easy to log out and log back in with a different name and so start afresh (p. 11). At the time it was the freedom implied in this possibility that seemed intriguing; we are now concerned by the social limitations it entails.

In this light the documentary nature of digital interaction becomes crucial. Virtual speech and action have the spontaneity and immediacy of traditionally undocumented social speech but also the indelibility of writing. On-line, we are what we write in a far more intimate and inflexible way than we are ever purely or merely what we say face-to-face. A primary characteristic of flame-wars—those intensely vitriolic exchanges that regularly erupt in on-line environments—is the speed with which individuals become polarized and fixed in their opinions. The often minute analysis of words that occurs on Usenet and in mailing lists causes the author of those words to become inextricably tied to defending what he or she said. It is all too easy on-line to find oneself becoming entrenched in a position that is increasingly indefensible or merely uncomfortable to maintain; it is equally easy to abandon that position by abandoning the persona through which it was projected. That done, community continuity suffers. The excessive fixity of words comes to fill the gap formed by the relentless fragmentation of the self in ways that hinder community formation.

Dispersed and Displaced Spaces

The dispersed nature of virtual geographies further imperils the fragile ability of the multiple and fragmented self to contribute to community continuity. A growing number of the criticisms leveled at virtual communities intimate a vexed relationship with virtual selves, and although the explicit relationship has yet to be detailed, many writers point to a socially and culturally unstable link between fragmented spaces and fragmented selves. Edward Soja's (1989) assertion that "spatiality cannot be completely separated from physical and psychological spaces" (p. 120), relates specifically to the connections we are drawing between the multiple, nonfixed self and the dispersed geography of cyberspace.

The fragmentation of the self is ultimately a dissolution of the internal psychological landscape. Nonetheless, the external terrain of virtual space is similarly displaced and fragmented. Because of this overlap, recent theoretical moves to integrate discussions of space in relation to social theory can provide guidelines for thinking about interaction and community formation in virtual space as embedded in both the development of self and place in cyberspace. In a critique of urban structures, M. Christine Boyer (1996) writes of nonvirtual realms:

> In the bodily disenchantment that haunts our postmodern era, if the self is unstable, dephysicalized, and thus beginning to disappear, making projections from it ambiguous and unclear, then the image of the city as a normally functioning or healthy body also begins to be undermined. Thus the corporeal analogies of body/architecture and body/city under posthumanist, poststructuralist thought are marked by zones of silence, estrangement, and emptiness. (p. 80)

Boyer's (1996) critique of city structures in light of how they accommodate a disappeared body relates significantly to cyberspace and the virtual structures that fail to define its boundaries. That is, as virtual communities similarly tend to displace but not efface the material, the categories of space and interaction with which we are most familiar dissolve. The zones of silence she names here are markedly evident in cyberspace, a telling estrangement of people from their words, from others, and from their communities. Boyer's pessimistic portrayal of the postmodern city is predicated on a belief that space correlates with function. A dispersed space allows only for the existence of dispersed subjects: too much dispersal and a self becomes solely a subject, not an agent.

Mark Lajoie (1996) is critical of virtual communities because they result in the elimination of public space. His argument is based on the assumption that virtual interactions reduce citizens to "the status of atomized entities, ill-equipped for collective politics or public life" (p. 154). Lajoie's critique here is predominately geographical; that is, the atomization to which he refers was a dispersal over time and space, a separation of the embodied self from the sensory consequences of physical space. We believe that his critique is well placed. Selves must be locatable geographically to be firmly embedded in a cause-effect relationship. As the tourist may behave destructively when removed from the social constraints and responsibilities of home ground, so the virtual persona lacks social responsibility when ties to place are displaced.

Dan Nguyen and Jon Alexander (1996) echo many of Lajoie's concerns. Nguyen and Alexander critique the political effects of virtual space, claiming that the public sphere that is being created on the Internet is a "conversational, demassified, non-representational democracy" (p. 111) that holds little potential for political efficacy. They acknowledge some of the positive potential of the medium, including the ways in which shifting subjectivities allow for a break from hegemonic structures. Ultimately, however, they see the geographical rootlessness and decentralization of virtual communities as destroying the concept of the polity and thus as essentially depoliticizing. They write:

> The wildly proliferating fields of cyberspacetime are . . . profoundly apolitical. In cyberspacetime, the social realm is engulfing and overwhelming the political realm. The "social" is decomposing the body politic. . . . Millions of people have made drifting in and out of digital realities a significant part of their everyday lives. This is a global retreat from our now empty public lives, from roles we once acted out in a real-life political realm. It is a retreat from nations, from nationalism and from politics itself. This is a retreat from civilization. It places millions in a tribalized fantasy culture, a theatre of the bizarre and the absurd. Fantasy culture becomes universal by making all the world a proliferation of cyberstages, an inauthentic virtual simulation of Shakespeare's *theatrum mundi*. (pp. 109, 116-117)

Nguyen and Alexander (1996) base their critique at the site of perceived emptied real-life interaction rather than on the flaws inherent in virtual communities. We have reservations about their claim that on-line activity is inherently effectless and that its growth signifies a reduction in "real" political interest or action. In light of the on-line political work of, among others, the Electronic Frontier Foundation and the ACLU, we are optimistic about the potential for the Internet to act as a realm for political interaction with concrete effects on the off-line world, even though issues of access continue to qualify claims regarding the widespread political potential of the Internet. Nevertheless, we are in sympathy with Nguyen and Alexander's perception of the drifting and shiftless nature of many digital realities and on-line personae. We would point to the geographical atomization described by Lajoie (1996) as the basis for this "tribalized fantasy culture," and add to it our own picture of psychological disjuncture leading to a nihilism that evokes fixed selves that are unable to negotiate the complex demands of their supposed humanity.

Jennifer Mnookin (1996a) adds a new dimension to this argument when she brings forward the idea that selves must be locatable within a legal landscape to be seen as consequential. Lajoie and Mnookin introduce two seemingly variant arguments that are reducible to a central claim—that is, a sense of place and permanence are necessary for selves to be conceptualized as implicated in surrounding communities. Nguyen and Alexander (1996) further refine this by distinguishing the virtual as that which robs the situated self of its power by creating spaces through which individuals float, seemingly oblivious to the consequences of their actions. Virtual spaces more often than not are precisely this—locales where participants, those multiple and fluid selves that Turkle (1995) delineates, move through the surface of virtual worlds, unable to burrow into the layers of the community and experience the idea of action and consequence. What evolves, then, is a case of temporary connections that do not hold any tangible consequences for those who are touched by such fleeting bonds. We would suggest, however, that this lack of intimacy rooted in reality is a psychological artifact of the fragmented nature of on-line spaces, rather than the cause of it.

Unification and Fragmentation: Space and Self

The missing sense of permanence of self is one component of this terminal surfaceness. Nonetheless, the construction of virtual communities, particularly the linguistic architecture of MUDs, reinforces this kind of relationship by creating atomized spaces as well as atomized selves. A dispersed architecture that gives individuals separable worlds that do not seek connection reinforces the sense that the multiple selves exist for one type of interaction alone. Multiplicity, in this case, resists fluidity as players see the power to create different selves as a reason not to integrate different kinds of actions and reactions into the same self. This results in a very particular singularity of the virtual self, and, ultimately, makes users unable to meaningfully contribute to the health and permanence of a virtual community.

When Lajoie (1996) critiques virtual communities it was in part because, as he argues, such social environments deny the physical realm and the physical self. Again, like Mnookin (1996a), he focuses on the importance of an embodied self. We would argue that Lajoie, Mnookin, and other critics' focus on embodiment is an acknowledgment of the importance of such characteristics as permanence and fixity of self in accomplishing meaningful social exchange. There is a point at which this argument teeters dangerously close to a reassertion of modernist conceptions of the self and a repudiation of the viability of a postmodern, dispersed self. Nonetheless, our claim rests not with either side of this great divide but, rather, with a kind of strategic use of both. In a modernist sense, we draw on the concept of accountability and persistence of identity, but from the lessons of postmodernism we have learned the importance of distributed presence, particularly with respect to the mediation of communication technologies and an overarching hope for political possibility. We would suggest that notions of unified and fragmented identity need not compete; that they can in fact cooperate to produce a conception of a self that consists of interrelationships between discrete personae, each of which contribute to a whole that none perpetually dominate.

Perhaps we might draw on the works of Donna Haraway (1991, 1997) and other postmodern feminists to explain how embodiment does not equal modernism, and how accountability does not negate the idea of play. Take, for example, the writings of Allucavère Roseanne Stone (1991, 1995). Stone posits a conceptualization of the self that is multiple, playful, and yet also embedded in consequences. At base, Turkle's (1995) argument in *Life on the Screen* is designed to make this argument, but by concentrating on the positive consequences to the exclusion of the negative she narrows the focus of inquiry. We assert that when virtual communities fail to create viable public spaces, we ought to seek explanation in that very distributed presence to which so many authors refer.

The architecture of cyberspaces pushes against traditional boundaries just as much as the construction of "cyberselves." Geopolitical affiliation is masked in much the same way as gender, age, or race. This is not to say that any of these characteristics can be wholly effaced, but there are ways to conceal them, and, the more one tries, the more such traces can be mediated. Nonetheless, the absence of impermeable walls within a virtual community, and the way such communities resist traditional space and time constrictions on human communication, have just as destabilizing an effect on exchanges within cyberspace as the fluidity of identity.

Place has always been tied to rhetorical authority; deconstructing space reconstructs our understanding of rhetoric. The structures of cyberspace consequently affect on-line lives from the standpoint of communicative ethics. The overlap of work and play in spaces has economic ramifications, and the reformation of domestic space effected by communication technologies has significant consequences from the perspective of feminist theory. But the arrangement of space within virtual communities wreaks havoc on a traditional understanding of communication, particularly with respect to conceptions of private and public space. Rhetoric is about relationships, the shifting connections among ethos, logos, and pathos. It is the relationship among these points that changes, but the points themselves are identifiable *in relation* to the others. It is the disruption of this very relation that is so disturbing in attempts to communicate with some authenticity in cyberspace. The fluidity of space combines with the fluidity of identity in cyberspace, further imperiling the ability to talk with any sense of familiarity, with any commitment to codes of the world we know and move through daily in real space. It is in the experiments in on-line governance that we can most clearly see the stakes of trying to carve public space out of the amorphous landscape of cyberspace.

Although we are dedicated to the idea that on-line communities can have tangible and positive effects on people's lives in real space, and that the boundaries between the two blur substantially, we are forced to make a concurrent argument that virtual communities seem to be less effective along other lines. As we cite the histories written of many on-line communities, including the work of Dibbell (1993), Mnookin (1996a, b), and Stivale (1995), our goal is to highlight the variety of communicative failures, incidents in which breakdown in the ability of the community to collaborate effectively interrupted daily routines. When William Mitchell (1995) raises the question of the civic character of cyberspace communities, when he says that we "will have to figure out how to make cyberspace communities work in just, equitable, and satisfying ways" (p. 160), he introduces an imperative that has yet to be met. Cyberspace may be William Gibson's "consensual hallucination," but for us to achieve just and equitable spaces we also need cyberspace to be a place of consensual discourse. It is the breakdown of such consensus that leads to the stories we see about LambdaMOO; it is the refusal to engage in consensual discourse that led to the tenor of the debates over governance on the professional MOO discussed earlier. We do not have consensual discourse in cyberspace; indeed it often seems that we do not have consensual discourse as a *thematic* of cyberspace. We hope that our chapter can aid the development of that thematic by reassessing the nature of the on-line selves engaged in that discourse.

Conclusion

Among the variety of possible explanations for failures in on-line communities, we would like to advance the claim that such breakdowns within virtual societies are tied to self, space, and the role of place with respect to rhetoric. What seems clear is that virtual selves can be paralyzed in a number of ways. Losing any notion of the continuity of the self threatens community development, and the displaced and dispersed nature of virtual space reinforces the psychological fragmentation of the on-line self. The cumulative effect silences and estranges inhabitants of on-line worlds. The body politic in cyberspace is as fragmented as the self. The fluidity of national boundaries overlaps the permeability of virtual structures, giving rise to amorphous spaces that leave physical situatedness a conceptual improbability. It seems that with the loss of the traditional nexus of place and power, we are left with the necessity of crafting an alternate way of viewing rhetorical relationships. Discursive resistance needs a place to act on, whether that place is a body or a space. The mediation of one and the blurring of the other within virtual communities stands as an unmet challenge in crafting such cyberspaces into viable public forums.

Given the fluidity of space in a virtual community, we lose those markers of place that confer rhetorical authority. It seems necessary, somehow, to find ways to contend with the messiness of virtual space, with the conflation of different purposes for the space, and with the myriad roles a virtual community takes on for individuals. Without recouping the idea of place and rhetorical authority within the virtual environment, we will be limited in our progressive uses of such media. Nevertheless, we believe that dispersed spaces and fragmentary projections of the self will remain integral to the on-line experience. Such facilities as anonymous remailers and pseudonymous MUD personae provide popular media through which individuals can explore previously hidden aspects of themselves; a popularity that seems unlikely to wane. It has been precisely the opportunity to project an unconnected multiplicity of selves into virtual spaces that has driven much of the growth of interest in the Internet.

Nonetheless, it is these opportunistic aspects of cyberselves that create many of the problems encountered in virtual communities. Individual psychological resilience stems from adaptability: the ability to change one's face to suit the moment and to devise new faces to meet changing circumstances, all the while maintaining coherence and continuity between those multiple faces. It is our very plurality, our multiple moods and changing opinions, that allows the creation of a vibrant and vital culture. It is the singularity of on-line personae that can be the greatest threat to on-line communities. It has been all too easy for virtual communities to encourage multiplicity but not coherence, with each individual persona having a limited, undiversified social range. This cultural schizophrenia makes the virtual community brittle and ill-equipped to evolve with the demands of circumstance. The human body cannot sustain increased growth of undiversified cells; that is cancer. The cultural body also demands diversity and adaptability. To have a multiplicity of facets to the self is singularly human, but if virtual communities are to be sustainable as communities they must allow and encourage a holistic projection of the self into the virtual landscape.

There are indeed signs that the nature of Internet tools that support social connections are changing to make possible the tracing of multiple links between individual personae. We offer as an example the facility of Dejanews that allows any Internet user to view a profile of any Usenet poster that includes a list of all the newsgroups that person has posted to and access to archives of each article. With this simple tool, Dejanews has put an end to the sense of anonymity that posting to the vast and unarchived bulk of Usenet once entailed. Extending this idea, Marc Smith of the Center for the Study of Online Community at UCLA is developing NetScan, a tool for analysis of social links and similarities between bodies of data, be they from Usenet, the World Wide Web, IRC or a MUD.

We hope that it will become more common for virtual communities to encourage the expression of multiplicity and situatedness within single instances of an individual's on-line presence. In pursuit of this we must try not to forget that although the virtual self may be disembodied and multiple it does remain tied to an embodied point: the place where access matters and bandwidth is a crucial variable, the place where RSI occurs, the place where laws regarding free speech and harassment collide not just with one another but also with the words that participants in the virtual community contribute. Whereas on-line space may be virtual, on-line expression is rooted in an embodied identity, and it is necessary to reach a coherent vision of this to understand how virtual communities can work and also why they often do not work.

Note

1. Curiously enough, attention was paid, however haphazardly, to the relationship of virtual spaces to the function of the MOO. We had virtual architectural spaces to facilitate the attempt at governance; we had a council meeting room that, when it was accused of Star Chamber overtones, was modified to log the meetings and, eventually, to allow one-way viewing of the council meetings by committee members. The meetings were not open to every- one for the particular reason the model of representative democracy was chosen. Through the very generous donation of programming time from one member, the MOO was equipped with a variety of structures that facilitated communica- tion.

References

Boyer, M. C. (1996). *CyberCities: Visual perception in the age of electronic communica- tion.* New York: Princeton Architectural Press.

Brodkey, L. (1996). *Writing permitted in designated areas only.* Minneapolis: Univer- sity of Minnesota Press.

Dibbell, J. (1993). Rape in cyberspace or how an evil clown, a Haitian trickster spirit, two wizards, and a cast of dozens turned a database into a society. *Village Voice, 38*(51), 36-42.

Haraway, D. (1991). *Simians, cyborgs, and women: The reinvention of nature.* New York: Routledge.

Haraway, D. (1997). *Modest_witness@second_millenium. Femaleman_ meets_onco- mouse*™: *Feminism and technoscience.* New York: Routledge.

Lajoie, M. (1996). Psychoanalysis and cyberspace. In R. Shields (Ed.), *Cultures of the Internet: Virtual spaces, real histories, living bodies* (pp. 153-169). London: Sage, Ltd.

Mitchell, W. (1995). *City of bits: Space, place, and the infobahn.* Cambridge: MIT Press.

Mnookin, J. (1996a, April). *Bodies, rest, and motion: Law and identity in virtual spaces.* Paper presented at *Virtue & virtuality: Gender, law & cyberspace symposium,* Cambridge: MIT.

Mnookin, J. (1996b). Virtual(ly) law: The emergence of law in LambdaMOO. *Journal of Computer-Mediated Communication, 2*(1).

Nguyen, T., & Alexander, J. (1996). The coming of cyberspacetime and the end of the polity. In R. Shields (Ed.), *Cultures of the Internet: Virtual spaces, real histories, living bodies* (pp. 99-124). London: Sage.

Poster, M. (1995). *The second media age.* Oxford, UK: Polity-Blackwell.

Reid, E. (1992). Electropolis: Communication and community on Internet relay chat. *Intertek, 3*(3), 7-13.

Rheingold, H. (1993). *The virtual community homesteading on the electronic frontier.* New York: HarperCollins.

Soja, E. (1989). *Postmodern geographies: The reassertion of space in critical theory.* London: Verso.

Stivale, C. J. (1995, Dec.). *"Help manners": Cyber-democracy and its vicissitudes.* Paper presented at the meeting of the Modern Language Association, San Diego, CA.

Stone, A. R. (1991). Will the real body please stand up?: Boundary stories about virtual cultures. In M. Benedikt (Ed.), *Cyberspace: First steps* (pp. 81-118). Cambridge: MIT Press.

Stone, A. R. (1995). *The war of desire and technology at the close of the mechanical age.* Cambridge: MIT Press.

Turkle, S. (1995). *Life on the screen: Identity in the age of the Internet.* New York: Simon & Schuster.

Index

About the Contributors

Philip E. Agre is Associate Professor of Communication at the University of California, San Diego. He is the author of *Computation and Human Experience* (1997) and co-editor (with Marc Rotenberg) of *Technology and Privacy: The New Landscape* (1997). He also edits an Internet mailing list, the Red Rock Eater News Service, which distributes useful information on the social and political aspects of networking and computing to 4,000 people in 60 countries.

Nancy K. Baym is Assistant Professor of Communication at Wayne State University (nbaym@uiuc.edu) where she teaches Computer-Mediated Communication, Discourse Analysis, and Interpersonal Communication, among other courses. Her research into the creation of the on-line social world of r.a.t.s. has been published in several journals and books. She is extending her research into the creation of social worlds in other on-line fan groups. She earned her Ph.D. in speech communication from the University of Illinois at Urbana-Champaign.

Lynn Schofield Clark is a post-doctoral research fellow in the Center for Mass Media Research in the School of Journalism and Mass Communication, University of Colorado, where she completed her Ph.D. on U.S. teens and their use of media in identity construction. She is coauthor with

Stewart M. Hoover of *Finding God in the Media* and coeditor of *Cultural Practice* and *Cultural Meaning: Explorations in Media, Religion, and Culture*, both forthcoming. She has published several book chapters and articles in several journals including *Critical Studies in Mass Communication*. She serves as a tutor to junior high students in her free time.

Brenda Danet (http://atar.mscc.huji.ac.il/msdanet) teaches sociology and communication at the Hebrew University of Jerusalem, and holds the Danny Arnold Chair in Communication. Her publications include an edited issue of the *Journal of Computer-Mediated Communication* (1995, 2(1)) on "Play and Performance in Computer-Mediated Communication," entries on digital communication for the *Encyclopedia of Semiotics and Cultural Studies* (Oxford, 1998), and her book, *Keybo@rd K@perz: Studies of Digital Communication* (in press).

Steven G. Jones (sjones@uic.edu) is Professor and Head of the Department of Communication at the University of Illinois at Chicago. His other books include *Virtual Culture* (1997), *CyberSociety* (1995), and *Rock Formation* (1992). He is editor of **New Media Cultures**, a series of books on culture and technology. In addition to his scholarly work, he has been providing Internet consulting services to many corporations and not-for-profit organizations. He also has been a featured speaker at numerous scholarly, government, and industry-sponsored seminars and conferences.

Beth Kolko (bek@uta.edu) is Assistant Professor of English at the University of Texas at Arlington where she teaches courses on rhetoric, cultural studies, and cyberspace theory. Her recent work includes articles on virtual communities, electronic discourse, gender and virtuality, and teaching with technology.

Cheris Kramarae (cheris@uiuc.edu) is Visiting Professor at the Center for the Study of Women in Society at the University of Oregon. She has authored, edited, or coedited 11 books, including *Technology and Women's Voices*, and *Women, Informaton Technology, and Scholarship (WITS)*, and has published a number of articles on the Internet, gender, and law. She is coediting, with Dale Spender, the *Women's International Sourcebook and Encyclopedia*.

Mark Poster teaches in the History Department and the Critical Theory Program at University of California, Irvine. His recent books include *Cultural History and Postmodernity* (1997), *The Second Media Age* (1995), and *The Mode of Information* (1990).

Elizabeth Reid (elizrs@mediaone.net) began studying on-line communities in 1990 at the University of Melbourne in her native Australia. She now lives in Los Angeles, where she works as a consultant on psychological and sociological factors in on-line system design. Her recent work includes articles on community formation in text-based environments and design issues in graphical virtual worlds.